Traveling with Pomegranates

Traveling with Pomegranates

A MOTHER-DAUGHTER STORY

Sue Monk Kidd

Ann Kidd Taylor

Viking

VIKING
Published by the Penguin Group
Penguin Group (USA) Inc., 375 Hudson Street, New York, New York 10014, U.S.A. • Penguin Group
(Canada), 90 Eglinton Avenue East, Suite 700, Toronto, Ontario, Canada M4P 2Y3 (a division of Pearson
Penguin Canada Inc.) • Penguin Books Ltd, 80 Strand, London WC2R 0RL, England • Penguin
Ireland, 25 St. Stephen's Green, Dublin 2, Ireland (a division of Penguin Books Ltd) • Penguin Books
Australia Ltd, 250 Camberwell Road, Camberwell, Victoria 3124, Australia (a division of Pearson
Australia Group Pty Ltd) • Penguin Books India Pvt Ltd, 11 Community Centre, Panchsheel Park,
New Delhi – 110 017, India • Penguin Group (NZ), 67 Apollo Drive, Rosedale, North Shore 0632,
New Zealand (a division of Pearson New Zealand Ltd) • Penguin Books (South Africa) (Pty) Ltd,
24 Sturdee Avenue, Rosebank, Johannesburg 2196, South Africa

Penguin Books Ltd, Registered Offices: 80 Strand, London WC2R 0RL, England

First published in 2009 by Viking Penguin, a member of Penguin Group (USA) Inc.

10   9   8   7   6   5   4   3   2   1

Grateful acknowledgment is made for permission to reprint excerpts from the following copyrighted
works:
"Ceres Looks at the Morning" from *The Lost Land* by Eavan Boland. Copyright © 1998 by Eavan
Boland. Used by permission of W. W. Norton & Company, Inc.
"The Music Master" from *The Essential Rumi*, translations by Coleman Barks with John Moyne
(HarperOne). By permission of Coleman Barks.
"When a woman feels alone, when the room" from *Collected Poems 1930–1993* by May Sarton. Copy-
right © 1984 by May Sarton. Used by permission of W. W. Norton & Company, Inc.
"Sweet Darkness" from *The House of Belonging* by David Whyte. Reprinted with permission of Many
Rivers Press, Langley, Washington. www.davidwhyte.com

LIBRARY OF CONGRESS CATALOGING IN PUBLICATION DATA
Kidd, Sue Monk.
    Traveling with pomegranates : a mother daughter story / by Sue Monk Kidd and
Ann Kidd Taylor.
      p.   cm.
    ISBN 978-0-670-02120-8
    1. Kidd, Sue Monk—Travel—Greece.   2. Kidd, Sue Monk—Family.   3. Mothers and
daughters—United States.   4. Authors, American—21st century—Biography.   5. Taylor,
Ann Kidd.   I. Taylor, Ann Kidd.   II. Title.
    PS3611.I44Z46 2009
    818'.6 B—dc22   2009009388

Printed in the United States of America
Map by Jeffrey L. Ward
Designed by Carla Bolte • Set in Granjon

---

*Penguin is committed to publishing works of quality and integrity. In that spirit, we are proud to offer this
book to our readers; however, the story, the experiences, and the words are the authors' alone.*

To Terry and Mandy Helwig with love

CONTENTS

NORTH CAROLINA

SOUTH CAROLINA

Columbia

GEORGIA

Charleston
(Home)

Atlantic Ocean

SIGHTS AND PLACES IN

Traveling with Pomegranates

Traveling with Pomegranates

LOSS

Greece / Turkey / South Carolina

1998–1999

Sue

National Archaeological Museum—Athens

❧ Sitting on a bench in the National Archaeological Museum in Greece, I watch my twenty-two-year-old daughter, Ann, angle her camera before a marble bas-relief of Demeter and Persephone unaware of the small ballet she's performing—her slow, precise steps forward, the tilt of her head, the way she dips to one knee as she turns her torso, leaning into the sharp afternoon light. The scene reminds me of something, a memory maybe, but I can't recall what. I only know she looks beautiful and impossibly grown, and for reasons not clear to me I'm possessed by an acute feeling of loss.

It's the summer of 1998, a few days before my fiftieth birthday. Ann and I have been in Athens a whole twenty-seven hours, a good portion of which I've spent lying awake in a room in the Hotel Grande Bretagne, waiting for blessed daylight. I tell myself the bereft feeling that washed over me means nothing—I'm jet-lagged, that's all. But that doesn't feel particularly convincing.

I close my eyes and even in the tumult of the museum, where there seem to be ten tourists per square inch, I know the feeling is actually *everything*. It is the undisclosed reason I've come to the other side of the world with my daughter. Because in a way which makes no sense, she seems lost to me now. Because she is grown and a stranger. And I miss her almost violently.

~ ~ ~

Our trip to Greece began as a birthday present to myself and a college graduation gift to Ann. The extravagant idea popped into my head six months earlier as the realization of turning fifty set in and I felt for the first time the overtures of an ending.

Those were the days I stood before the bathroom mirror examining new lines and sags around my eyes and mouth like a seismologist studying unstable tectonic plates. The days I dug through photo albums in search of images of my mother and grandmother at fifty, scrutinizing their faces and comparing them to my own.

Surely I'm above this sort of thing. I could not be one of those women who clings to the façades of youth. I didn't understand why I was responding to the prospect of aging with such shallowness and dread, only that there had to be more to it than the etchings of time on my skin. Was I dabbling in the politics of vanity or did I obsess on my face to avoid my soul? Furthermore, whatever room I happened to be in seemed unnaturally overheated. During the nights I wandered in long, sleepless corridors. At forty-nine my body was engaged in vague, mutinous behaviors.

These weren't the only hints that I was about to emigrate to a new universe. At the same time I was observing the goings-on in the mirror, I came down with an irrepressible need to leave my old geography—a small town in upstate South Carolina where we'd lived for twenty-two years—and move to an unfamiliar landscape. I envisioned a place tucked away somewhere, quiet and untamed, near water, marsh grass, and tidal rhythms. In an act of boldness or recklessness, or some perfect combination thereof, my husband, Sandy, and I put our house on the market and moved to Charleston, where we subsisted in a minuscule one-bedroom apartment while searching for this magical and necessary place. I never said out loud that I thought it was mandatory for my soul and my creative life (how could I explain that?), but I assure you, I was thinking it.

I felt like my writing had gone to seed. A strange fallowness had set in. I could not seem to write in the same way. I felt I'd come to some conclusion in my creative life and now something new wanted to break through. I had crazy intimations about writing a novel, about which I knew more or less nothing. Frankly, the whole thing terrified me.

After being crammed in the tiny apartment for so long I began to think we'd lost our minds by tossing over our comfortable old life, I was driving alone one day when I took a wrong turn that led to a salt marsh. I stopped the car by a FOR SALE sign on an empty lot, climbed out and gazed at an expanse of waving spartina grass with a tidal creek curling through it. It was low tide. The mudflats glinted with oyster shells and egrets floated down to them like plumes of smoke. My heart tumbled wildly. *I belong to this place.* Perhaps living here, my creative life would crack open like one of those oyster shells. Or sweep in like the tides, brimming and amniotic. In those moments, the longing I felt to bring forth a new voice, some new substance in myself, almost knocked me down.

I called Sandy. "I'm standing on the spot where we need to live."

To his everlasting credit he did not say, "Don't you think I need to see it first?" Or, "What do you mean you don't know the price?" He heard the conviction and hunger in my words. After a pause, a fairly long one, he said, "Well, okay, if we really need to."

Later I went to the store and bought a red leather journal. I carried it, blank and unchristened, to the lot beside the salt marsh where we now planned to build our house. Construction hadn't started, wouldn't start for a few months. I sat on a faded beach towel beneath a palmetto palm and began making a list of 100 Things to Do Before I Die. It started off with a 10K race and riding a hot-air balloon over Tuscany. I didn't like running and really had no desire to travel by balloon. I turned the page.

Finally, I began to write about becoming an older woman and the trepidation it stirred. The small, telling "betrayals" of my body. The stalled, eerie stillness in my writing, accompanied by an ache for some unlived destiny. I wrote about the raw, unsettled feelings coursing through me, the need to divest and relocate, the urge to radically simplify and distill life into a new, unknown meaning. And why, I asked myself, had I begun to think for the first time about my own mortality? Some days, the thought of dying gouged into my heart to the point I filled up with tears at the sight of the small, ordinary things I would miss.

Finally, I wrote a series of questions: *Is there an odyssey the female soul longs to make at the approach of fifty—one that has been blurred and lost within a culture awesomely alienated from soul? If so, what sort of journey would that be? Where would it take me?*

The impulse to go to Greece emerged out of those questions. It seized me before I got back to the minuscule apartment. *Greece.* That would be the portal. I would make a *pilgrimage* in search of an initiation.

A few days later, flipping through a small anthology, I stumbled upon four lines in May Sarton's poem "When a Woman Feels Alone":

> *Old Woman I meet you deep inside myself.*
> *There in the rootbed of fertility,*
> *World without end, as the legend tells it.*
> *Under the words you are my silence.*

I read it a half-dozen times. I became entranced with the verse, which attached itself to the side of my heart something like a limpet on a rock. The image of the Old Woman haunted me—this idea that there was an encounter that needed to take place at the "rootbed" of a new fertility. Who *was* this Old Woman who had to be met deep inside oneself? Sometimes I woke in the middle of the night thinking about her. About her dark fertility. About the silence beneath the words.

When I made my first trip to Greece in 1993, I'd inscribed a quotation on the first page of my travel diary—words by theologian Richard Niebuhr: "Pilgrims are poets who create by taking journeys." Recalling this, I recopied the words in the new red journal. What I wanted—at least what I was trying hard to want—was to create in myself a new poetry: *the spiritual composition of the Old Woman, not through words, but through the wisdom of a journey.*

I imagined the trip as a pilgrimage for Ann, too. She had gone to Greece almost a year and a half ago on an academic trip and fallen in love with the place. Returning would be the graduation gift of gifts for her, but I also wondered if it might become an initiation for her as well. She was officially exiting the precincts of girlhood and stepping into young womanhood—another threshold that wasn't all that defined and acknowledged—and she did seem daunted lately. Not that we talked about it. When I inquired, she said she was *fine.* But on the flight over, during the hours she sat next to me, she stared out the oval window, at the *SkyMall* catalog, at the movie playing on the monitor over our heads, and there was an emission of sadness around her, like the faint dots and dashes of Morse code blinking secret distress.

I realized it was conceivable that Ann and I both, in our own way, were experiencing a crisis, which according to its definition is: (1) a crucial stage or turning point, and (2) an unstable or precarious situation. At the very least, Ann was struggling to figure out the beginning of being a woman, and I, the beginning of the ending of it.

~ ~ ~

Now, though, I sit on the museum bench and consider this *new* epiphany, how surprising it is that for all these months I've thought traveling to Greece was basically a pilgrimage about crossing borders into foreign regions of the soul. About meeting the Old Woman. I haven't considered it has anything to do with mothers and daughters. With Ann and me. With *us*.

I watch Ann hone in with her telephoto lens on Persephone's face, the nose of which is partially missing. If you asked me to describe Ann, the first thing I would say is: smart. Her intelligence was never just scholastic, though; it has always had a creative, inventive bent. When other eight-year-olds were busy with lemonade stands, Ann set up a booth for dispensing "Advice for People With Problems": minor problems cost a nickel; major ones, a dime. She made a killing.

On the other hand, it must be said that Ann's defining quality is kindness. I don't mean politeness so much as tenderheartedness. Growing up, she railed against animal abuse and was unable to bear even the thought of a squashed bug, insisting we carry all insects from the house in dustpans. Indeed, whatever her sensitive and fiery heart attached itself to, she was passionate about it: bugs, dogs, horses, books, dolls, comic strips, Save-the-Earth, movies, Hello Kitty, *Star Wars*.

The list of attachments revolved continually. Her constant testaments to these passions were the poems and stories she wrote throughout her childhood, filling one composition book after another.

The only thing that seemed to curb her fervency was the other predominant thing about Ann—her natural diffidence and the way it often veered off into self-consciousness.

I wrap my arms across my abdomen and look away from her

toward the room we just left, which like this one is a cluttered boneyard of sculptures and myths. I have the most absurd impulse to cry.

I've had intimations of this feeling of loss before, but it was a shadow passing in the peripheries, then gone. After Ann left home, I would wander into her room and catch the scent of dried prom corsages in the closet, or turn over an old photograph of our beagles and find myself staring at her handwriting—*Caesar and Brutus 1990*—or come upon her poem "Ode to a Teddy Bear," or open a cookbook to her perfected horse head sketch in the margin, and I would feel it, the momentary eclipse.

I tell myself it's natural for the feeling to surface now, with the two of us captive in each other's presence, brought together in a way we haven't experienced in . . . well, forever. Once, when Ann was twelve, we'd traveled—just the two of us—to San Francisco, but that was hardly comparable to this. At twelve, Ann had not been away for four years during which time she transformed into a young woman I barely know.

Her backpack is plopped open between her feet while she copies something from the sign beside the bas-relief into a blue spiral notebook. It has not escaped me that Demeter and Persephone have captured her attention.

We have by this point tromped by a few thousand antiquities at least—frescoes from Santorini, gold from Mycenae, bronzes from Attica, pottery from every nook and cranny of ancient Greece— but *this* is the spot where I told Ann my feet are in abject misery and I need to take a break: before Demeter and Persephone. At the intersection of mothers and daughters.

I wander over to the marble canvas and stare at the two robed women who face one another. Their myth is familiar to me.

The maiden, Persephone, is picking flowers in a meadow when a hole opens in the earth and up charges Hades, lord of the dead, who abducts Persephone into the underworld. Unable to find her daughter, Demeter, the great earth Goddess of grain, harvest, and fertility, lights a torch and scours the earth. After nine futile days of searching, Demeter is approached by Hecate, the quintessential old crone and Goddess of the crossroads and the dark moon, who explains that her daughter has been abducted.

In a rage and too dejected to keep up her divine duties, Demeter lets the crops wither and the earth becomes a wasteland. She disguises herself as an old woman and travels to the town of Eleusis, where she sits beside a well in despair. Zeus tries to talk some sense into her. Hades will make a nice son-in-law, he says. She needs to lighten up and let the crops grow. Demeter will not budge.

The earth becomes so desolate Zeus finally gives up and orders Persephone returned to her mother. As Persephone prepares to leave, however, she unwittingly swallows some pomegranate seeds, which ensures her return to the underworld for a third of each year.

Mother and daughter are reunited on the first day of spring. Interestingly, Hecate shows up for the occasion, and the myth says from that point on, she precedes and follows Persephone wherever she goes. (A curious piece of the story that rarely gets noticed.) When Demeter learns about the fateful pomegranate, her joy is tempered, but she stops her mourning and allows the earth to flourish again. After all, her daughter is back. Not the same innocent girl who tripped through the meadow picking flowers, but a woman transfigured by her experience.

Later, I would learn there's a name for this mother-daughter reunion. The Greeks call it *heuresis*.

I dig through my travel tote for my map and unfold it across the bench. I find Eleusis, the ancient site of Demeter's temple, located just outside of Athens in what's described as an "industrial area."

Contemplating a visit before we leave Greece, I stuff the map back in my bag and wander off to find Ann, who has disappeared into the next wing.

I want my daughter back.

~ ~ ~

I find Ann circling a tree rack of postcards in the museum gift shop, and notice she has plucked off a card depicting a statue of the Goddess Athena.

"Isn't she beautiful?" she says, holding it out to me and digging in her purse for the drachmas we exchanged for dollars in the airport.

A few moments later we step into the blare of sun and car horns and walk in silence, or possibly in stupefying shock at the heat, which was a hundred and five degrees when we left the hotel earlier. It's like slogging through pudding. Athens in high summer is not for the fainthearted, but I love how it spills into the streets, with sidewalk markets bulging with apricots, loquats, nectarines, and melons; the bougainvillea hanging in hot-pink awnings over the outdoor cafés; the white apartment buildings etched with grapevines.

We plod several blocks in search of a cab and are rescued on the corner of Voulis and Ermou. The taxi is an air-conditioned Mercedes-Benz. Ann and I fan ourselves in the backseat with museum maps. When we get out, I ask for the driver's card.

Inside our room, we joke about making an offering on the Altar of the Air Conditioner Vent. We order room service and eat Greek salad, which is a Pisa-like tower of sliced tomatoes, cucumbers, and feta. Then we draw the curtains and go straight to bed. It is 3:30 in the afternoon.

Lying on the twin mattress, I stare at the edge of light oozing under the curtain and I think about my relationship with my daughter. Congenial, warm, nice—those are the words that come to me. We've never had one of those pyrotechnic relationships that end up being written about so often and famously in books.

We've had our moments, naturally. The period of mild rebellion when she was fourteen springs to mind, a phase when the door slammed a lot. Beyond that, we had the typical antagonisms and disagreements. I suspect like most mothers and daughters we've participated in the classic struggle: the mother, trying to let her daughter go while unconsciously seeing her as an appendage of herself. And the daughter, enmeshed in her mother's power, compelled to please her and pattern herself in her mother's image, but straining at the same time to craft an identity separate from her.

Mostly, though, our relationship has been full of goodness. I would even say, given the natural constraints of adolescent girls and their mothers, we've been close. And yet I feel my relationship with Ann now exists largely on the surface. There is distance in it that I have trouble characterizing. We talk, for instance, but nothing really heart to heart. It's as if the relationship has fallen into a strange purgatory. For so long our roles were strictly defined as mother and daughter, as adult and child. But now as she leaves college, we both seem to sense some finality to this. She is changing and I am changing, too, but we don't quite know how to shift the conversation between ourselves. How to reforge our connection.

I feel traces of guilt about the growing distance between us. I toss on the bed, remembering that while she was away at school metamorphosing into the young woman I barely know, I was too busy with a book project to notice she was gone. Her leaving was not a problem. At least not in the maternal trench where these things are usually battled out. What's more, I was *proud* of this. I chirped to my friends: "I don't know what the big deal is about the empty nest. It's kind of wonderful, actually."

It seems now I said this with smugness, as if I were somehow immune because I, after all, had a life of my own, creative passions, a spiritual journey, a career separate from my role of mother. Ann was rightly abducted from me by her own separate life and I was too self-absorbed to come to terms with it, to figure out what it meant, what it should mean.

I sit up. Ann is sound asleep.

I tiptoe to my suitcase, retrieve my journal, then crawl back into bed where I write down the streams of awareness that began in the museum. When I drift to sleep, I dream.

I am in my kitchen, stirring a pot on the stove. I turn around and find a large, mystifying crevice in the center of the floor. It is jagged and gaping and looks as if an earthquake has taken place. As I stare down into the darkness, I realize with horrifying certainty that Ann has fallen into the hole. I drop onto my knees and call into the blackness. I scream her name until the sound clots in my throat. I don't know what to do. Finally I search for a flashlight so I can see down into the opening.

I wake with a dry, achy throat, throw off the sheet, and go stand by Ann's bed, taking in the sight of her. My heart still thuds a little. It awes me that the myth has moved into the intimate space of my dreams.

At this point in my life, I've been recording my dreams for twelve years. I think of them as snapshots floating up from a mysterious vat, offering metaphoric pictures of what's going on inside. Sometimes the images suggest where my soul wants to lead me and sometimes where it does not, giving me input and guidance about choices I might make. I am not thinking of the soul in the typical sense, as an immortal essence like the spirit, but rather as the rich, inner life of the psyche, the deepest impulse of which is to create wholeness.

Unlike most of my dreams, this one is not enigmatic. Its associations to the myth are obvious, as if the dream choreographer is being lenient, trying to make sure I don't miss the point. It intrigues me that the opening through which Ann falls is in the foundation of the kitchen—one of the more nurturing, feminine rooms in the psychic house. For me, the kitchen represents the hearth, a symbolic heart-center. I feel as if the dream is exposing a hole in my heart.

I wonder if dropping to my knees—helpless and grief-stricken—foreshadows the collapse of my old relationship with my daughter. *Ann, Ann, Ann.* In the dream, I shout her name as if Demeter herself has showed up in me at the height of her raging. The dream ends with my confusion, then a hint about what to do: find a flashlight. In other words, find light, a new consciousness—a very unsubtle allusion to Demeter lighting her torch in the myth.

~ ~ ~

Eight years before I had this dream revealing the growing separation between Ann and me, I had an experience that also made a small explosion in my life. And it, too, was about my daughter. One afternoon, I walked into the drugstore where Ann had an after-school job. She was on her knees, stocking toothpaste on a bottom shelf. She was fourteen. As I spotted her, I noticed two men stop beside her. One nudged the other, saying words that fairly pivoted my world: "Now that's how I like to see a woman—on her knees." The other man laughed.

I watched the expression that floated across Ann's face as she looked up. I would describe this moment later as Kafka's "ice axe," which broke a frozen sea inside of me. Ann seemed more than my daughter. She was my mother, my grandmother, and *myself*. She was so many daughters. I confronted the men, trembling with anger. "This is my *daughter* . . . ," I began. They had tapped Demeter's passion.

I only vaguely understood at the time the ways that I myself was on my knees, how in need I was of taking back my soul as a woman. The episode propelled me into a collision with the patriarchal underpinning of my church, my faith tradition, my culture, my marriage, and, most illuminating of all, me. It sent me in search of the feminine dimension of God. It began a spiritual cataclysm. My old life dissolved and a new life, a new consciousness, rose up.

I wrote about that experience in my book *The Dance of the Dissident Daughter*, which had come out in 1996, just a couple of years before the trip. Now, as I slip into the bathroom to wash my face, I think about that juncture of my life, about the book. One particular line from it swims back to me . . . about a certain music that comes from the feminine soul, how the strands of it pulled me unceasingly into awakening.

In the hotel bathroom, I stare at myself in the mirror over the sink, bewildered about why such thoughts are coming to me now. Except—perhaps I'm hearing the music again.

~ ~ ~

I return to Ann's bedside and pull the blanket over her shoulder, tucking it about her like she is six or ten or fourteen. It's a regression to a ritual of mothering I enacted almost every night of her childhood. From the time both of my children were babies until they became teens who stayed up watching David Letterman, the last thing I did before going to bed was to slip into their rooms and observe them asleep on their pillows. Sometimes the moment extended to the tucking of covers, sometimes not. I told myself the visits were a way of checking on them, but in reality they were small benedictions of love—a way to let myself feel for a moment the immensity of what was in my heart, to be intimate with a tenderness that often went missing during the strained, conflicted days of motherhood and writing.

It is possible I've kept company with Demeter more than I've thought. I'd imagined myself traveling more in the orbits of the so-called "virgin" Goddesses like Artemis and Athena, whose forms of the feminine are about the search for an independent self. They are the ones who could bring home the bacon *and* fry it up in the pan. I haven't much pictured myself as a "mother goddess" type. My children have always existed at the deepest center of me, right there in the heart/hearth, but I struggled with the powerful demands of motherhood, chafing sometimes at the way they pulled me away from my separate life, not knowing how to balance them with my unwieldy need for solitude and creative expression. Is it possible I also *valued* motherhood less?

Once in an art gallery, I came upon a painting of the Madonna holding her toddler in one arm and an open book in her opposite hand. Her eyes are turned toward her child as if she has just been torn from her reading. Heavily lidded, they exude a look of sweet adoring, but they also carry a wistful expression, the sigh of interruption, the veiled craving for her book pages. It was like observing a conflict at the hub of my existence. *Baby or book. Children or writing. Motherhood or career.* I bought the painting and hung it prominently in the living room. In secret, I sympathized with the self-actualizing side of the Madonna, feeling her perturbation at the child's demands.

My own post–World War II mother, still alive and well, worked for a time doing secretarial work in my father's business, but she was a consummate Demeterian woman. Growing up, I didn't witness expressions of feminism in her. Indeed, not even in my adulthood. The image she conjured in me was not the Madonna in

Conflict, but *Maria Lactans*, the breast-feeding depiction of Mary contentedly offering her child the milk of her life. I asked her once: "When you were a girl, what did you dream of growing up to be?" She did not hesitate. "A mother," she answered. She had four children, and if there was ever conflict in her mothering, none of us glimpsed it. It seems revealing of my mother and me, and maybe of our generations, that she was the one who got the "Mother of the Year" award, while I got the "Career Woman" plaque.

I'd always adored my mother. I soaked up her plush maternal spirit. Yet I wanted to differentiate myself from her. In the sixties, as I was coming of age, I knew I would be a mother—yes, absolutely. But *differently.*

~ ~ ~

I walk to the hotel window and peer through a slit in the curtain at Syntagma Square directly across the street, then east to the Greek Parliament House where I can just make out the Presidential Guard. Ann informed me earlier that the short, white skirt they wear is called a *foustanella.* I imagine she read that once in a book, probably two years ago. Ann forgets nothing. Her mind clicks like a camera, storing memories and fine details. *Remember when we were at the beach when I was three and you had on a red bathing suit and I almost stepped on a jellyfish?* Hearing such a careful rendering, I stare at her, thinking what red bathing suit, what jellyfish?

A flock of pigeons takes off from a grassy area in the square and, watching them, I think of Ann with everything before her, everything becoming, the white moon perched over her head waxing in grandeur, and it reminds me that my moon will start its long wane any day now. This comparison with its darker implication of enmeshment and envy repels, then humbles me. It is an awful truth.

Noticing my journal on the bed, I sit down and record my dream. As I write the part about dropping to my knees, my thoughts reel back to the museum, to Ann's little dance with her camera, the way she dipped to her knees before snapping the shutter. At the time, it reminded me of something I couldn't call to mind. Was it rustling the memory of Ann on her knees in the drugstore?

Suddenly I understand my dream in a new way. Just as I saw my own self in Ann's kneeling figure in the drugstore aisle, I now see myself in the daughter who has fallen through the hole in the kitchen floor. The dream is about Ann and me, yes, but it's also a snapshot of me on the eve of my fiftieth birthday, bereft over the loss of my younger self. That *other* Persephone in danger of being wrenched away.

To borrow a phrase from Dylan Thomas, Persephone is the "green fuse" in the soul, the regenerative energy. She's the bright, invisible sap within that must rise after fifty. But just how that happens I have no idea.

Without warning, my mother's face blazes up. It crosses my mind that I'm not only Demeter in search of Persephone, but—God help me—I'm Persephone in search of Demeter, too. When *The Dance of the Dissident Daughter* was published, I sent my mother a copy. I didn't hear back from her about it for two months. I had no idea what to make of that. I knew the tumultuous journey I described in the book would seem alien to her. Oddly, that was what concerned me most about writing the book—not so much taking on an entire religious tradition, but the reaction of my mother down in Georgia.

Then a letter arrived. She never wrote me *letters*. Inside, I found her account of reading the book. She told me that my "dance of dissidence and search for self" had proved difficult for her at first, but she had felt its truth. I've committed her last sentences to memory: "I am seventy-five years old," she wrote, "and all I can think is that I want to take care of myself so I can live long. Oh, Sue, I don't want to miss the 'dance.'"

I have to tell myself what is true, that I didn't follow up on that bright opening the way I might have. My relationship with my mother, like the one with my daughter, has no history of fireworks, only the necessary loss and then the loving congeniality. Yet I wish for a deeper connection with her, too.

~ ~ ~

Outside, the heat of Athens dissolves into dusk. It sifts from yellow and gold and parched brown into the colors of the sea. On the other side of the room my daughter naps. Across the world my mother is probably sleeping, too. I sit still on the bed and let the longing fill me.

Ann

———

The Acropolis–Athens

As we climb the path to the top of the Acropolis, my mom stops every five minutes to admire something in the distance—the Temple of Olympian Zeus, the Theater of Dionysus, the Hill of the Muses. She has the guidebook out and a red leather journal tucked under her arm. A pen is wedged between her teeth, so when she asks, "Is that the Hill of the Nymphs," it sounds like "Is that the Will of the Wimps?"

"Yep, the Will of the Wimps," I tell her, and we laugh.

Yesterday when we left the archaeological museum, the heat had been so awful we'd retreated to the hotel and gone to bed. Today is better, but not much. I look toward the crest, trying to judge how long before we get to the top. I'm in no hurry. The thought of being up there again unnerves me.

Seventeen months ago I came to Greece as a twenty-one-year-old history major participating in a college study tour—an experience that changed me. I realize everybody says that, but I promise, something deeply altering happened to me during that trip. It was supposed to be about earning college credit but instead turned into a kind of unraveling of myself. The culmination had taken place on top of the Acropolis in what I still refer to as *my moment* because I don't know what else to call it. I do know that when it happened, it seemed like all the dangling wires of my future came together to throw a spark I thought would last forever. I came down from the Acropolis with a vision for my life, destiny in hand, a big, jubilant fire warming my insides.

Recently, though, all of that had more or less fallen apart. Now, not only have I not explained any of this to my mother, but my feelings around it are so confused and filled with pain, I've been unable to face them myself. At this moment they are stuffed in a small, lightbulb-less closet in the back of my chest. Trudging up the hill with Mom, I wonder how I can be up there again without the door bursting open and everything falling out.

Near the peak, the steps leading up to the Propylea become clogged with people, a huge throng of multicolored fanny packs. We shuffle along, forced to take baby steps. Finally, squeezing through the colonnade, I catch a glimpse of the Parthenon glowing fluorescent in the sunlight, throwing long, symmetrical shadows, and I go a little weak in the knees.

"I think I'll wander around for a while by myself," I tell Mom, not wanting her to see how sad I feel all of a sudden. She gives me a look, so I add, "You know, like it suggests in the guidebook." There's an entire paragraph in it about the "necessity" of a moment alone to let the sight of the Parthenon break over you.

"Sure," she says. "Good idea." She starts to walk away, then stops, turns around. "Are you happy to be back?"

"You must be joking!" I smile at her.

All my life I'd been *the quiet, happy girl*. Now I'm the quiet girl *pretending* to be happy. Every day is an acting class.

Hurrying toward the Parthenon's western pediment, I glance once over my shoulder and see Mom headed in the opposite direction. *Who am I kidding? She's on to me.*

With surprising ease I locate the same slab of marble I sat on when I was last here. Until recently I'd kept a photograph of it on my desk. The marble is long and narrow and tilts slightly upward, reminding me, as it did then, of a surfboard that has just caught a wave.

I sit on it, feeling the coolness hit my bare legs.

~ ~ ~

Right before I left on that college study tour to Greece, my boyfriend of four years, the one I thought I would marry, called and broke up with me. Out of nowhere.

"One day you'll find someone and he'll be the luckiest guy in the world," he told me. I think he intended for this to make me feel better, but come on, the *luckiest guy in the world* and he didn't want to be that guy. So, when I should've been making big Xs on a countdown calendar, buying travel-size shampoo and watching *Shirley Valentine* and *Zorba the Greek*, I sat on the blue sofa in the apartment I shared with my best friend Laura in a state of shocked disbelief—what birds must feel after flying into windowpanes. That was followed by a period of pure heartache. I abandoned mascara and retreated into class lectures, cafeteria gossip, and the absurdly watchable *Days of Our Lives* that played in the student lounge, feeling my life rub against routine, against the lives of other people, but oddly disengaged from it. Laura gave me postbreakup pep talks, attempting to pull me back into the living world.

At the apex of this pathetic state, I called my mom and told her I didn't think I wanted to go to Greece. "Why should I go halfway around the world and be lonely, when I can do that here?" I said with complete irrationality.

I couldn't imagine tromping around Greece with my heart fractured. I didn't mention to her that I barely knew any of the other girls who were going, which felt more than a little scary. I'd made my peace with being an introvert. It only meant that my natural inclination was to draw my "energy" from within instead of seeking it outside of myself, plus my mom was an introvert, and so were a lot of normal people. The problem was I was shy on top of that. And we all know how the world loves a shy introvert. The combination trailed after me like the cloud of dust and grunge that perpetually follows Pigpen around in the *Peanuts* cartoon. The only thing harder than being around forty girls was thinking up what to say to them.

Mom was sympathetic, but told me, "I know this must be hard for you, Ann, but I have a feeling you'll look back and regret not going. Think about it, okay?"

The minute she said this, I knew it was true—I would always regret it if I didn't go. It was so like her to hone in on the truth where I was concerned and then leave it to me to decide. Mom had never been one to offer unsolicited opinions about what I ought to do. Which is why when she did give advice, I tended to listen.

So I went.

Somewhere over the Atlantic, sitting with an entire row of seats to myself in the back of the plane, I watched as a few of the girls in our group started a party with nothing but a bag of jelly beans and a quiz out of *Cosmopolitan* magazine. From that moment, I thought of them as the Fun Girls.

I told myself if I couldn't be a Fun Girl, I could at least be a Diligent Student.

When we boarded the chartered bus to Delphi, our first stop, I settled (again) in a seat to myself, spreading out maps and books and making copious notes as our Greek tour guide, Kristina, lectured. "Delphi is situated on the steep, craggy slope of Mount Parnassus. It was the navel of the world for ancient Greeks, and a pilgrimage site for thousands of years."

Apparently people had flocked here to consult the Delphic

Oracle, a priestess of Apollo who answered everyone's most pressing questions while in a trance, or, as Kristina noted, while probably intoxicated on "fumes."

"Like sniffing glue?" one of the Fun Girls said.

Kristina actually nodded.

Despite the source of the oracle's prescience, she was apparently good at what she did. It was she who told Oedipus he would murder his father and marry his mother, and we all know how that turned out. I decided I would've lined up with the rest of the world to hear what she had to say about my future: *Will anyone ever love me again? Will I ever get over my withdrawn and tentative way of being in the world? What am I supposed to do with a bachelor's degree in history? Better yet, what am I supposed to do with my life?* I didn't have a clue.

We piled out of the bus and followed the Sacred Way that snaked up to the temple of Apollo. It was March; cold, thick vapor drooped over our heads. The entire side of the mountain was strewn with white ruins. I moved among them feeling a little spellbound. Halfway up, it began to snow. The flakes floated through the cypresses out toward the watery blue line of the mountains. I turned 360 degrees trying to take it in, and I could feel something inside of me start to open like a tiny flower. I think that's when I stopped thinking so much about my poor, cracked heart and succumbed to the magic of Greece.

I'd been studying its history, culture, art, architecture, and myths for weeks in classrooms, but now that I was here, those subjects felt alive and vividly present. They brought into sharp focus all the life I had not lived, all the places in the world I had not yet seen, how large it all was. Being here made me feel alive and vividly present, too. There were things, it seemed, that could only happen to me in Greece.

We scrunched down in our jackets as Kristina pointed out where the words KNOW THYSELF were carved prominently into Apollo's temple, and suddenly I had a "palm-slap to the forehead" moment. The inscription must've been the more ulterior meaning of the oracle: to find the answers inside oneself. What if the oracle was a metaphor for a source of knowing within?

As I treaded toward the amphitheater with the group, wondering whether I possessed my own source of self-knowledge, I had a thought which seemed to have originated from just such a place: *I forfeited way too much of myself as a girlfriend.*

I don't know how I knew it to be true—and in fact, to be vital—but I did. Maybe it was because I was far from home, far from my ordinary circumstances, and more or less alone for the first time in my life, feeling like I was on an awkward first date with myself. I'd known who I was with my ex-boyfriend. I'd invested years in the girlfriend role, in the ways of accommodation, being what I thought he wanted me to be, moon to his Jupiter, quietly organizing my psychological orbits around him. But in Greece, I existed in a kind of solitude, and in this quietness I realized I'd lost my self.

In the Amalia Hotel in Delphi, I woke several times during the night, and the truth of this knowing was still there in the darkness. And there was longing there, too. For myself.

The next day, we wandered along a gravel path to a small, circular ruin known as the Tholos. Built as a temple to Athena, its shape was mysterious to archaeologists, who were still guessing what it had been used for. All forty of us reverted to whispers as we moved among its remnants.

One of the papers I'd chosen to write to fulfill the study requirements for the tour was about Athena. I'd become fascinated with her. I'd tended to think of her only as a soldier, but long before she was given a helmet and a spear, she had been a nurturing Goddess of fertility, wisdom, and the arts. I liked both sides of her—the wise nurturer and the fierce warrior. But what I loved most was that she was a virgin Goddess. Her virginity was about much more than the fact that she never married. It symbolized her autonomy, her ability to belong to herself. I'd included a section about this in my paper, unable to see then how I had given too much of myself away.

Standing in a lump of marble fragments, I found a plaque on which the words TEMPLE OF ATHENA were engraved in both Greek and English, and lying on top of it were two yellow wildflowers. Someone had carefully knotted the stems together. *An offering to Athena.* I felt sure of it. Seeing the flowers, I understood that some people still loved and revered Athena. Time moved on. The whole world moved on. Athena, and her potent meaning, had not gone anywhere.

Searching the ground, I picked up one of the millions of pebbles scattered around the site. I turned it over in my hand and began to pray for the things Athena was revered for—wisdom, self-possession, bravery.

I didn't want anyone to notice what I was doing, and thereby become known as the Weird Girl, so I placed the tiny rock by the yellow flowers as inconspicuously as I could. *Don't ever lose yourself again*, I told myself.

A short time later in the Delphi Museum, I stood mesmerized before a bronze statue from the fifth century BCE known as the Charioteer of Delphi, realistic down to his wiry eyelashes. The story goes that while a French team was clearing a village for excavation, an old Greek woman, who'd previously refused to abandon her house, dreamed of a trapped boy calling to her, "Set me free!

Set me free," which finally convinced her to leave. When the archaeologists dug beneath the house, they found the Charioteer.

"Do you think he's seeing anyone?" one of the Fun Girls joked, and I laughed, but I also got her point. He was gorgeous. The white of his eyes appeared alive and his mouth seemed about to break into a smile. Kristina explained that his expression depicted the first seconds after his chariot victory. He was on the cusp of elation and the anticipation of it—set in stone—was eternal. When I walked away from him, from Delphi, from the navel of the earth, I felt his voice rumbling down inside me. *Set me free, set me free.*

A few days later, however, when Kristina summoned all of us to a footrace on the ancient Olympic track in Olympia, all I heard was the racket of my own panicked self-consciousness. The stadium was packed with tourists. *This is so juvenile.* Turning to Dr. Gergel, my faculty advisor, I asked if the race was a requirement. "You'll regret it if you don't," she said, smiling. *Why were people always saying that to me?* I lined up with the others and stared 633 feet to the end. Even with the throng around us, the world seemed to get very quiet. "You are standing exactly where the athletes in ancient times stood; you are breathing in the same space," Kristina called out. When she blew the whistle, I ran with my whole heart. I hadn't run like this since my brother, Bob, and I raced barefoot on the beach in South Carolina. I honestly couldn't believe it when a girl passed me, kicking up dust with her Keds, but by then I had so surprised myself it didn't matter. I was breathing in the same space. The first- through fourth-place winners stood on the four stone pediments where the athletes had once been crowned. I finished in second place.

Kristina placed an olive wreath on each of our heads while the rest of the group sang the American national anthem. Someone took our picture. In it, I am smiling like the Charioteer, a cluster of black olives hanging over my right eye.

Other than a couple of writing contests in my early teens, I had never won anything. Winning second felt as good as finishing first. I didn't know I had it in me. It made me wonder what else I could do that I wasn't aware of. I wore the Nike Air sneakers that had carried me across the finish line everywhere for a long time, and when I finally retired them, I couldn't bring myself to throw them away.

The stirring and surprising events of the trip slowly began to unravel my old self. Strolling beneath the Lion Gate in Mycenae, teetering over a footbridge a thousand feet in the air in Meteora, eating pita and *tzatziki* like chips and salsa—again and again I felt the intensity of being alive, as if my destiny was pooling in around my feet. The experiences I was having seemed to be refashioning me. They were returning me to myself.

"There is a name for what happened to you," Kristina told me at the end of the trip. "It's called the Greek Miracle."

On the last day, in a small shop in the Plaka, the oldest quarter in Athens, I bought a silver ring with Athena's image carved on it, then climbed the hill to the Acropolis, where I found the slab of surfboard-shaped marble near the Parthenon. Sitting on it, I unceremoniously slid the ring onto the finger on my left hand, the one reserved for wedding rings. The ring was about Greece and staying connected to the fire this place lit in me. It was a way to be reminded of Athena's qualities and the potential to find them in myself.

As I lingered there, an awareness that had been growing in me throughout the trip coalesced and I knew what I wanted to do with my life. I decided I would go to graduate school and study ancient Greek history.

On some level this made practical sense—I was a history major and graduate school seemed a smart choice. But it wasn't just pragmatic. I had, by now, been swept off my feet by Greece in every way. When the idea presented itself, I felt a snap of brightness inside. Later it would remind me of the click inside a kaleidoscope when all the tumbling pieces merge suddenly into a pattern of radiance. That was *my moment.*

That same night, three Fun Girls and I walked blocks through the Plaka, searching for a restaurant, but all the tables at the outdoor cafés were occupied. Finally, huddling on the sidewalk, we discussed options. Should we go back to the hotel to eat? I was ready to buy gyro meat on a stick from a walk-up counter, but the Fun Girls insisted we find a sit-down restaurant. "Couldn't we just ask a local?" one of them suggested. She nodded at a tall, dark-haired guy standing behind us. He looked about our age, his hands stuffed in his jacket pockets. "How about him?" she said. They looked at me. Why me?

"Just ask him," she said, and they all piped up in agreement.

He seemed harmless enough. As I walked over to him, it occurred to me he might not even speak English.

"Excuse me," I said.

He pulled his hands out of his pockets and looked at me. He was—how shall I put it?—a breathing Charioteer. "Hello," he said.

"Um, my friends and I were wondering if you could tell us where we might find a place to eat." I pointed to the clump of girls.

He glanced over at them. "I'm Demetri," he said to me with a thick Greek accent.

"Oh, hi. I'm Ann." Then, for some reason, we shook hands like it was a formal occasion.

"I'm waiting on my friend," he said, pointing to a guy on a pay phone. "We're meeting a group for dinner. All of you can join us, if you like. It's not far."

I motioned the girls over.

When his friend hung up the phone, he found Demetri surrounded by four American girls. *Man, what did you do?* his look suggested, and Demetri smiled at him and shrugged.

The restaurant was packed with locals, pulsing with syrtaki music and Greek dancing. It wasn't long after the rest of their friends arrived that the young women in the group began to ask what American "boys" were like, which I left to the others to explain, this being a complex subject for me at the moment. Demetri slid his chair toward mine and asked what I studied at school. "History," I told him. He asked about my family, my life, what I thought of Greece. I discovered he attended the Ikaron School, Greece's Air Force Academy. He had a younger brother. And ever since his parents divorced, his mother worried about him more.

Plates of pastitsio, moussaka, salad, bread, and feta went around the table while we talked, just the two of us, for what seemed like hours. He was intelligent and polite with a quiet, intense way about him. He translated the lyrics of songs the band was playing, most of them about love—losing it or finding it—then held out his hand to me. An invitation to dance.

I looked at the dancers with their arms clamped on one another's shoulders, at the complicated steps they performed, at the tables jammed with people watching and clapping. I felt myself sweating under my gray turtleneck. I'd been blending in fine at the table, a lot like the curtains hanging behind me. The girl who'd run like beach wind around the track in Olympia seemed like another person.

"I'll teach you," Demetri said. His hand still stretched out.

The great dancer Isadora Duncan, who was, coincidentally, deeply influenced by Greek myths, spoke of dance as a manifestation of the soul. I'd been dedicated to invisibility for such a long time that I did not dance, not in public or private. I did not want my soul out there expressing itself. Who knew what it would say?

Demetri leaned down, his mouth close to my ear. "Life is short."

If you don't dance with him, you'll regret it. The line had been used on me so often, now I was using it on myself. Besides, if I was going to live the kind of life I wanted, I would have to be less like the draperies.

I took Demetri's hand and he pulled me onto the dance floor. At some point, bouncing along in the Greek dance line, the thought of my ex-boyfriend popped into my head, accompanied by the dull pang that had followed his rejection. It had not completely gone away. I pictured myself boxing up the photographs of him that lined my desk and dresser back home. I told myself I would be okay.

We kept dancing, song after song, and when the other dancers climbed up on the tables, I was right in the middle of them. Finally, laughing and exhausted, Demetri and I slipped outside into the cool night air. He wrote his address on a piece of paper and handed it to me. I opened my eyes when he kissed me. The Acropolis was lit up just over his shoulder.

After the Fun Girls and I got back to the hotel, I was too excited to go to bed. I persuaded one of them to go up to the rooftop, where we waited for the sun to come up. We watched as light spilled over the city of Athens.

The next night Demetri met me in the lobby of my hotel. We walked for blocks, and when we got back, I was surprised when he gave me a necklace, a simple chain with a blue stone. He'd gone out and bought it earlier that day. To remember him by. We promised to write and said good-bye. The last thing he said to me was, "Ann, learn some Greek."

Once I was back home in South Carolina, Demetri and I exchanged letters. I bought Greek language tapes and listened to them in my Toyota Corolla, practicing phrases like *Pou einai i toualeta?* (Where's the toilet?) The word I loved the most was *kefi*. It means joyous abandonment.

My plans for the future took on weight and detail. I pictured myself with a doctorate, teaching Greek history, writing during sabbaticals, and continuing my studies in Greece, maybe even working there. My parents and friends encouraged me. I applied to the master's program in history at the University of South Carolina, the one affordable place I knew that had a program with an emphasis on the ancient world, including Greece.

~ ~ ~

Two months after my return from Greece, not long before my senior year, I met Scott. I spotted him in a pizza place near campus. A recent graduate of the University of South Carolina, he sat at a table with a group of friends. He looked familiar.

Wearing a maroon Carolina baseball cap, he had a handsome, tanned face, brown hair, and blue eyes that were glued to a golf tournament playing on a television set over the bar. Somebody missed a putt and he groaned. In an act of boldness that was so unlike me I can only attribute it to Greece, I walked up to him.

"I think we went to the same high school," I said.

He stared at me, squinting a little. Clearly, I did not look familiar to him. "I'm Ann. Ann Kidd." I wished I had not said my name like James Bond.

"What was your last name?" he asked.

"K-I-D-D." I readied myself for the questions that always followed: Any relation to Captain Kidd?

No.

Billy the Kid?

But he didn't ask me either of those.

"Any relation to Bob Kidd?" he said.

"He's my brother."

Scott smiled. "Bob and I played Little League together on the
Perk's Car Wash team."

We'd grown up in the same town.

I sat down and we talked baseball. I think it surprised him that
I *could* talk baseball. More so, that I wanted to. I told him I owned
a baseball signed by Hank Aaron and that I'd watched the Braves
play the '95 World Series alone in my dorm room and called—who
else but—Bob when they won.

On our first date we almost went to a Bombers (Columbia's
minor league team) game, but due to extreme hunger, we ended
up at an Italian restaurant called Mangia, Mangia, which roughly
translates as Eat, Eat. We've been dating ever since.

Scott's degree was in sports administration—he was a brilliant
tennis player, a golfer, a surfer, and stored baseball statistics in his
vault of a brain—but his day job was in real estate. He had an
outgoing, affable nature—he could sell ocean water on the beach
if he wanted to—but in private, his warmth and openness was just
as real. I learned quickly that he was a grounded, dependable person I could count on, but he also had an independent way of view-
ing the world—not conforming to conventional ways of thinking,
but making up his own mind. He was both a people person and
his own person—the perfect combination. I loved how much he
cared about his interests and how hard he worked to achieve his

goals and the running stream of wisecracks that always made me laugh. I fell hard for him.

As my relationship with Scott developed, I sometimes thought about the tiny offering I left at Athena's temple in Delphi and the words I told myself: *Don't ever lose yourself again.* And I was vigilant. If I wanted to browse a bookstore or walk the beach instead of watching his tennis match, I did. I realized that not losing myself wasn't only about how we spent time, though; it was about the way I *valued* myself within the relationship. I felt I'd left the accommodating girlfriend role behind. I had only to look at Athena's face on my ring to be reminded to keep it that way.

~ ~ ~

When Mom called and asked if I wanted to go to Greece with her, it was early spring and I was in the thick of my senior midterm exams, my future seemingly locked in place. I'd missed Greece from the moment I'd left. There were times I wondered if I could possibly wait years and years to go back.

"Really? Seriously??" I shouted into the receiver.

Mom said we were going there to celebrate her fiftieth birthday and my graduation. A celebration. No problem.

I called Scott with the news. He showed up an hour later holding a plastic grocery bag. Inside was a jar of Greek Kalamata olives.

Curled up on my sofa a few weeks later, I opened a letter from the University of South Carolina, informing me that I'd been rejected from the graduate program to study ancient Greek history.

At the time I lived alone in a one-bedroom apartment after Laura moved to pursue her studies in Charleston, and I could have wailed if I'd wanted and no one would have heard, but I couldn't muster anything so forceful. Everything drained out of me. I stared at the television, which was not on. I stayed like that for a while, then folded the letter back into its creases. I slipped it into the back of a drawer, covering it with gym socks and underwear. I told no one.

In the weeks that followed, the drawer became a receptacle of so much hurt and disappointment, I couldn't walk past it without my eyes welling up. I fell into what I can only describe as despair. It simply had not occurred to me that I wouldn't be accepted. I had the grade point average, a decent list of extracurricular activities, all the bells and whistles you supposedly need. I probably didn't dazzle anybody with my GRE score, but still, it wasn't *that* bad. I'd figured that, if nothing else, the sheer force of my wanting would get me in.

It took me two days to tell Scott, two days throughout which he kept asking if I was okay.

Finally I just said it. "I didn't get in."

"You didn't get in? You mean, to *graduate school?*" He was shocked and upset. I wished he would just do the water-off-a-duck's-back thing that he was so good at and go back to watching *The X-Files.* He was usually so laid-back, but suddenly he was riled up, determined to peel the lid off my feelings.

"They're crazy," he yelled. "You need to call them."

"And say what?"

"That they made a mistake."

He could not be serious.

"It happens, okay? I'm fine."

But it was not okay and I was not fine, and worse, I feared the school was not crazy, that they knew exactly what they were doing.

I had the benefit of telling Mom over the phone, adding that it was not that big a deal, trying to downplay my embarrassment.

How could she and Dad not interpret the letter the same way I had—as an official pronouncement that I was not academic material, not bright enough, not good enough? Of course, my parents refuted that, but somehow their reassurance made me feel even more ashamed. I decided I did not want to talk about it. Ever.

After I was accepted into the graduate program in history at the College of Charleston, my precautionary "backup" school, I decided to go, not out of desire, but out of duty and desperation. My emphasis would be *American* history. I told myself it was my best and last option.

Once again, I called Mom, this time to tell her I was moving to Charleston. I tried to sound excited about graduate school, then steered the conversation to the news flash that we would be living in the same city.

"What about Scott?" she asked.

"He's moving to Charleston, too. He's already looking for a job."

"Things are pretty serious then."

"They are," I told her, keeping it short and to the point. We'd been together almost a year. We simply did not want to be apart.

It seemed strange that my pain about the rejection letter and my happiness with Scott could exist inside of me at the same time. He observed my sadness, and his willingness to allow my feelings made me care for him more. There was never the unspoken question: aren't I enough to offset those feelings? He seemed to understand they came from another part of me.

Graduation came and went. I found an apartment in Charleston. With three months left before the fall semester started, I spent my mornings slumped in a lawn chair on the beach, skimming the classifieds for a part-time job. Inevitably, I ended up anchoring the newspaper under my chair and staring blankly at the water, wanting to tuck myself away where life could not find me again. I

observed flotsam on the ocean and fantasized about floating off
with it.

What happened should not have thrown me like this, I reasoned. Nevertheless, instead of dissipating, the pain had grown,
solidifying itself around the rejection letter. I'd never been depressed
before and I didn't quite understand what was happening to me. I
told myself a thousand times to get over it, to regroup, but the sadness became intractable, eventually accompanied by anger at the
turn my life had taken. It was odd how abandoned I felt by the
future, by my own self, by the promise of the life I'd discovered in
Greece. I was not proud of any of this, how things had imploded,
the way depression had taken over, how I'd retreated. My world
became an unforgiving place. It scared the daylights out of me.

I feel like a failure, I wrote in my journal. I was twenty-two.

Luckily, I got a job as a part-time assistant to the editor of *Skirt!*,
a local women's magazine, which I gathered would mostly involve
answering the phone and being the all-round gofer girl, a position
I would begin when I returned from Greece. When I left the inter-
view, I stopped in the salon next door and made an appointment
for a haircut. A week later, in what may have been a small act of
grief or a reach for newness, or maybe both, I had my long hair cut
off. When Mom and I left for Greece, I looked like Tinkerbell.

~~~

Now, here in Neverland, sitting beside the Parthenon on the same
slab of marble as before, I spot my mom in the distance. She stands
by the Erechtheion, taking pictures of the sculpted columns of
women on the Porch of the Caryatids. She wrote about the Caryatids in her book *The Dance of the Dissident Daughter*. She described
them as an embodiment of "strong women bearing up." Women
who bear the weight of opposition, she wrote, create a shelter for
the rest of us.

The Dance of the Dissident Daughter was published during my sophomore year in college. When I opened it and saw it was dedicated to me, I read it like a mother's letter to her daughter, sometimes forgetting her story was being read by thousands of other people. At times it seemed beyond weird that we'd lived in the same house during those years—I'd known so little about what she'd struggled with inside. There had been hints—bits of conversation, the piles of feminist theology books that were suddenly in the house, moments when it was apparent some kind of awakening or ripening was going on in her. Mostly, though, I knew her as my mother—the one who stayed up half the night decorating my Raggedy Ann birthday cake, who indulged me by creating the Coke/Pepsi Challenge in the kitchen for Bob and me, who helped me pick out my black cotillion dress, who taught me how to parallel park at the DMV—but when I finished *Dissident Daughter*, I glimpsed her, for the first time, as a woman, like one of those beautiful Caryatids she's standing with now.

Catching my eye, she waves and begins to wind her way toward me through the other tourists. I wonder why I can't tell her what I'm going through. When it came to the letter back home, still in the drawer with my gym socks (why did I keep it, this evidence against myself?), certainly I didn't think she'd reject me. Perhaps the shame of failing is not my only reason for not talking to her about it. We've been close since childhood, but I feel a kind of partition between us now, not anger or aloofness, but a room divider that properly marks the space: this is your territory, this is mine. I did not confide intensely personal matters to her. Are the particulars of your own darkness something you describe to your mother or your best friend?

But it wasn't just the darkness I secreted, was it? Why did I give her only the postcard version of my first trip to Greece? *Ran a race in Olympia, visited Athena's Tholos, saw the Charioteer, sat beside Parthenon, danced in a restaurant with some locals, bought a pretty ring . . . having a great time—wish you were here.* Obviously she knew I'd been affected enough to want to spend my life teaching ancient Greek history, but I'd left her to sense for herself the deeper imprint those experiences had made on me. Maybe it was the particulars of my soul—the experiences, feelings, and inner thoughts I held close—that I kept from her.

As I sit here, I feel the depression closing in.

"Help me," I pray, barely moving my lips.

I suppose I sought out this spot again in the hope I would have a revelation, like before—that lightning would strike twice and I would know what to do with my life. Or, that something inside of me would get completely rearranged and my depression would evaporate.

None of this happens.

The last thing I want is to seem ungrateful or make my mother feel like bringing me here was a mistake. How can I possibly tell her the whole trip feels mournful? And if I do tell her that, how can I possibly expect her to believe the other side of that truth— that there is nowhere else I'd rather be.

"Let me take your picture," Mom says. She focuses the camera. *Click.* I already know I'll put the photo on my dresser and compare it to the one that was taken of me on this spot the year before, the one in which I am grinning with abandon while massive chalky columns beam up behind my head.

I'm afraid of becoming invisible again.

We walk in a dusty loop around the Parthenon toward the Acropolis Museum. There is a sculpture relief inside I want to see called the *Mourning Athena.* In it, Athena holds her spear upright with her head bent against it as if she's mourning. The other name for the relief is *Contemplating Athena*. When I saw the image in a book, though, Athena did not appear to be in deep thought. To me, she appeared to be grieving, like the fight had gone out of her.

The museum, we discover, is closed for renovation. I stare at the notice on the door, twisting the Athena ring on my finger.

"Next time," we joke.

Mom glances at her watch. "Ready to go?"

I nod and suddenly my eyes fill with tears.

"Ann?" Mom says. "What is it? Are you okay?"

"It's—it's just my hair," I say, putting one hand on the back of my bare neck and managing a smile. "I miss it."

Sue

The Cathedral of Athens

꧁ Ann and I wander through the Plaka, threading the convoluted tangle of shops and restaurants. The streets twist and coil, occasionally doubling back on themselves. I realize we're lost the third time we pass the bearded young Orthodox priest in black robes standing outside a jewelry store.

"If we loop by him one more time, he's going to think we're stalking him," Ann says.

I smile. Like her brother, she has always been funny, cracking us up with her wry observations. It's a relief to hear her making a joke. Earlier today on the Acropolis she had been distant and pulled into herself, even tearing up for a moment when we left. As we walked down the path the word *depression* came to me for the first time. Could she be . . . depressed? I pushed the thought away. But now as we move through the narrow, stone streets of the Plaka, the word darts again at the edge of my thoughts. *Depression.*

A corkscrew of alarm twists in my abdomen. I have a ferocious urge to swoop in like a mother hen, gather Ann under my flapping wing, and say, *Look, I'm not oblivious. I'm your mother. Something's wrong. Talk to me. Let me fix it.* But I know my impulse to tear open the closed, secret place in my daughter comes from a need to stave off my own fear. When is the impulse to help an adult child a wise intervention and when is it self-serving and prying? I have an uneasy feeling I will have to carry the question around for a while like some grating pebble in my shoe.

I tell myself Ann is a young woman who needs to find a separate sense of herself in the world, who's trying to stand fully in her own life. Let it be. For now.

As we pause before a shop window, a cluster of shining red baubles catches my eye. No, not baubles—what are they? Leaning closer, squinting into the glare, I realize I'm looking at glass pomegranates. They're piled like ruby eggs into a nest of twigs. "Look," I say.

"They're in a bird's nest," says Ann.

It appears to be a real one. I imagine the shop owner finding the nest on a limb in her garden and thinking: *Oh, perfect for displaying pomegranates!*

I think of Persephone eating the fruit in the underworld. How the flesh splits open to reveal a small, secret womb and the seeds spill out like garnets.

The door to the shop is locked. Closed for lunch. Ann and I cast one last look at the pomegranates and walk on, famished now, ready to find our way out of the maze. After consulting several shopkeepers—one of whom follows us to the door holding a plaster-cast statue of Poseidon, cajoling, "You buy, yes?"—we emerge into a familiar, open square that buzzes with tourists, spared another lap around the priest.

We slip into an outdoor taverna and are barely seated when two scrawny cats appear and stare at us with pleading eyes. They lick their paws like they've sized us up perfectly and are preparing for a banquet. "So what would the cats like us to order?" I ask.

"*Kotopoulo.* Or *psaria*," says Ann, then translates: "Chicken. Or fish."

She has been studying Greek. It began over a year ago after her college trip. She came back full of purpose, with a plan to teach ancient Greek history. You couldn't have missed the new vividness about her, as if being over here had flipped on a light inside of her that no one had quite noticed was off. Before the trip, her own pursuits had seemed overshadowed by her relationship with her boyfriend, a subtle eclipse I noticed only in retrospect. Even Sandy, a professional counselor, didn't have a name for what had happened to her in Greece. "She seems to have 'found herself,'" he remarked. And this "finding" had not faded, not for all this time. Until now.

"Listen to you," I say, trying to appear lighthearted. "You speak Greek."

"Just Greek *food*," she says.

I remember at thirteen she went through the refrigerator and pantry, calling out the contents in Spanish. I remember her then— the perm that didn't work, the braces on her teeth, giggling as she recited *la leche, el pastel*. It shocks me how I wish for all of that again, for what is lost and cannot come back.

We eat roast chicken and Greek salad in silence. Idly, I begin to feed the last of the *kotopoulo* to the cats and instantly a dozen or so other cats materialize out of nowhere. They swarm around our table, mewing, jockeying, possibly multiplying. Waiters rush over, waving trays, snapping crisp, white napkins, and shouting in Greek. Cats hiss and scatter. It's a dazzling eruption that hushes the taverna. Everyone turns. And there we are, Ann and I—stupid, cat-loving, American women—smiling sheepishly, bits of roast chicken sprinkled about our table.

"Check, please," I say.

We slink out, head straight to the nearest bench, and collapse in laughter. We laugh until it's not about the cats anymore. Our laughing takes on a life of its own, making us cry. Every time we think we've composed ourselves, one of us looks at the other, her mouth twitches, and we're gone again.

Gradually, though, we get hold of ourselves, and gazing around the square, I see a large church the color of oatmeal. It has two bell towers, three arched entrances, and one shining, cinnamon-tinted dome. We resort to our guidebooks and discover we're staring at the Mitrópoli, the "Annunciation cathedral."

"It's Athens' largest Greek Orthodox church," Ann says, reading from the book. "'Dedicated to the Annunciation of the Mother of God in 1862 by King Otto and Queen Amalia.' Hey, listen to this—the bones of St. Philothei are in there. She was martyred in 1589 for rescuing women enslaved in Turkish harems."

"Well, the least we can do is go in and pay our respects to somebody who did *that*," I tell her.

~~~

Entering the narthex of the cathedral, I consider the extreme laughing Ann and I have just done, how buoyant I feel, and I see how laughing can become a "narthex" in its own right—a space of divesting. The laughter has cracked the heaviness that formed around us like tight, brittle skin, and even now delivers me peeled and fresh to this moment, to Ann, to myself.

Standing near the entrance, I watch a young woman bend over and kiss an icon of Jesus, leaving a firm, heart-shaped blotch of lipstick on the glass. She licks the back of her thumb and rubs the cherry smudge as if scrubbing ink off a child's face. When it's spit-cleaned to perfection, she drops a coin into a wooden box, lights a candle and drones her prayer, half-whispered, into the bronze light. I have left so much of traditional religion behind, but the scene tugs at me, the whole lovely encounter.

Inside the sanctuary, the air is dusky. A sweet, acrid scent drifts like vapor. I notice the altar screen at the end of the aisle holds a series of icons. From this distance I cannot tell whose images they portray; I can only see the shining swatches of jeweled colors. I'm drawn to them almost magnetically. Ann slips into a pew near the back while I head down the aisle toward the icons.

In recent years my understanding of God had evolved into increasingly remote abstractions. I'd come to think of God in terms like Divine Reality, the Absolute, or the One who holds us in being. I do believe that God is beyond any form and image, but it has grown clear to me that I need an image in order to relate. I need an image in order to carry on an intimate conversation with what is so vast, amorphous, mysterious, and holy that it becomes ungraspable. I mean, really, how do you become intimate with Divine Reality? Or the Absolute?

Maybe in the end, the big thing we call God can only be experienced in concrete particulars, not unlike William Blake's vision of the whole world in a grain of sand.

Was there an image—a mere grain of sand—that could be a symbol for me of this ineffable, divine presence? What amazes me, what makes me almost break down and cry in the aisle of the cathedral, is how much I hunger for this.

I think suddenly about a crude little icon of Mary that a stranger gave to me several months before. I was sitting in a bookstore in Atlanta signing copies of *Dissident Daughter* when an Episcopal priest introduced himself with a shy, reluctant look, like a boy delivering a note to his mother about his behavior in school.

"I imagine this will sound peculiar," he said, "but many years ago, a Greek woman gave me this icon from her home on the

island of Tinos. She said she'd gotten the overwhelming sense she
was supposed to give it to me, and one day I would meet someone
and get the same feeling. When I saw you, that's what happened.
I actually drove back home to get it."

"Me?" I looked at him, startled and wary.

He set the icon on the table in front of me. It was a rectangular
piece of wood no more than two by three inches with a tin figure
of Mary hammered onto it.

His story seemed bizarre, but I thanked him. I sensed he was a
forward-thinking man who loved life's mysteries and tried to follow his nudges even when it made him uncomfortable.

Later, while searching for information about icons on Tinos, I
found a peculiar story about a nun named Pelagia who had dreams
in which the Virgin Mary begged for her icon to be dug up from
a certain uncultivated field on the island. When the excavation was
carried out, an ancient icon of Our Lady of the Annunciation was
discovered. Numerous stories like this exist in Greece, where Mary
has a habit of coming up from the underworld like Persephone,
pushing her way into consciousness. I had no idea what to make
of the mystifying way my Tinos icon came to me. I wondered if it
was a replica of the icon Pelagia dreamed about. Nevertheless, I
slipped it into the bottom drawer of my bedside table and forgot
about it.

Am I thinking about the icon now because I'm in Greece where
it originated? Or perhaps it's something deeper. Perhaps I feel compelled finally to try and understand the strange experience in the
only way such things can be understood—as metaphor, as life
speaking in parables. If so, what do I do with the idea that the
Mary presented to me might be the same one who pleaded for her
image to be dug up from an uncultivated field or at the very least
that my icon came from the same island as the excavated Mary?

Was I being prodded to dig up Mary from a neglected place in myself?

I walk to the icon screen, straight to her image.

In Greece, she is known as the *Panagia*, the Virgin. Her skin is dark, the color of almonds, though considering how often she rises out of the depths, you have to wonder if it's the darkness of the earth she wears on her skin. She gazes out from the icon with uncompromising authority, her eyes alert and undaunted. The look of her resurrects Margaret Atwood's novel *Cat's Eye* that I read just before we left home. Atwood has her character, an artist, paint Mary with the head of a lioness while envisioning a gnawed bone at her feet. The peculiar vision, so different from the typical Mary with downturned eyes, dipped chin, and tentative demeanor, stuck in my head for days.

Is it just me, or are there traces of the fierce, untamed Mary in the *Panagia* in the cathedral icon? I stare at her so long I see motes of dust floating in the air—dark gold, pulsing crumbs. I sit down in the closest pew. I don't know how I feel about this. Parts of me don't want it to be Mary—the feminist part, the theologically correct part, the pragmatic, demythologized, leached-of-mystery part, the teeny part where the old Protestant tapes groan "Mary, just a woman, just a woman. . . ." I feel like I'm suddenly going in the wrong direction on a one-way street. Everybody knows you don't go this way. Who makes Mary an icon of devotion these days? How could she possibly be suited to twenty-first-century feminine experience?

But I can't let it go.

It has been easy to admit to myself recently that I need some new aspect within my spirituality, one that could take me into the next phase of my life. Uncovering this need has been like finding an empty room in the center of my house, one I didn't know was there, one I couldn't pass without feeling its vacuity and wondering how it should be filled. I know I came to Greece in part to try and fill this vacancy in myself. I just didn't think it would have anything to do with Mary.

Leading up to the appearance of the Tinos icon in my life, my history with Mary was relatively short, a series of unexamined stories. I have a sudden, overpowering need to remember, to rough them out on paper. Twisting around in the pew, I locate Ann still in the back, her nose buried in a guidebook. I pull out my red notebook and a pen.

~ ~ ~

Growing up Baptist in a small town in Georgia, I was virtually unaware of Mary except at Christmas, when she turned up life-sized in the outdoor nativity scene beside the church, wearing a sky-blue scarf and kneeling over the manger. When the nativity caught on fire one year, our minister dashed in to save baby Jesus and left his mother behind, a story that was retold at the dinner table for years. That sums up how expendable the Baptist Mary was. I, too, acquired the habit of slighting her. Of leaving her behind.

I took no notice of her until my late thirties. It was not a cheerful meeting. I came upon a drawing in which Mary's hands were amputated—a reference to the fairy tale "The Handless Maiden," about a docile daughter whose father asks for her hands. This got my attention. It caused me to contemplate how Mary and sacred feminine images in general had become wounded, diminished, and sacrificed. Why was Mary so often portrayed as an obedient and submissive "handmaid of the Lord," all her power sublimated to the male aspects of the deity? I was put off by the meek and mild look. I wanted to shake her.

My next brush with Mary went better. It came around age forty when I noticed a print of Leonardo da Vinci's cartoon sketch, *The Virgin and Child with St. Anne and St. John the Baptist* hanging in Mercy Center in Burlingame, California. As I gazed at the Madonna and her child both sitting in her mother Anne's lap, a tuning fork went off in my chest. Admittedly, I was struck mostly by Mary's mother, Anne—by her great, extravagant lap and her burning, unapologetic gaze. She looked for all the world like the Great Mother who births, contains, and encompasses everything, even the male savior. That was probably the first time I grasped that the image of a female could be a symbol of the divine. And Mary was her mother's daughter. I amended my opinion of her, coming to understand that she'd inherited the role of the ancient Goddesses, however sublimated their earthiness, grit, and author-ity had become in her. The human soul needs a divine mother, a feminine aspect to balance out the masculinity of God, and yes, Mary had carried it off the best she could.

A year or so later, I had a dream which would become strangely prophetic. I wrote it down but didn't explore it at the time except for a chalk drawing I made on black paper, then rolled up and deposited in the back of my closet, where it remained like a lump of dark leavening. In the dream I'm riding on a train. It slows down as it passes through a quarantined slum area, and looking out the window, I see a rundown house where a black woman in a red African scarf weeps on the porch. She seems bereft. I turn to the other passengers: "Look! Do you see her?" No one does. As the train rumbles by, she fixes her eyes on me—a riveting, heart-stopping look—and in a flash I realize: this is Mary! I beat on the train window and shout over and over, "I will come back for you."

The next time I met her was a year later in the Tate in London.

Coming upon Rossetti's annunciation painting *Ecce Ancilla Domini!,* I stared at the angel, tall and oddly wingless, standing beside the Virgin Mary's bed with tendrils of fire licking around his feet. He thrusts out a long white lily and announces to Mary that she will give birth to a divine child. Mary appears startled out of sleep, startled out of her wits, in fact. Wearing a white night shift, her auburn hair tumbling around her, she shrinks against her pillow in terror.

I gazed at the painting for twenty minutes, stirred by it, as if I, too, were being shaken awake to some mysterious knowledge I couldn't take in. The painting triggered a longing in me that was maternal and aching. It struck a raw nerve inside that had to do with unfulfilled creative desires, conjuring up my dormant and unacknowledged wish to write fiction.

Many years before this, when I first set out to be a writer, I had entertained a dream of writing fiction, then quickly banished it—I thought forever. In the museum that day, I realized the aspiration had never really left, it had merely gone underground to wait its turn. The dream had been turning up recently dressed as whimsy, hope, impulse, and silly conceit. I'd refused to take it seriously. It felt beyond my power and courage, the sort of thing that made me shrink against my pillow late at night.

As I stood before the Rossetti painting, however, my desire to write fiction crystallized into a pursuit that I saw as authentic, necessary, and even sacred. I now understood that writing fiction was a seed implanted in my soul, though I would not be ready to grow that seed for a long time.

What had happened, of course, was that Mary's annunciation became a metaphor for my own creative potential. It became a means to confess the truth to myself, to understand and interpret this quiescent potential in a way that would begin to bring it to life.

I didn't bump into Mary again until an October afternoon in 1993 during my first pilgrimage to Greece. After traveling for several days with a group of women on Crete, we stopped at Palianis Nunnery, a tiny, walled-away place so ancient its name comes from the word *palaia*, which means old. Supposedly it goes all the way back to the first Byzantine period.

When I stepped through the gate, I had the sensation of time slowing. A whitewashed church sat in a courtyard filled with fuchsia oleander, red hibiscus, date palms, lime trees, and terra-cotta jars overflowing with feathery orange flowers. Several nuns sat outside their apartments making what appeared to be lace. The serenity was narcotic. "Greek Eden," someone in the group said, and sure enough, behind the church, we found the Tree of Life. It was an immense myrtle sacred to the nuns, purportedly a thousand years old. It held itself in an elaborate yoga posture, its serpentine limbs bent into mind-boggling contortions. I noticed crutches piled near the trunk, with a back brace and other orthopedic apparatuses that looked like they, too, might go back to the first Byzantine period. Rosaries were tied to the branches next to hundreds of tin votive offerings or *tamata*, hanging like drooping garlands. Ribbons, cards, jewelry—even wedding rings—dangled from the limbs. No one spoke—all of us a little dumbstruck by the sight of a massive, old tree decorated with so many inventive prayers.

Catching the smell of beeswax candles, I wandered around the tree to find tapers burning in a metallic shrine box. That's when I saw the huge, glass-plated icon perched in the branches. *Panagia Myrtidiotisa*, the Virgin of the Myrtle.

Her legend holds its own among the most lavish Greek stories of miraculous, walking, talking icons. It's said that after the Turks destroyed the convent in 1821, the surviving nuns heard a voice calling from the tree and discovered the Virgin of the Myrtle. They carried the icon into the church, but that night she escaped back to the tree, where they found her the next morning wedged happily in the branches like a tomboy returned to her true element. This went on and on. Eventually the nuns gave up and left her out there.

A short, black-clad nun found us staring at the icon. She greeted us in labored English. "You ask her for the thing at the bottom of your heart, yes? The Virgin will give it. Then you give to her something."

As I studied the dark-skinned Madonna, her face as brown as the tree bark, her headdress bright red, I had a flash of the Mary in my dream with her red scarf and dark skin. Even the thick glass covering the icon reminded me of the train window. In the spirit of pilgrimage, we all decided to ask the Virgin of the Myrtle for what lay discarded at the bottom of the heart, the thing half-known and half-allowed. When I stepped beneath the limbs into green, phosphorescent light and tingling *tamata*, I was unsure what I would pray for.

To my surprise I blurted: "I would like to become a novelist."

~ ~ ~

Hunched over my journal in the wan light of the cathedral, I look over the experiences with Mary that I've collected—the motif of leaving her behind; the recognition she could be larger than the human Mary, unconfined by religion and imbued with meanings that have long been associated with the ancient Goddess; how she showed up as a dark, feminine divinity, a Black Madonna; and finally, the way she was connected to my desire to write fiction.

I will come back for you.

Mary crying in my dream, living impoverished and quarantined in my soul, reminds me suddenly of Mary in the Tinos icon, begging to be dug up from the uncultivated field. I can't deny the inner behest in all this. It seems more than possible that the piece I'm missing in my spiritual life is a single image of devotion. Is Mary my "grain of sand"?

If I penetrate to the center of Mary's image, perhaps I will find a new center of myself. Isn't that what iconic images are meant to do—bring us into encounters with our own deep selves? My heart and my gut tell me that the night-skinned, fierce-eyed, tree-loving Mary will help lead me to the inner sanctum of the Old Woman, that she has something to do with my rebirth as an older woman. I can't explain this to myself. I only feel in intuitive, indeterminate ways that she will have a part in whatever renaissance might lie in my aging, perhaps opening me to the deeper, more primal layers of creativity I yearn for, and at the same time, taking me down to an irreducible essence, all the way to the severity of my own dying. Down to the gnawed bone.

Light sweeps across the slits of windows in the dome of the cathedral, sparking the air with bits of coppery brightness, and I look up for a moment and feel the spaciousness of wonder. And then a kind of guilt. How long have I been sitting here? An hour? Where is Ann? As I jump up, I see her walking toward me. "Did you see the bones?" she says.

I must have looked at her quizzically.

"St. Philothei's bones."

"Oh." I shake my head.

"They're over there," she tells me and points to a silver reliquary on the altar.

We stand beside it and stare at the bones. We stand with our shoulders touching, without saying anything, and I can think of nothing now but Ann.

I have one of those stabbing, crystalline moments when it's as if I'm outside of myself, observing. I see myself almost fifty and my daughter unrecognizably grown, and I wonder: *How did this happen? Where did all the time go? Where did* we *go—those other selves?* Then the moment passes and I'm back, staring again at the bones, these tiny sticks of enduring.

Ann

Restaurant–Athens

❧ The hotel concierge recommends a restaurant in the Plaka. He writes the name on a piece of paper bearing a watermark of the Grande Bretagne and tears it off the tablet.

"We need good directions," I tell him. "We've been lost in the Plaka once today."

"All the streets there look alike," he says and pulls a map from behind the desk. Using a yellow highlighter, he draws a spiraling path from our hotel to the restaurant.

"The yellow brick road," I say. For no apparent reason.

"The road isn't brick," he explains.

Mom smiles.

"Right," I say, deciding to stop while I'm not ahead.

"There is music and dancing," he informs us as he marks the destination with a big star.

"Oz," Mom says.

I give her a look that says *very funny*, as the concierge hands her the map. Everything on her face—mouth, eyes, eyebrows, especially her eyebrows—turns up as she looks at it, and I know she's thinking this is a great way to spend the evening: music and dancing, a real Greek experience. She's right; it's a tradition that goes back centuries and there's nothing more Greek than dancing—but I feel the wary beginnings of a stomachache.

We follow the swath of yellow on the map until Mom stops suddenly on the sidewalk. I'm already a few paces ahead of her when I hear her say, "Look, this is the same store. And it's open." When I turn back, she's pointing into the window at glass pomegranates in a bird's nest. We'd passed by them earlier today, but the shop was closed.

The place sells just about everything: key chains, worry beads, Byzantine icons, Zeus beach towels, miniature statues of the Olympian family members. Mom goes over to the nest and plucks out a pomegranate. It has an eye on top to slip a chain through. On the bottom, the glass is fluted out like the knotted end of a tiny red balloon.

I learned about Persephone and the pomegranate reading Edith Hamilton's *Mythology* in middle school. As I recall, it boiled down to three things: Persephone ate the pomegranate seeds that Hades offered her in the underworld; this guaranteed she and her mother would be separated a third of every year; and that was how winter came into the world.

"I'm going to buy a pomegranate for each of us," Mom announces.

"Thanks," I say, but frankly I'm wondering, *why pomegranates?*

At the register, Mom fingers through the colorful bills in her wallet—cream, aqua, and orange. Our new charms cost 1900 drachmas, about seven or eight American dollars. I pull out several hundred-drachma bills, but Mom tells me to save my money for something else. As I slide the money back, I notice the lavender-tinted Athena on one of the bills, wearing her plumed helmet. In Greece, she is everywhere. At home, with the exception of my left ring finger, she is nowhere to be found.

I dreamed about her once. She emerged from a dark nowhere, a distant black hole in the universe, growing bigger and closer until she was right beside me. She wore a robe that was lit with actual stars from the cosmos. "You can see me anytime you want," she said. "All you have to do is dream." Then she was gone. It was one part divine, one part Everly Brothers. That was over a year ago; I hadn't been able to conjure her again.

I've been reading about her, though. I think for a moment about her unusual birth story, how she emerged fully grown from her father Zeus's head. It's interpreted as having cut Athena off from her feminine roots. She's described as a "father's daughter" who portrays masculine traits. But I think of Athena's qualities of bravery and autonomy, even her warrior energy, as inherently feminine, right along with her wisdom and creativity. I always return to the idea of her virginity, how it symbolizes self-belonging. I believe the possibility of that exists in a woman. It's the territory I keep trying to define for myself.

I wander through the shop, inspecting the T-shirts displayed on the wall, thinking I'll buy one for Scott. I try to picture what he's doing right now. Probably tracking tropical storms, looking for the beach with the best surfing. He has promised to teach me to surf one day. Scott has a way of pulling me into the *Wide World of Sports* . . . and maybe into the wide world itself.

I spot a T-shirt with Aphrodite laid out like a fish on ice, completely naked. "Why not just put some bunny ears on her?" I say to my mom, who looks at the shirt and rolls her eyes. I pick a blue one with HELLAS printed in white letters.

As the clerk rings it up, Mom hands me a small plastic bag with my pomegranate inside. I watch as she takes off the silver chain around her neck and slips her pomegranate onto it. Her chain already has a bee charm on it. I'm not sure what the bee is about, but it's not unusual for my mother to find inspiration in nature. At the moment, I'm not wearing a necklace so I slip my pomegranate inside my shoulder bag along with Scott's shirt.

A block later, we stop again so I can sign a petition requesting that the British Museum return the Elgin Marbles to Greece. I write my name and where I live into the thickly bound book sitting on a wooden stand on the sidewalk, then glance at the addresses of the other names recorded on the page: Frankfurt, Barcelona, Houston. Now, Charleston. I love the place, but I walk the rest of the way trying not to think about how I ended up there.

I spot a body shop with rolling garage doors, then across the street, a restaurant. Mom points at it. "That's the one."

"I don't believe it. I've been to that restaurant before!"

"No kidding," Mom says, sounding surprised.

How is it possible that in a city the size of Athens we've come to the very restaurant I ate in when I was here before? It's so unlikely it feels almost purposeful, and for a few seconds I have the feeling I will walk inside and bump into the ghost of myself seventeen months ago—the girl who came to Greece and figured out how to belong to herself and feel at home in the world. The doorway is low. Mom and I duck our heads as we slip into a waiting area the size of a walk-in closet. *Yes, the same place.*

"Is this where you danced with . . . what's his name?" Mom says.

"Demetri." I'm slightly embarrassed that she's brought him up. "I met him somewhere else," I explain. "*This* is where Dr. Gergel brought a few of us on the first night we were in Athens."

I'd told Mom about Demetri before we left home. I had to—in the last letters that Demetri and I exchanged, we had arranged to meet during the trip. The plan is for him to call me tomorrow afternoon at the hotel and for us to go back to the place we met. The name of that place is about the only detail from my first trip that I can't remember. It's not like me to forget, and it drives me crazy because that was one of the happiest nights of my life.

"Maybe we'll dance again," Demetri had written. Maybe we will, but it won't be in the same way. We may have started with a romance, but now there is Scott. Through our letters, through time and distance, Demetri and I are developing a friendship. That is all our relationship can ever be.

I keep indulging in the hope that being in Greece, and only that, will solve everything for me. Even when I woke this morning, before I opened my eyes, I lay in bed luxuriating in that particular fantasy. *I'm going to walk out of the hotel lobby onto the sidewalks of Athens and that alone is going to make me happy.*

There's relief in moments like those, but when they're gone I always return to my New Normal—a state of semiterror at the thought of failing, looking stupid, getting hurt, or being rejected. For me, normality has become the act of retreat, of being afraid the world will find me and slip like smoke beneath the door. All of which fills me with sadness that I'm missing out on my own life. I know girls from my graduating class who are starting new jobs, MBA programs, law school; girls with five-year plans; girls who want to take on the world. Post–rejection letter, I've preferred hiding in plain view, like one of those insects camouflaged as a stick.

A man greets us, holding an armful of menus. *"Yassas, kalispera!"*

His name, Yiannis, is embroidered in red thread on the front pocket of his shirt. We follow him into the dining room where a band is playing "Lara's Theme" from *Doctor Zhivago.* It is just as

I remember: The stage with the oversized painting of the Parthenon hanging behind it. Long, narrow tables, plates of cucumber, tomato, feta, bowls of *tzatziki*, platters of chicken souvlaki, moussaka, shish kebabs, black olives. Wine the color of dark cherries. Pastry drowned in honey. I have lost all direction for my life, but I have not lost my appetite.

Yiannis leads us to two seats directly in front of the stage, then hops up to the microphone to introduce the next performer. A heavyset woman wearing a blue sequined gown with tassels on her shoulders walks into the spotlight and sings a song that seems to be about losing someone and hoping he'll come back.

She is followed by a belly dancer with a sword. Her outfit is a shimmery bra and a sheer purple skirt that falls to her ankles with slits cut to her hips. Her spine is an octopus tentacle. When she balances the sword on a spot above her belly button, I think to myself, *I could never be this woman.* Finally, the room explodes with lively Greek music. Everyone claps. Some stomp their feet. Men shout and let out long, curling whistles. Women roll their shoulders and snap their fingers over their heads.

Our food arrives just after the band takes a break. Mom and I have barely spoken, but I really think it's because the party has been so loud. I stab a piece of the pork souvlaki on her plate and she spoons *tzatziki* from mine. "You can't have too much of this," she says, spreading the yogurt sauce onto a piece of pita, and in this uncomplicated exchange I think I might tell her everything.

I want to say: Did you know that Dr. Gergel asked me if I wanted her to find out why my application to graduate school was turned down and that I said *no*? I don't want to know the reasons because the reasons are my defects. And did you know she suggested I reapply? But how do you go through getting turned down

by the same school twice? There are other ancient history programs out there, but I haven't looked into them. What are the odds
of another program accepting me if the first one didn't? It's as if
the rejection letter has uncovered a terrible truth about myself that
I didn't know, don't want to know.

I glance at my mother unable to form any of this into words.

I haven't done the things Dr. Gergel suggested because I'm
afraid—okay, I gave up. I tell myself that studying ancient Greek
history in graduate school is my road-not-taken thing, so get over
it. But there have been times lately when I've asked myself: *Is a
person meant to do only one thing in this life? What if I leapt at that
road too fast? Should my love of Greece translate into a career? And
if not, what do I do with that love?* I don't know where this devil's
advocate voice comes from or why I wonder about these things
when I still feel so attached to the dream.

Mom reaches for the carafe of water, fills her glass and then
mine. And another thing, I want to tell her, it was a big mistake
for me to enroll in graduate school in American history, but I didn't
know what else to do, and I had to do something.

I don't say any of that either.

There's nothing in our history to make me believe my mother
would respond to me as if I were a disappointment. She didn't do
it when I was ten and quit piano. And not when I forfeited a full
college scholarship my freshman year to transfer to the school I'd
really wanted to go to all along. My heart starts to jog the second
I think about the school switch.

I had been miserable that first semester of college, but I'd stifled
that, too. For four months. How do you tell your parents you want
to give up a four-year academic scholarship worth a zillion dollars
in pursuit of your own unreasoned happiness? At the end of

Christmas break, Mom found me sitting on my bed next to my open suitcase, crying. That's when I finally told her, explaining the obvious—that what I wanted was selfish and insensible. She surprised me by saying the sensible thing would be listening to my heart. Within two weeks I was enrolled at Columbia College, the school I had wanted to attend.

This was so like my mother. She had a generous spirit, but it wasn't only that. It was the respect she had for feelings, how she believed it was inimical to the soul to deny them. I've watched her follow her own heart countless times in her life, most recently when she convinced Dad they should leave their home of twenty-two years and move to Charleston. I feel a little cheated out of that gene.

I turn and look at her, wondering what I'm so afraid of now. "What?" she says. "What is it?"

The music kicks up again and I shake my head. "Nothing," I mouth.

Six dancers—three men and three women—move across the stage, holding hands and forming a circle. The men wear *foustanellas* with white wool tights underneath, sashes, vests, and red clogs with big black pom-poms on the toes. They take turns leaping into the air from a crouching position, kicking one leg and slapping their ankles. Each time, the crowd shouts, "Hey!"

This is the men's show.

Suddenly the dancers fan out into the dining room. My stomachache returns. I know what is about to happen—*audience participation.*

One of the female dancers pulls a man, who looks about seventy-five, out of his chair onto the stage. He makes a small show of resisting, then throws up his hands in a what-the-hell gesture.

Everyone laughs. The troupe pulls others from their seats—a teen-age girl, a forty-something man. I hold my camera up to my face and stare at the scene through the tiny glass square. Then the square goes black. I lower the camera to find one of the dancers leaning over me, holding out his hand. He is asking me to join the others.

It's as if my fear of this very thing has turned on me and sum-moned him over. His face is sweating. He smiles at me.

I can't move. I want to want to.

I shake my head. "No."

He looks at me like no one has ever turned him down before.

It's not you, it's me, I want to tell him.

He moves on to another girl with long brown hair. I pick up my camera. Through the lens I watch this girl take his hand and fol-low him to the stage. She studies the dancers' feet, stepping left when she should go right, laughing at herself. I think maybe she is the ghost of me seventeen months ago, that she's here after all. But, sadly, I don't think I could be this woman either.

God, I'm draperies again.

"You didn't want to dance with him?" Mom asks. Her tone matches the expression I saw on his face. It has a slight "that's too bad" ring to it. I taste the tanginess of pennies and realize I've bit-ten the inside of my cheek. It is actually bleeding a little.

"Not really," I say, shrugging it off.

I can tell she's worked up about me. I'm worried she might ask me what's wrong and I'll have to lie, or worse, tell her the truth.

When the dance ends, I muster all the energy I have just to clap my hands.

We take a taxi back to the hotel. In the backseat I can see the Acropolis lit up, the Parthenon floating at the top. I reach inside my bag for the room key and feel the small lump of the glass pome-granate.

The Parthenon slips out of view and I'm left staring at my reflection in the window. I look like a girl, once wild, who's been utterly tamed.

Sue

Sanctuary of Demeter–Eleusis

⥺ Last night, we ended up at a restaurant that Ann had gone to on her first trip to Greece, a considerable coincidence that seemed to excite her at first, but as the evening wore on and the Greek dancing grew more delirious, I could feel her retreating to some unreachable place. I had the impression it had to do with her being in the same restaurant again, with the overlap of then and now, but I could make no sense of that.

She remained quiet all the way back to the hotel, staring through the car window seemingly at nothing. "You okay?" I asked, hoping I did not sound like a broken record.

"Just tired," she said.

Now, this morning, she stands on the sidewalk outside the hotel with guidebooks and camera, appearing refreshed and eager, but something is off. I feel it.

Our taxi pulls up at 10:15—the same white Mercedes that rescued us from the heat a couple of days earlier. I read the driver's name on the card I'd saved. Alexander. From the moment I stumbled into the myth of Demeter and Persephone in the museum, I knew we would have to make this trip, but when I tell him we want to go to Elefsina, the modern-day name for Eleusis, he balks.

"I can take you anywhere in Athens," he tells us. "Olympic

stadium, the Agora, the statue of Harry Truman. We will go up the Hill of the Muses. You can see everything from there."

"But we really want to go to Elefsina," I say.

He is not impressed with our sightseeing skills. From the driver's seat, he twists around to face us. "It is twenty kilometers. There is nothing much to see."

"But there's the Sanctuary of Demeter. And the museum—"

He shakes his head and turns to stare over the steering wheel, as if waiting for us to remove ourselves.

It occurs to me *no* taxi will take us there, that we will not get to Eleusis at all. I offer Alexander more money. He politely refuses. As Ann and I open the doors to climb out of the car, he watches us in the rearview mirror, noticing the newly bought pendants that dangle from chains around our necks.

"You are wearing pomegranates," he says abruptly. "You are mother and daughter?" I pause halfway out the door. "Yes," I tell him. "Mother and daughter."

"Demeter and Persephone. All right, then." He motions us back inside and starts the car.

We drive northwest out of Athens into a yellow-gray haze. Elefsina/Eleusis is wreathed with ugly industrial slums, cement factories coughing up white, phlegmlike smoke. The sky droops with pollution. Ann reads from one of a half-dozen guidebooks that we have lugged across the Atlantic Ocean, while I stare through the window at the sun being swallowed into grainy clouds, disintegrating into pinpoints.

The Demeter-Persephone myth had been enacted at Eleusis annually for around eighteen hundred years. Thousands of initiates came from around the Panhellenic world to go through secret rites of death and rebirth known as the Eleusinian Mysteries.

These involved a symbolic going down into the underworld, called the *kathodos*, and a rising up to new life, known as the *anados*. Eleusis had been one of the greatest religious centers in all antiquity, and at the heart of it was not a divine father and son, but a divine mother and daughter. *How extraordinary is that*, I thought when the notion of visiting Eleusis popped up. What I did not consider, not even when I woke from the dream of Ann falling through the cavity in the kitchen floor, was that traveling here would evoke my own version of *kathodos* and *anados*. I lean my head back on the seat and close my eyes.

Ann conveys a stray piece of information from the book. "The earliest of the ruins go back to the fifteenth century BC. That's," she computes in her head, "*more than three thousand years.*" A couple of miles later, she says, "Did you know that everyone who went through the Mysteries at Eleusis experienced a secret that made them no longer afraid of dying?"

The air is brighter once we reach Eleusis, some of the Attic blueness of Greece breaking through the foul crust. As I step from the car, I drop my unzipped bag in the street and out rolls the big red pomegranate that had been on the breakfast buffet at the hotel, part of the decorative centerpiece. To Ann's embarrassment, I had convinced the server to wrest it from the display and give it to me. Alexander stares at it lying beside the car tire.

Ann's look says *UN-believable.*

I grab the fruit and stuff it back into my floppy purse.

"I'll wait for you," Alexander tells us. "You cannot get a taxi back to Athens from here on Sunday. How long do you need? One hour?"

"Three," I say.

"Two," he tells me firmly, and I don't argue.

~ ~ ~

I am floored by the vastness of the ruins. They are strewn across the slope of a hill which is hedged by the Bay of Eleusis on one side and mountains on the other three. It's as if there has been a volcanic eruption of stone and marble—toppled columns and rooftops, remnants of temple walls, chunks of altars and statues. Ann and I clutch the brochures and maps we picked up at the gate and stare into the morass of sacred debris. An abandoned mother-daughter continent. We are the only ones here.

I chatter to Ann as we wade into the remains, postulating about the style of the columns—Doric? Ionic?—pointing out engravings of eggs, flowers, and Demeter's wheat, trying hard to be an animated tourist. But almost immediately we come upon a well from the sixth century BCE—now called the Kallichoron Well—and I stop, plunged back into the myth—Demeter scouring the earth for her lost daughter and coming to Eleusis, where she plops down beside a well and mourns for Persephone. Something is over for her, really over.

The well is encircled with flat stones, cut in the shape of petals, giving it the appearance of an age-pitted flower. We walk around it, peering inside. It is empty except for a few tattered spiderwebs. Once, long ago, it was called the Well of the Beautiful Dances. Initiates gathered around it to commemorate Demeter's grief, dancing in solemn circles. The guidebook suggests you can see the path of their dance worn into the courtyard pavement. Ann makes an earnest search, but cannot find it.

"Do you see it?" she says.

I shake my head and sit down, feeling heavy, like one of the ponderous, blue-gray Eleusinian stones, coming to rest in a dark gravity I cannot reverse. I pull out my journal, and Ann drifts off with her camera.

Our aloneness in the ruins engulfs me. Quietness rises. The ringing of a church bell. Wind slapping the chain on a distant flagpole. What is the conversation that needs to go on inside of a woman at this juncture in her life? Is it really the one about relinquishment, grief, and return? I look around, and for a moment I think I will forget all of this. Just be a tourist again. But sitting in the compost of this demised world, I know I'm here to enter that very conversation. To face irrevocable truths and grieve a little . . . or perhaps a lot. Then start to let go.

Something is over.

I watch Ann in the distance as she moves toward the Plutonian, a large, cavernous rock that represents the spot where Persephone disappeared into the underworld. Now and then as she walks, she turns and watches me back. Once I see her lift her camera and take a photograph of me, unaware she is capturing a surrender, a caving-in of my heart. I sit in the passing of our old relationship, the one in which she was the little girl and I was the grown-up mother, and I try to finish what I never did when she left home for college—letting her go into her own life. And my daughter unwittingly preserves it.

In what seems like a cruel trick of timing, women often find themselves letting go of their daughters around the same time they must let go of their identities as younger women. I am clearly in the vestibule of menopause, otherwise known as perimenopause—a strange foyer where you find yourself waiting around to be ushered into the real room, the final room. In the beginning, I spent a fair amount of time telling myself I didn't belong in there. Then the small jolts of truth began. I had my first bone density scan a few months before the trip. My doctor gave the results to me over the phone: osteopenia, the prelude to osteoporosis, spots where the bone was just starting to leach away. This had to be an appalling mistake: I took calcium capsules. I exercised.

"This can't be right," I blurted.

"Bone loss can begin around menopause," the doctor said. I didn't hear much after that. I heard *bone loss*. Then *loss*.

Why does the approach of menopause feel momentous and sad somehow? It certainly doesn't bother me that I won't have more children! *Please.* I only know there's something unsettling about a door that closes forever. I feel a vague lament about the changing of my body, the alterations in my appearance, the bleeding out of motherhood, the fear that I will not find the mysterious green fuse again. As I listen carefully to myself, I overhear a confused murmuring inside: *What now? What will be born in me now?*

My mind goes to the pull I feel to write fiction. Ever since I stood in the Tate before the painting of Mary receiving news of her pregnancy, I've framed this inner pull in the imagery of birth—of a *creative* child.

But despite whatever intellect I try to apply to the situation, I cannot deny that when the womb folds its red tent, at some level it becomes a primal confrontation with limitation. There seem to be deep, archaic, often unconscious beliefs about the womb as *the* place of fertility and feminine fruition, and when the womb is spent, all kinds of illogical feelings can surface, feelings that one's creativity and identity are over, too.

I have not wanted to admit the small sorrow I feel. No one is supposed to lament about menopause anymore—fifty being the new forty and all. Turning fifty is about freedom and hitting your stride, and I do believe this. But everything has its opposite, its shadow, a darkness that defines the light. Rebirth is almost impossible without that darkness; I have at least learned that over the years. I tell myself I am experiencing the death of myself as mother, the death of myself as a younger woman—precious old lives going by the wayside. Of course, I should let myself grieve. To deny the grief is to squander a transforming and radiant possibility. Everything in me knows this.

I find my yellow Swiss Army knife near the bottom of my bag. Wasn't cutting hair a symbolic act of grief in some cultures? Without thinking about it too much, because that would surely stop me, I cut off a small lock of my hair. I snip it spontaneously, spurred by a desire to ritualize the moment, to etch it indelibly into myself. I stare at the short, dark curl in my palm, then toss it into the well.

~ ~ ~

When I leave the well, it is past noon, the sun a small lemon near the top of the sky. Following the site map, I wander into the remnants of a temple dedicated to Hecate. Apparently her supporting role in the myth earned her an impressive monument.

For a long time, Hecate was a powerful divinity in the Greek pantheon, but gradually, as patriarchy took hold, her status deteriorated. She went from magnificent crone Goddess to gargoyle-y hag, the harbinger of nightmares. By the time Homer wrote the myth, the metamorphosis was already under way. I gaze at the ravages of time on her lost temple and wonder if there are any divine, postmenopausal figures left anywhere.

In Christianity, the image of God as an elderly man with a white beard has presided over art and religious imagination, but there has never been an image of an old female God. Not even Mary, who came down to us through the centuries as a young Virgin and Madonna. An ingenue. True, her darker features in the icon in the Athens cathedral conjured the *feeling* of the Old Woman for me, but I've never actually seen Mary pictured that way. No Marian wrinkles and sagging cheeks.

I roam about in Hecate's pile of rocks. In the myth, no one dares to tell Demeter her daughter has been abducted. It's fearless old Hecate who hears Demeter's cries and breaks the news to her. She lights a torch and joins Demeter in the search and rescue. And, in what I've always thought to be a cryptic end to the story, Hecate shows up at the reunion and afterward accompanies Persephone wherever she goes. For the first time, I wonder if this isn't an allusion to the old woman's rightful place in the Goddess trinity of maiden, mother, and crone—a feeble attempt to restore her past.

A flight of steps leads up to a rectangular terrace where prickly cacti grow wild in the stone crevices like an incarnation of the crone Goddess herself—vexing, unbridled, subversive, tough, and vibrantly green. I look around for shade, finally sitting with my back against a rock in a shrinking puddle of shadow. I fan the neck of my white sundress, trying to stir a breeze.

Coming to Greece seems to have split open a strange, nocturnal piñata full of nettlesome dreams. Last night I dreamed about digging up a bone. At first I'm thrilled, the way a paleontologist might be at unearthing a dinosaur bone. I'm sure the bone is rare and probably valuable. But as I turn it over in my hands, I'm seized with trepidation about it. I have an urge to shove the bone back in the hole.

This is the Old Woman's bone.

Naturally, any time you stray into the landscape of feminine age, menopause, or the exodus of children, the archetype of the Old Woman turns up, arriving like cactus from rock. In the dream, I can't decide whether to keep the Old Woman's bone or bury it again. It's revealing to me that I revere the Old Woman *and* am repulsed by her.

One of the more provocative lines in Carl Jung's book *Memories, Dreams, Reflections* is his assertion that finding the image concealed in an emotion calmed and reassured him. Obviously, the Old Woman is the image concealed in my emotions. Knowing this does reassure me, filling me with clarity and hope, but now the dread has surfaced.

The reason is suddenly plain to me. She holds my dying inside of her.

I look around for Ann and see her fifty yards away staring at a bust of Marcus Aurelius on a fallen tympanum. The shimmer of heat falls over everything. I feel my small life, impossibly brief. Tears float on the edges of my eyelids, then recede.

Simone de Beauvoir was of the opinion that if, at menopause, a woman gives her "consent" to growing older, she is changed into a "different being," one who is more herself, one who is complete. I get to my feet and climb down the temple steps, picking my way through the cactus, wondering why we do not have ceremonies of consent.

~ ~ ~

Ann and I promenade along the Sacred Way, the path of the initiates, moving through the gates of the Lesser Propylea, into the Telesterion where the faithful were initiated into the Eleusinian Mysteries. We end up in the small museum on top of the hill.

Inside it is a small orgy of beauty—black and toffee-colored vases; curving statues of the fleeing Kore; votive carvings of torches, pomegranates, flowers, and wheat; marble sculptures of women with big, elaborate baskets balanced on their coiffed heads; terra-cotta vessels that once held honey and wine, layered and decorated like russet wedding cakes.

I pause before a plaque that portrays Demeter holding her grown daughter in her lap. It is a depiction of the reunion, the *heuresis.*

I motion Ann over and together we stare at the tenderness that has somehow been chiseled into their embrace. In the back of my mind, I see Leonardo's sketch of *The Virgin and Child with St. Anne and St. John the Baptist*—the grown-up Mary sitting in her mother's lap.

"What's the hardest thing about being my daughter?" I suddenly ask Ann. I don't know where this abrupt question has come from or why I've asked it.

"I don't know," she says blankly, then frowns in an effort to at least try and think up an answer. She shakes her head, shrugs. "Really, I can't think of anything."

Then she turns the tables. "What would you answer if Grandma asked you that?"

"*Oh*. Well . . . I would probably say . . . the Easter rabbit cookie tin."

As I form the words, it seems entirely possible that what I wanted all along was to answer the question myself.

"You mean the cookie cutter Grandma makes the bunnies with?"

"Yes, that one."

It is *the* cookie cutter, practically the size of an actual rabbit, hand-forged and revered. It belonged to my grandmother, who passed it to my mother, who each year rolls out scarves of dough, stamps the cookies, ices them white, affixes pink jelly-bean eyes, and personalizes them with everyone's name. To date I have received fifty bunny cookies with SUE on them.

What I most remember about this opus was my mother's timeless absorption in it, humming and singing as she worked, lost in a domestic ecstasy that I could only try to imagine. The ancient Greeks had a Goddess for every sphere of life. Jean Shinoda Bolen, a Jungian psychiatrist and author, introduced me to the idea that these Goddesses also represent patterns and gravitations inside every woman. And one or two of them will always find dominance. The home and hearth belong to Hestia, who was at the bottom of my psychic totem pole but who, I was pretty sure, was at the top of my mother's. Even more of a Hestia woman than a Demeter one,

Mother seemed happiest when making and tending home, the sewing machine whistling and the Mixmaster whirling. Her deepest impulse was to nurture, to simply dwell; it had nothing to do with ambition and achievement in the world. The bunny tin must have grown into an emblem of that in my mind, a kind of Hestian scepter. And yes, I realized now, it was the hardest thing about being my mother's daughter, because it symbolized how we were *different*.

I once remarked to Mother that if the Easter bunnies were to live on, she would probably have to pass the cookie cutter on to Ann instead of me, and we both laughed, but there was a tacit judgment in my little joke, an unintentional refusal of her satisfied, unhurried labor. How had I come to believe that my world of questing and writing was more valuable than her dwelling and domestic artistry?

Standing in the deserted museum, Ann scrutinizes me, trying to figure out what the cookie cutter has to do with anything. I say, "Your grandmother's gift has been different than mine. It's not just that she makes the bunny cookies, but she finds the depths of herself in doing it. Do you know what I mean?"

Ann nods and I realize I'm only now understanding it myself. In some way her cookies remind me of the sand mandalas I've watched Tibetan monks spend hours meditatively creating then sweeping away—a sacred art that is more about process than product, more about being than doing.

"I wanted to go out and do things—write books, speak out," I tell Ann. "I've been driven by that. I don't know how to rest in myself very well, how to be content staying put. But Mother knows how to *be* at home—and, really, to be in herself. It's actually very beautiful what she does—"

I stop, grasping that I've just articulated a split in the fabric of myself. My longing to meet my mother in a deeper way has never been a matter of love or closeness, but has come from an invisible rift in *me*, from my unknowing diminishment of Hestia and her world. My mother's world.

"What *both* of you do is important," says Ann, holding my gaze, and I see she is moved by my outpouring. This telling of secret things.

I look at Persephone in her mother's lap. "I know," I say. "I think part of me just longs for the way Mother experiences home."

~ ~ ~

Ann has already explored the Plutonian, where the faithful memorialized Persephone's descent and return, but she comes again with me since I haven't seen it yet. As I step into the gaping mouth of a cave, cool, thick shade drops over me, then the smell of old, dank earth. Looking up, I inspect the stone arched over my head, crenulated in white, umber, and charcoal-gray colors. It's not hard to imagine being swallowed and spit back out.

I try to focus on the reunion—not the one in the myth, or even the one with Ann, but with the more mysterious Persephone in myself. It occurs to me that Ann and I may each be searching for something that resides naturally in the other: Ann, seeking her true self, her autonomy and voice, her place in the world; and me, looking for the sap of spring, the ability to conjure a new dream of myself and bring it forth. Ann is new potential in search of ripening and I am ripening in search of new potential.

My initiation into my fifties seems to have as much to do with the Young Woman as it does with the old one. In the myth, Persephone and Hecate *both* show up at the reunion and become inseparable—the Young Woman accompanied by the Old Woman—suggesting a new coupling in a woman's psyche.

I notice that several niches in the rock have been turned into improvised altars, holding offerings left by visitors. Standing on tiptoe, I examine a collection of dried flowers, snail shells, a pile of stones, bouquets of wheat, a small scroll of paper, and the peelings of a pomegranate.

This will sound outlandish, considering my age, but I've never tasted a pomegranate. Not in my entire life. I have no idea why this is so. It has simply never entered my mind to eat one. Now, in the space of days, I am wearing them, begging them off waiters, dropping them in the street, consumed with their mythological meaning and engrossed in their symbolism.

They are lavish symbols of fertility. When opened, they look for all the world like ovaries engorged with seeds, their insides bloodred. In some parts of Greece, a groom hands a pomegranate to the bride when they cross the threshold; in others, farmers break the fruit against their plows before planting. As I contemplate the fertility I hope for in my fifties and beyond—the regeneration of my creativity, the refinement of my spirituality, a new relationship with my body, the rediscovery of my daughter, indeed an inner culmination I cannot fully articulate to myself—I realize it cannot be plotted, orchestrated, controlled, and forced to bloom. It can only germinate naturally out of my experience . . . or not.

I retrieve the pomegranate from my bag and slice it open with my knife.

The pomegranate in the myth symbolizes both death and life. When Persephone ate the seeds Hades gave her in the underworld, she ensured her return to it, initiating what impresses me now as an astonishing process: dying and being reborn. *The secret of fertility.*

Maybe it is a feminine thing, I don't know—but whenever I've managed to find new consciousness and renewals of my work, my relationships, and myself, it has been by going down into what seemed like a holy dark. It has come through a deep metabolizing of my experience and moments of metaphoric dying. The old cycle: life, death, rebirth.

"I'm going to eat some of the seeds," I tell Ann. "Do you want some?"

Of course, this is what I've had in mind all along, ever since I spotted the leather-skinned fruit on the breakfast buffet. The idea was more innocuous then, an interesting thing to do at a sacred site. Now, it is personal, serious, and makes my heart thump in my chest. I feel like Eve in the garden about to bite into an undreamed-of hazard. I will look up the word pomegranate when I get home and discover it comes from the Middle French *pomme grenate*, literally "seedy apple," and I will wonder if maybe the fruit in Eden wasn't a pomegranate all along.

I pick out a handful of seeds and eat them one by one. I let the tart, acidic sweetness saturate my tongue. It becomes an initiation. A ceremony of consent. Traveling now with bones. Traveling with pomegranates.

~ ~ ~

As we leave, a single sheaf of wheat lies on the ground, blown from the cleft in the rock. Demeter's wheat.

Ann picks it up and hands it to me. "Happy birthday," she says.

Ann

Sanctuary of Demeter–Eleusis

❧ Walking toward the Plutonian at Eleusis, I stop to take a picture of a column that lies on the ground like a fallen tree trunk, arranged evenly in seven pieces. If a column falls in a Greek ruin and there's no one around to hear it, does it make a sound? This is the kind of thought I distract myself with.

I love how remnants of the past overlie everything here. I am moved by the way history is folded right into the present, where it can remind people of who they are, where they come from, and how they were shaped. My feelings for Greece haven't changed since I was here before, only the question of what I will do with them.

I flip my journal open to the photo log I've created and write "Eleusis" at the top of the page, then list everything I've photographed so far: cypresses growing between power lines; a Greek flag hoisted on a clock tower; four smokestacks puffing behind the ruins of a temple dedicated to Artemis; the bust of a man who has lost his forehead but not the curl in his beard. Finally, I scrawl: *marble column in seven slices.*

I left Mom beside a well, a journal in her lap and a pen behind her ear. Somehow I know she came here to sit by that well. What I don't know is why, and I can't help but wonder if it has anything to do with me. I don't want it to have anything to do with me, seeing as how she's at the spot where Demeter grieved for her daughter.

"I'll be in hell," I told her, pointing toward the Plutonian with my site map. It was an obvious joke about the entrance to the underworld, and I manufactured a smile to conceal how much my joke had revealed.

"You've been dying to say that, haven't you?" she said. Her laugh sounded as put-on as my smile. I look back now to see Mom still by the well, and I lift the camera and take her picture. I label it: *Demeter Sue.*

I can't keep her in the dark much longer about what's going on with me, and I don't want to anymore—well, more or less. Once the words are out there, they start to live and breathe in unpredictable ways. Another person will know what I do, and that will make the whole thing somehow truer and irreversible. It will crush my mother to know how unhappy I am. Besides, this is her birthday trip, so why would I lay all this on her now?

If a column falls in a Greek ruin and no one is there to hear it . . .

I move along the path, consulting the map as I walk, tripping on clumps of grass which sprout from seams in the pavement, passing steps that once led to the threshold of a temple but now end in midair, a capital ornamented with winged lions and bulls, and the *Agelastos Petra* or Mirthless Stone, where Demeter supposedly took a rest, apparently without delight.

I don't need the map to tell me I've arrived at the Plutonian. A cave is hollowed into the rock, its entrance bulging with deep blue shadow. When I step into it, chill bumps break out across my arms. Several clefts and cavities are lined with flowers, stalks of wheat, pomegranates, buttons, and ribbons—little altars scooped in the rock. I photograph them from different angles.

The holes seem to tunnel back endlessly, disappearing into

darkness. I put the cap on the camera lens and force myself to sit down on a stone ledge inside the grotto and take in the fact that I'm at the mythical spot where Persephone returned. *I should do something.* Pray for answers. Make an offering. I lift the pomegranate charm on my necklace and roll it between my fingertips, thinking for a second that I'll make a grand gesture and leave it at one of the altars. But gazing at it around my neck, I notice it gives off a tiny glow against the skin of my chest, just a smudge of rose light, and I decide I can't part with it.

What I do is sit here and think about last night in the restaurant—the dancer waiting for me to get out of my seat, the way his face dropped when I didn't. I wonder if my dancing would have broken an impasse inside of me and made everything better. The fantasy du jour. Why had I sat there like that? Now the evening will haunt me until I can't remember the details anymore— not the music, the dancer's face, or how helpless I felt when I was up against my own resistance to living out there in the world.

My mind bounces from one self-recrimination to another, settling finally on the rejection letter, the doorstep where I usually end up with my load of blame and self-loathing. Sometimes, in an attempt to sidestep reality, I binge on memories of how it was before that letter came, and on my daydreams about the life I'd envisioned—silly things like wearing jeans to teach my classes, carrying a brown leather briefcase, updating my passport, planning my next sabbatical in Athens, writing papers on Greece at an antique desk. When I think about those reveries now, though, they seem infused with romance. There is nothing in them about a fervent interest in students, grading stacks of papers, chiseling out lesson plans, or sitting through faculty meetings. I'm not enthused by these facets of the job—the nitty-gritty parts—and this sudden revelation both disconcerts and embarrasses me.

I think about the weird moment in the restaurant when it crossed my mind that the evaporation of my career plan was not the real source of my depression. I do realize the letter has become far more than a rejection letter. Somehow it has gotten attached to much deeper things, turning into a catchall for everything that seems wrong with me: "Ann: the Official Document." Could my depression come from my belief that the document is true? These thoughts create a lump of anxiety in my stomach. I don't want to venture any further into them.

I sit on the stone ledge as depression floods in. I try to hold myself there, to not jump up and take more pictures, to not run away. I remember when I was around nine, playing rodeo in the ocean waves with my brother, straddling a raft, and how a large wave unexpectedly knocked me off and shoved me under. Before I could surface, another wave pushed me down, then another. But this is not a game. This is my life. The darkness tunneling back and back.

I could lose myself to depression.

Fear flushes through me and for a moment I border on panic.

This is when I land on the ocean floor, and I don't know how to surface, or if I will. Simply facing that truth, grim as it is, alleviates the alarm inside. I take a slow breath. I don't know how many minutes pass, but gradually the crest of anxiety subsides.

I rummage through my backpack for a guidebook and turn the pages till I find the myth of Demeter and Persephone that I'd scanned earlier in the taxi. This time I pore over it slowly, and it dawns on me that the myth tells *my* story.

Persephone never saw Hades coming. She was jerked out of her nice, sweet life and plunged into a dark underworld. On one level, she was abducted into her own depths, forced into a deep and painful confrontation with herself. Yet the time she spent in the underworld is precisely what transforms her from a naive, untested girl into a mature and conscious young woman. I reread the part of the myth in which Persephone eats the pomegranate seeds. Is that the moment she accepts the complexity of her experience and really takes it in? I wonder: instead of retreating and hiding, instead of pining for the way it was, what if I accept the way it is? This strikes me as both the most obvious thing in the world and the most profound.

It occurs to me then that Persephone came back. I could come back, even if at this moment I don't understand how. *There is an end to this.*

Seeing my experience mirrored in this mythical context reassures me. I take out my journal and write three words on a piece of paper, then scroll it up and place it on one of the altars inside the cave. I stare at it, wanting to memorize what it looks like sitting between a mound of pebbles and a sheaf of wheat.

~ ~ ~

When I leave the Plutonian, Mom and I wander through the museum, where she surprises me, and I think herself, too, by opening up to me about a struggle she has long had between her writing ambitions and her desire to . . . how did she put it? To just dwell, to be. Her confession flabbergasts me. Growing up, I never saw this private tension of hers. What touches me most about the conversation is that Mom has revealed this to me at all, that she has let me see how human she is.

When we leave the museum, we return to the Plutonian. She hasn't been there yet. Standing beneath the overhang of rock, I watch as she inspects the altars. She gazes right at my piece of paper and has no idea.

She pulls out the pomegranate she confiscated from the hotel, cuts it open, and offers me some of the seeds. The myth, I realize, is her story, too. It's not hard to see that being here is full of meaning for her. It's like she's inwardly grieving. It could be because of her birthday. Turning fifty has clearly gotten her attention. But maybe, too, she feels she has lost me in some way. If I'm aware of how our relationship has changed, of the room divider that marks her world from mine, of the way I withhold, then she must be aware of it as well.

I watch Mom eat several of the pomegranate seeds.

I take a handful and swallow them.

~ ~ ~

Back in Athens, Mom and I go shopping. We spend the whole time in one art gallery. Mom goes back and forth between two museum replicas—a white Cycladic statue and a black Minoan vase. She says it's a gift for the new house she and Dad are building, a house-warming gift . . . for herself. She has been known to buy herself birthday presents and wrap them.

As she studies the amphora, I wander through the gallery, trying not to think about Demetri. This is the night I'm supposed to meet him, and already I'm reluctant about the prospect. It feels like the same resistance that gripped me in the restaurant when the dancer held out his hand and I felt powerless to move, the same resistance I have to talking to my mother.

While Mom debates about her purchase, I have a conversation with myself about how disappointed I'll be if I don't see him. I tell myself it's probably the last chance I'll get for the rest of my life. Dancing with him all those months ago drew me out of myself into a world where I felt like I belonged. We wrote letters, traded pictures, became close. How could I not go?

"Which one, Ann?" Mom says, pointing at the two replicas.

"I like them both."

"Good idea," she says, and turns to the clerk. "I'll take both of them."

I do not know how to have both things I want. To see him *and* to stay safely disengaged in my hotel room. I want to know how a person can be happy *and* isolate herself from most everyone on the planet.

Maybe I hesitate because I don't want to be reminded of who I was when I was with him—I'm so far from that person now.

On the way back to the hotel, we watch the changing of the guard at Parliament House from across the street.

"It's been a long day," Mom says. "Let's eat dinner in the room."

"Okay."

"Oh, wait, I forgot. You're meeting Demetri tonight."

"I can still eat with you," I tell her, but I know what I'm doing. I'm steeping myself in an alternate plan. An escape plan. One about a picnic in the room.

At a small grocery, we buy cheese pie, a spinach calzone, two bottles of Coke, and a chocolate pastry. When we get to the room, I fall across the bed with my feet dangling off the side. All I can think about is the phone.

It rings while I'm washing my face at the sink.

Mom calls into the bathroom, "That must be Demetri. Do you want me to get it?"

The depression comes, one black wave after another. I look at myself in the mirror. "Let it ring," I say.

I close the bathroom door. He will not understand. He will think he means nothing to me.

I sit on the side of the tub and wait for the phone to stop ringing. When he finally hangs up, I sob into the washcloth.

Right now, I wish I were someone else. I will have to come out

of the bathroom and explain to Mom why I didn't answer Demetri's call. I have no idea what I'll tell her. I want to go out there
and sit beside her on the bed and quietly lay my head in her lap.
That's all. I'm twenty-two and that is what I want.

I open the door. I tell myself not to think about anything except
the three words I wrote down on the scroll of paper I left in the
cave: *I will return.*

Sue

Mary's House–Ephesus, Turkey

೨ In the Turkish bazaar at Kuşadasi, Ann and I meander through a bright maze of rugs, evil-eye bracelets, coffee grinders, hookahs, silver jewelry, leather purses, and old pots. To see her now, you would not know she's depressed. I watch her photograph trays of golden and magenta spices—sumak, kekik, kimyon—and marvel at how her melancholy comes and goes. Back in Athens, her sobs landed like soft, muffled explosions against the closed door of the hotel bathroom, while I sat on the bed feeling their detonations inside my chest, and now she circles objects with her camera, engrossed in pleasure, cracking up at the dark-eyed toddler who pretends to smoke a hookah and his mother who puts on a show of scolding him but keeps lapsing into laughter.

We left Athens two days ago, desperate for air temperature less than ninety-nine degrees. Boarding a ship at Piraeus for an excursion to several Greek islands and the coast of Turkey, we sailed into the cool blue colors of the Aegean, clinging to the rail of the deck like wind socks, filling up with fat, glorious breezes. Yesterday, as we hiked around Mykonos, the island was brimming with windmills and zephyrs, and when the sun slumped toward the horizon, we floated back to the ship in small boats, shivering in the tinted light.

"Oh great, now we need *sweaters!*" I told Ann.

I behave as if she's fine, as if I did not hear her grief spilled out in the bathroom, but I no longer doubt her depression. When I wake—at all hours of the night—that is what first breaks the surface of my thoughts. Then the sinkhole of fear opens. I know I should talk to her, intervene, do something . . . but it's so easy to go on acting as we are, giggling at goose bumps on our arms.

A particular memory has come to me twice since we boarded the ship. I am a new mother for the first time, barely twenty-four years old, and it is the day my own mother returns to her home, leaving me alone with my six-pound newborn son. I look over his crib and a paroxysm of fear grips me. *Maybe I will be terrible at this; I will do something horribly wrong—sleep through his hungry crying until he grows emaciated or overfeed him until he spits up and aspirates.* There are a thousand ways to screw it up, and I feel ripe for all of them. Alone, terrified, swimming in postpartum, hormonal soup, I sink straight down onto the floor and cry.

Sometimes memory has the purposefulness of dreams. The second time I recollect that long-ago day, I realize it's because I've arrived at the moment again—the scared new mother, not of a newborn, but of a grown, floundering daughter—feeling alone, afraid, the hormonal soup turned menopausal. There are a thousand ways to screw it up.

Inside the coils of the bazaar, we wander into a small shop where sitar music whines from a tape player on the counter. I stare at a wall of shelves lined with identical ceramic statues of Artemis, as if she has been cheaply cloned at the goddess factory. I pick one up. Once Artemis flourished here. Her temple, one of the Seven Wonders of the Ancient World, is just up the road in Ephesus. Her symbol, I notice, is a bee. It is engraved all over her dress.

I slide my hand to the hollow of my neck and feel the sterling

silver bee charm on my necklace, resting beside the glass pomegranate. I bought the bee six or seven months ago for no reason
except that I felt drawn to it. Maybe the pull I felt was simple nostalgia. When I was growing up, bees lived inside a wall of our
house, making honey that sometimes leaked out onto the floor.
The wall would hum. Sometimes the house would hum. After I
told Mary in the myrtle tree that I wanted to be a novelist, I went
home and wrote a first chapter about a girl whose bedroom wall
is full of bees that slip through the cracks and fly around at night.
I even took it off to a writer's conference, where the teacher pro-
nounced it "interesting"—the despised, dreaded word—suggesting
its potential as a novel was "small." *Small.* At times, I still hear his
voice in my head, saying the word.

On his advice, I turned the chapter into a short story, but for a
long while now I've felt nudged to go back and write the novel after
all. Despite my nudges and prayers, though, I don't much believe
in myself as a novelist. I tell myself I'm wearing the bee charm
because it expresses something about the fertilizing power of
women moving into their fifties, but I don't know.

"How much for the statue?" I ask the young man who has
materialized at my elbow.

"Twenty dollars," he says.

"Five," I tell him.

He throws up his arms as if halting oncoming traffic. "Lady!"
he cries. "Do you have a gun in your purse?"

I blink at him, while Ann tugs on the back of my dress and
takes a step toward the door.

He grins. "You must have a gun, lady, because you're *killing*
me!" he says, and to prove it, he staggers backward a few steps, his
hand flying to his chest, feigning a mortal wound.

Ah, the drama of bargaining!

"All right," I tell him. "Ten dollars."

He bows—the Thespian Merchant of Kuşadasi—and takes the money.

~ ~ ~

South of Ephesus our tour van begins a spiraling ascent up Nightingale Mountain to *Panaya Kapulu*—Mary's House. Until we boarded the ship and saw the list of tour outings, I was not aware the Virgin Mary had a house anywhere, much less in the woods on the summit of a mountain in Turkey. Supposedly she lived out her days there as an old woman. I found this fairly stunning in itself, but the fact that I would stumble upon a chance to visit the house after what transpired between Mary and me in the cathedral in Athens—well, it seemed uncanny. I felt like I was *supposed* to go.

Not that I believe it's *really* her house. I'm guessing the whole thing is another lovable "fictoid" of the Catholic Church. As we jostle along on the seat of the bus, it doesn't matter that much to me whether the ruins of the house belonged to Mary or not. In some way, I am going to the house of Mary as an old woman.

As the van crawls around the steep curves, the plain of Ephesus slips in and out of sight. On the seat in front of us, an American woman hums "the wheels on the bus go round and round." Ann writes in her journal while I gaze through the window. For a moment, I consider asking if she's okay, wondering if this is the right time to coax her into a conversation about the sadness I sense in her.

"Round and round . . . round and round."

Laying down her pen, Ann cuts her eyes at me and whispers: "I'm going to ask her if she has a gun in her purse, because . . . she's killing me!"

I smile. For the rest of the trip, we speculate on whether this person or that has a gun in their purse, depending on their ability to irritate us. There's something unbecoming about it, but it makes us laugh, and any thoughts I have about delving right now into Ann's hidden distress dissipate.

Rifling through the tour material in my expandable bag, I find the little booklet on Mary's House I bought in the market in Kuşadasi. It was on a table marked GUIDE BOOKS in English, but I discover it's not so much a guidebook as a story.

It begins with a mystical, bedridden German nun named Anne Catherine Emmerich. In 1822, the forty-eight-year-old nun began to have vivid and highly detailed visions that described the house in which Mary died, along with its precise location near Ephesus. The accounts were transcribed verbatim by Clemens Brentano, the German poet, and published around 1874, fifty years after the nun's death. They sparked a series of scholarly expeditions and excavations that led to the remains of an ancient house identical to the details in Anne Catherine Emmerich's visions. It was *Panaya Kapulu*.

The story leaves me spellbound. I start to wonder if maybe the house is for real. One writer pointed out that if the ancient city of Troy vanished for three thousand years until Schliemann rediscovered it by following clues in the *Iliad*, then why not believe that a two-thousand-year-old house could disappear and be recovered by following clues in the visions of a saintly nun?

Yes, why not?

Actually, there are two equally probable theories about where Mary lived out her life: in either Jerusalem or Ephesus. While on the cross, Jesus entrusted Mary into the care of his disciple John, an event recorded in the Scriptures. A strong and enduring tradition holds that later, when the persecutions in Jerusalem began around AD 37, John fled to Ephesus, taking Mary with him. A number of historical and ecclesiastical documents support the possibility. For sure, Ephesus came to be a thriving center of Christianity by the second century, and at the epicenter of it was the spiritual presence of John and Mary.

I lower the booklet, drawn back to the van window, squinting into the shadowed green valley. The ruins of the ancient city of Ephesus are spread below, glinting and ivory, diminutive as Lincoln Logs, but still discernible. Using an aerial map in the back of a guidebook, I pinpoint places we visited earlier in the day: the Great Theatre; the Odeon; the Library of Celsus; columns lining Harbour Street like rows of jagged teeth. Somewhere down there amid all of that rubble and lost glory, Mary was declared *Theotokos*, the Mother of God.

~ ~ ~

I did not remember this strange piece of history until last night. I sat awake in the dark berth of our cabin, staring at the moon, at the bowl of the night lit up like a stadium and the sea swishing past, lunar and shining black, and it suddenly came to me—Mary became the Mother of God *in Ephesus.*

I got up and searched the guidebook by flashlight, finding a passing reference: *In 431 AD the church officially proclaimed Mary* Theotokos, *"God-bearer," more commonly referred to as "Mother of God," at the Third Ecumenical Council in Ephesus.*

What happened to Mary at Ephesus seemed deeply related to how my own experience with her was unfolding. In one spiritual and theological swoop, Mary went from human Jewish mother to a divine Mother Goddess. Or—as scholar Charlene Spretnak describes it—from biblical to biblical*plus.* She became "big Mary."

How did something like that happen—a young woman from Galilee ending up enthroned and gloried in the art and cathedrals of Europe? How did she land at the center of icons, rose windows, liturgies, music, miracles, healings, processions, offerings, shrines, and feast days? How did "little Mary" come to be worshipped as a full-blown Goddess in everything but name? And frankly, she'd come pretty close with the names, too. They roll through my head like lavish floats in the Rose Parade: Queen of Heaven, Mother of All Living, Star of the Sea, Merciful Intercessor, Mystical Rose, Mistress of the Angels . . .

I could not go back to sleep. I'd been thinking about Mary since those moments in the Athens cathedral. My encounter with her there had set off a backlash of feeling. If I pursued her, it would mean a whole compass-change in my spiritual life. There were people who would think it was fatuous, if not theologically egregious. I suppose some part of me thought so, too.

Part of the problem was that the larger-than-human Mary had fallen on hard times. Not only had she been expelled from the Protestant world, but a strong "progressive" movement to downsize her had been under way in the Catholic Church since Vatican II. Feminists had taken up the cause of getting Mary off her pedestal. I had been right there among them, at least ideologically, insisting we take Mary's humanity back.

So why did this astounding magnification of Mary's at Ephesus excite me? How much of Mary's humanity did we have to take back before we could handle the grand, cosmological Mary? Was it crazy to think I could reclaim that part of her, too? I stared at the lacquered surface of the water, torn with doubt.

~ ~ ~

Eighteen months ago, when I ended seven years of Jungian analysis, my analyst's farewell gift to me was a picture of a woman making her way through a forest. Surrounded by an entourage of wild animals, she follows a dove, which flies just above her head.

Nervous about leaving the relationship, I tried to make a joke. "Are you telling me it's a jungle out there?"

"I'm telling you that you'll be fine if you follow your spirit and travel with your instincts."

Her words became a distillation of wisdom squeezed from those fruitful seven years. I framed the picture and hung it in my study.

Now, sitting on the bus to Ephesus, my head lolls against the warm, vibrating window. As my eyes sink closed, the picture of the woman in the forest floats against the thin membrane of my lids.

~~~

As we arrive on top of Nightingale Mountain—known as *Bulbul Dagi*—our Turkish guide divides up the passengers on the van and explains in her venturesome English that the first group will "propel" into the house, and when it has "exhausted itself," the "terminating group" will enter. Ann and I are assigned to the "terminating group," along with a teenage boy in a Bart Simpson T-shirt who mortifies his mother by shouting, "Yeah, we're the *terminators!*" pronouncing it like Arnold Schwarzenegger. This prompts the guide to offer a little talk about how "overcome with holiness" the place is, not just for Christians, but Muslims. "We revere Mary, too," she says.

The path to the house is lined with olive trees and thick emerald woods. It curves up a small knoll and disappears into patches of light, loamy smells, tiny dollops of wildflowers the color of butter. As we step onto the walkway, the entire group grows subdued and whispery, our revved-up tourist motors—the rushing to get somewhere, the grasping for experiences, checking them off like items on a grocery list—becoming eerily still. Perhaps, like me, the group has flashed back to the guide's comment about the place being overcome with holiness. Surprisingly, there *is* a palpable serenity in the air, that immense feeling in which everything returns to itself, just as it is, just as it should be.

Then I hear Gregorian chanting. It wafts down the hill from the direction of the house. Ann and I follow the sound to a spot where four monks and two nuns are singing their prayers. Their rosaries swing from their fingers, catching the light. Behind them, swathed in olive trees, Mary's House is tiny, L-shaped, made of sand-colored stone, with high windows and two petite, rounded domes on the roof. As the chant rises and falls, we sit on a stone wall beside the door to wait our turn to enter.

"Do you ever think about Mary?" I ask Ann.

She regards me with serious eyes, blue like her father's. "I guess the first time was when I was here before. We went to this monastery—Varlaam—and I saw her painted on a wall. She sat on a golden chest and had stars on her forehead and shoulders. Our guide, Kristina, said it was Mary's ascension into heaven. I didn't even know what that was." Ann looks over my shoulder and squints, as if focusing on the details. "The room was dark, so we shined our flashlights on the wall so we could see her better. When she lit up, I got teary. I bought a postcard of the painting and for a while I kept it by my bed."

"I didn't know that," I say, thinking of how much I do not know about my daughter, moved by the image of her standing before the Queen of Heaven ablaze with flashlights. "What was it about her that got to you?"

Ann looks into her palms that sit on her lap like small, empty cups. "I think it was how majestic she was. I can remember what Kristina said: 'Mary ascended to heaven and became a queen and the connector between heaven and earth.' Part of me was shocked, thinking, how could *all that* happen without me knowing? The other part wanted to cry because of how beautiful it was."

We are quiet for a moment—the small, awkward aftermath of revelation. She looks away and I wonder if she has retreated, but she says, "What about you; do you think about her?"

I relate my own accumulated moments with Mary more or less as I recorded them in my journal in the Athens cathedral. When I tell her what I asked Mary beneath the myrtle tree at Palianis convent, Ann's mouth drops open a little. I hear myself tell her about the image I can't shake—the girl who lies in bed while bees fly about her room in the dark—and the idea of writing a novel around it, but I gradually begin to feel uneasy that I brought it up, that I exposed it like this.

I drop the subject and try instead to explain the pull I feel to relate to Mary as an expression of the Divine Feminine. This feels awkward, too. "It's . . . disconcerting," I say.

"But *why?*" Ann asks and I realize how free of baggage she is when it comes to Mary. Is the difference generational?

Like me, Ann was raised in a traditional Protestant church that put little emphasis on Mary. I tell her about Ephesus and Mary as *Theotokos*. "That's more or less when Mary became the feminine face of God," I say. "Not officially, but for a long time people experienced her like that."

My mind congests with ways Mary's symbol has functioned. How she took on God's tender side, "his" mercy, becoming the one everyone went to. The way she mediated the big thresholds in women's lives—conception, birth, suffering, death. And because Mary possessed so much power as a female, it had to trickle down and empower women at least some, giving them new ways to see themselves.

Ann frowns, waiting. "So, I don't get it—what's the problem?"

I hesitate, realizing I've never tried to put it into words before. "Well, basically, the church reined in Mary's influence by typecasting her as a virgin and a mother, completely sexless and selfless. So naturally, that's what became the vision of perfect womanhood." I let out a sigh. "It was really a way for the church to control women and keep them in their place."

"Oh, nice," Ann says.

"Yeah," I say, "and a lot of women, not just feminists, got fed up. Some of them threw Mary out. Anyway, there's a push to get rid of the old Mary stuff and rediscover her purely as a human being."

I want to hold on to the moment, to the conversation, not just because of what's being said, but because of the intimacy it's creating between us. We are *talking*.

"I'm all for Mary being human," I say. "Especially if we reinstate it in new ways."

"What do you mean?"

"I mean, this whole thing about Mary being a virgin—we could reclaim the ancient definition of virginity—"

"Like a woman belonging to herself, being autonomous?" Ann asks.

I give her an impressed look, and she says, "I read your book. And the definition applies to Athena, too."

I smile at her and go on with my rush of thoughts. "And I don't see why the meaning of her motherhood couldn't be opened up to include all kinds of mothering—birthing *creative* children, including ideas, yourself, God . . ."

My voice trails off as the split in me widens. It's as if my head wants human Mary and my heart, divine Mary.

The chanting stops. The drone of insects rises around us, followed by the soft whir of voices from the group starting to congregate near the door.

"Yeah, I like all that," Ann says, nodding.

"But I'd hate to see her divine nature stripped away—that's what moved you in Varlaam."

The tour guide appears at the front door of the house and motions the "terminating group" to enter.

Ann is saying, "All I know is—if Mary wants to be the feminine face of God for you, why don't you just let her?"

~ ~ ~

The main room is large and austere, divided by a wide archway. As the last person to enter, I wander to a table that's covered with candles and wait my turn to light one. Their flames throw a yolky glow against the stone wall. Everything smells like candle smoke and veneration.

Ann wanders off to read a plaque on the opposite wall, while I watch the little swarm of people in front of me, how urgent they look pressed together in the candlelight, jockeying for an unlit votive, wanting to believe in a loving mystery. The boy in the Bart Simpson shirt has morphed into an altar boy. I wonder what mercy he is reaching for over there.

Standing here, I feel the sadness of everything. The way life moves on through its courses—the leaving behind of so much. Ann's depression. The hole in the floor. The lock of my hair fluttering into the well. The taste of pomegranate. . . . In a couple of days we will sail back to Athens and fly home and I will end up taking all of this back with me.

Tears prick at my eyes. What did I think? That I would come over here and meet the Old Woman and return home a new older woman? I fight a fleeting impulse to hurl myself out the door and down the hill, though I know it is not this house I want to flee—it is beautiful in the frail light and thick with Presence. It is the necessity of loss.

The crowd around the candles has thinned away. I take a taper and light it, watching the flame sprout before I anchor it back in its holder without any prayer at all.

Beyond the archway, an altar sits beneath an apse in the wall, holding the statue of Mary that was found in the ruins when the house was discovered. The place has been a site of worship for centuries. A coin was unearthed here from the reign of Anastasius I, who ruled only sixty years after Mary was proclaimed the Mother of God. In all this time the house has been restored numerous times, but, it's said, always over the original foundation.

People approach the altar and stand there looking momentarily lost. Some cross themselves and make a quick genuflection. One woman, whom I'm guessing is non-Catholic like me, nods to the statue as if to say, Hi, how are you? They are all having their moments with Mary.

Right about now, if I let myself, I could get yanked into skepticism. I could entertain thoughts about the efficacy of what they're doing, what I'm doing. Sending prayers into the universe. Are they heard? Can they change anything? Are our supplications a form of magical thinking? I don't know the answers. In recent years, my praying has grown more meditative, a kind of sitting in silence. It has been a long while since I've made a concrete petition, but as I linger, waiting for my own moment with Mary, it is faith I wish for. I wish to shape my needs into specific, well-considered words and offer them to my own particular image of the Loving Mystery, believing like a wise child.

Poised beneath the arch, I look down to find myself standing on a dark, gray tile different from the others. Identified as the spot where excavators uncovered charred fragments of marble and stone, it is the location of the original fireplace.

Mary's hearth.

Perhaps she once stood here, tending it. Mary-Hestia.

I decide I will make my prayer right here, standing on the hearth, the center of the house, the center of me. The place of my mother. I can picture her stamping out her Easter cookies, and I feel again the hunger to let go of my striving and find the ability to become content and still, intentionally "superfluous," as writer Helen M. Luke puts it. I want a refuge from my old conquering self. *Let it be.* Mary's words at the annunciation come to me, and I realize this, too, is part of the passage into my fifties—the cultivation of being.

But how in the world do I reconcile it with my fierce need to write, the deep clamor to bring forth a new creative flowering in myself? It almost bereaves me to think of unrealized potentials dying inside, the small miscarriages of self. *I want to be a novelist.* It has been five years since I made that pronouncement to Mary beneath the myrtle tree, and it is not happening. I think of the image of the girl and the bees and I don't know what to do with it.

The two most powerful impulses in my life have been the urge to create and the urge to be—a set of opposites—and they have always clunked into each other. How very like them to do so right now.

I am good at pushing things into either-or corners. A moment ago it was faith or rationality. Now, being or creating. I close my eyes and try to shift how I come at it. Both, I think, and start to imagine the hearth not only as a place of being but as one of creating. Why couldn't it stand for tending the present moment and also for the fiery combustion of my work? The words *contemplative writer* form in a slow, measured way across my mind, as if being arranged on a Scrabble board. They give me the barest glimpse of a wholeness shining behind my divisiveness, the possibility of union.

I pray in a silent stream of words. Help my daughter. Help me hold the losses I feel inside and not run away. Show me the ways of being. Give me courage to find a new creative voice. When I look up, I am alone in the house.

I walk through the last room and out the side door. The brightness hits my eyes, a shattering kind of light after the dimness in the house. Ann waits beneath a tree. "I was about to come look for you," she says, very motherly, strapping on her backpack and striding toward me across the yard.

As we walk toward each other, a honeybee lights on my left shoulder. I come to an abrupt stop, watching it from the corner of my eye. Perhaps this visitation is nothing, but it feels purposeful. As Ann approaches, she reaches out reflexively to wave the bee away and I put up my hand, shaking my head, as if to say, no, it's a bee. A *bee*.

She steps back as she remembers our conversation and the connection dawns in her face. "Oh," she says.

We stare at the bee, trying to be stock-still, glancing at each other, making surprised faces. The bee is a mystery, a metaphor, a pure synchronicity. I tell myself it is the imaginative eloquence of Mary.

It does not make the ache inside me go away. Or change the necessity of loss. It does not mean I do not have to go dig up the Old Woman's bone. I know this even as I stand there. I know the bee probably has multiple meanings which will unfold with time. The real awe now is how personal it feels, how intentional. The awe is that the bee has come at all. Minutes go by. Five, six, perhaps more.

It occurs to us we could miss the tour van. We walk down the hill to join the rest of group, who are drinking the holy water that flows into taps from a nearby spring. The bee rides along.

"What's with this bee?" Ann says, genuinely affected. "It's like it has adopted you!" Not until I stoop over and scoop spring water into my hands does it fly away.

I look at Ann. "I'm going to write the novel about the bees," I tell her.

Ann

Aboard Ship–Patmos, Turkey

❧ Our ship, the *Triton*, is docked at the port of Skala just off the island of Patmos in the southeastern part of the Aegean Sea. Outside on the Apollo deck, we sit at a round table, our journals in front of us, shielded from the glare by a cerulean umbrella which flaps steadily in the breeze. Even from far away, the island of Patmos appears rugged, its edges unsmoothed by the sunlight crashing against its steep slopes. White churches and villas are scattered brightly across the hills. The whole of it looks a little golden, as if dusted in curry powder.

Mom and I have three excursions to choose from: a tour of the town of Chora, an afternoon swimming off the shores of Patmos, or a tour of the monastery of St. John the Divine and the Grotto of the Apocalypse. We sift through the brochures that were provided for us in our cabin. We're intrigued by the Grotto because supposedly it's where the apostle John received his visions and wrote the Book of Revelation. We kid around that maybe if we go there, we'll have a revelation, too, though it seems to me Mom has already had one.

The pictures of Chora look inviting except that they show tourists riding donkeys up a hill. "I think we could tour Chora without you having to ride a donkey," Mom jokes.

My one stipulation for seeing any of the islands was that I would not have to ride a donkey, a mode of transport that seems to be like the Gray Line bus tour over here. One of the first things Scott and I did after moving to Charleston was take a carriage ride downtown and I'd spent the entire time worrying about the horses. Were they tired? Did they need a drink of water? Wasn't it too hot for them to be laboring for the sake of my entertainment?

"Let's skip Chora," I say.

"Okay," she agrees.

The sound of the water smacking against the ship is slightly hypnotic. I feel as though I've been poured into my chair and rendered shapeless.

"I don't really want to swim either."

"Me either."

"And I'm fine not going to Patmos," I tell her.

She eyes me. "Okay." She glances around. "We'll have the whole ship to ourselves."

She's right. It looks abandoned. We decide to take in Patmos from the Apollo deck. We sit there. Mom draws in her journal while I stare at the water. Pieces of myth that Kristina had told our group back in '97 wander in and out of my thoughts. *Poseidon has a crystal palace sitting on the ocean floor. . . . Apollo travels the sea riding on a dolphin.* It's funny how often her words come back to me. "When you look at the light shining on the water's surface," she said, "you are seeing the reflection from Poseidon's palace. The whitecaps are the manes of his horses pulling his chariot. The dolphins are Apollo's favorite creatures, which he believed were guides to other worlds and the embodiment of undisguised joy."

Kristina didn't expect us to believe any of this was fact, of course—only to believe it was part of the Greek story, another way to experience the world, a poem filled with metaphors. Whitecaps, dolphins, and spangles on the water. Even the pomegranate seeds we swallowed at Eleusis.

A waiter comes by and hands us menus. "You are not going on the island today?" he asks.

"We've decided to stay on the ship," Mom says.

"Well, you have a beautiful view." Stepping back, as if to take in both of our faces, he says, "You are sisters, no?"

Mom laughs. "No." I can tell what she wants to say is "*Yeah, right.*" Instead she explains politely, "This is my daughter."

I smile at him to acknowledge the fact, one he seems intent on disbelieving. "Ah, well," he says, "you have the same faces."

And we dressed alike this morning. I showered and put on a black sundress in the small bathroom of our cabin, and stepped out to find Mom wearing *her* black sundress. We laughed, and I changed clothes.

From behind my sunglasses, I study my mother's face. I look for the resemblance, but I can't see it. As a little girl, I wanted brown eyes and black hair like hers. She has always been dark and beautiful to me, the unique onyx in our family of blue eyes and brown hair that Bob and I inherited from my dad. I got the freckles from him, too—a heavy sprinkle across my nose. As I grew up, I accepted my eyes and hair. I'm still working on the freckles, which carry a cuteness I would just as soon shake off. I don't feel cute.

We order tea. The waiter brings a platter of cookies along with it. I reach for the cigar-shaped one dipped in chocolate on one end. Mom puts her pencil down to unwrap her tea bag and I notice she's sketched a bee on a page of her journal, its wings small and gray. I'm still in disbelief—make that awe—about the bee yesterday. She prayed and Mary gave her a sign. It helped her finally decide to write her novel about bees. I've heard of muses before, but this one takes the cake.

"I don't think things like that can happen to me," I blurt. Mom releases the tea bag from between her fingers and it plops into her cup.

"Things like what?" she asks, looking up at me.

"Things like that *bee*," I nod toward her pencil sketch on the page. I realize, too late, I've started something and maybe that's what I wanted when I weaseled us out of the tours, but the words have tumbled out unexpectedly, slipping like a glass from my hand, the slivers lying there for me to step around and clean up.

Mom adjusts her chair so her eyes are out of the sun, then takes off her sunglasses. She looks at me. Seriously looks at me. Her eyes are locked on mine, the expression of someone who knows she has happened upon a moment of impending truth and is not about to retreat from it.

"What do you mean, Ann?" she says.

I stall, looking past her toward Patmos in the distance, scanning for the other Dodecanese islands. The lightness I felt moments ago thinking of Poseidon's crystal palace and Apollo's dolphins drains out. I fight the urge to say that I don't know what I mean. I know good and well what I mean.

I say, "Bees don't land on me. I don't get signs—except I half expect a bird to shit on my shoulder. After I got back from Greece last year, I had a dream about Athena. She told me I could see her any time, if I dreamed about her. I can't even do that."

I press my fingers against the corners of my eyes and decide I will not cry. I stare at my napkin, blue like the umbrella. As soon as I look up, a silent transmission will pass between us that could only happen with her. She will finally know how sad I am, and I won't be able to spare her anymore. I force myself to meet her brown eyes.

She gives me a small, sad smile. For one or two seconds, I can tell she sees me in a way I cannot see myself. My eyes fill and her face goes blurry. I fight for composure. I'm afraid that if I start to cry, I won't finish till the ship docks again in Athens. I get it together, but I can't look at her. I cut my eyes to the platter of cookies and stare at them in what looks like an ardent attempt to memorize every crumb and crystal of sugar.

She reaches for my hand. I could go on and on without saying anything, but right now it feels like staying quiet would be more painful than talking.

"It's okay, just tell me," Mom says.

Suddenly the words are in my mouth and I'm saying them. "I—I'm just depressed."

Her fingers tighten on mine. Like I've fallen overboard and she's determined to hold on. "I knew something was going on. I'm sorry; I should've asked you about it."

She loosens my hand, and I pull it free and take another bite of cookie. Eating a cookie—how normal.

"When did all this start?" Mom asks.

"When the letter came," I tell her.

She wrinkles up her forehead. "The letter . . ."

"The grad school letter. The one confirming my inadequacies." I hear the smart-ass tone in my voice, but for some reason it helps to keep me from falling apart.

"But that was last March," she says and her eyes widen.

"Yep."

For the next hour it all pours out, the whole miserable thing: what it was like the day I got the letter, how I hid it in my sock drawer, the way things went from bad to worse, the depression taking over. I tell her that I went over it in my head a thousand times—whether to reapply to the University of South Carolina or to look for another school that had courses in ancient Greek studies, but I always came back to the fact that no matter how much I wanted that life, it didn't seem to want me, and now I'm having my own doubts about it, not sure I want that life at all. Half the time, I feel like what I'm saying doesn't make sense, but Mom just lets me talk, and I go on and on, laying my confused thoughts on the table. They are like the toothpaste you can't get back in the tube, but I feel a huge relief having it out there despite how messy it is. For the first time since this all started, I don't feel completely alone.

Finally I say, "I guess I'll just stick to the plan and go to the College of Charleston."

"Is that what you really want?" she asks.

"What else am I going to do?" I say, even though I know attending a grad program in American history feels plain wrong. Why can't I just say that? Why am I always easing into the truth like it's a scalding bath? What's true is true and it's not going to change whether I admit it now or twenty minutes from now. Deep down, I think I belabor it for Mom's benefit. Shocking her in little increments instead of all at once seems kinder. And I do it for me. Because I don't have the courage to just jump in.

Mom says, "I don't know, but your heart needs to want it."

It's true. I've always wanted to do something with my life that I feel passionate about.

"Remember how you felt after you transferred to Columbia

College? It was the best move in the world for you because your whole heart was in it." Mom grins. "So what if you lost a full scholarship?"

The wind whips up around us and Mom slides her jacket on. I rest my head against the back of the chair. I know I shouldn't aim my life in a direction I don't want to go, but I've indoctrinated myself with the idea that studying American history is better than nothing. It is at least a plan. Without that plan, I would be back at square one. Back to "nothing."

We are silent for several moments, but I feel her watching me. Finally she says, "The dream you mentioned about Athena—it's beautiful. I figured she's important because of your ring."

I've worn the ring every day for the last seventeen months. Athena, and all those things I love about her—her bravery and wisdom, her fierce independence—have been like a North Star for me. "Yeah, I guess she was what I needed to find in myself."

"And you did."

"For a while, anyway." I look at the wind dissolving into the water. All I can think is *underworld*. I say, "I'm begging for Athena or Mary or God or somebody to help and it's dead silent." I take a breath and hear it stutter through my chest like it might turn into a sob. "I think it took me seeing the bee to realize it's not that miracles don't happen, they just don't happen to me. I don't deserve them."

I tell my mother how afraid I am inside, how lost, how *rejected* I feel. When I say the word *rejected* out loud, something snaps into place, a truth that has eluded me. Yes, I had a dream and it didn't work out, and while that may have started my slide into depression, it is hardly the whole story. The real story is the rejection itself. It had unearthed my own self-doubt and feelings of unworthiness.

Then the anger started, along with the shame that I was not good enough.

This is the moment when I realize I've been hating myself for a long time.

I cannot hold back anymore. I drop my head on the table and cry. I feel Mom's hand on the back of my head and I cry harder.

It is whole minutes before I can stop. I use the napkin to wipe my nose. The waitstaff is having a whispered conversation that I can only imagine: *Crazy girl on deck. Call the ship's doctor.* Mom scoots forward in her chair. *Now she knows.*

"Ann, listen to me. I understand how the rejection letter snow-balled into a rejection of yourself and how depressed you became. It's hard to feel like you deserve anything when that happens. But all those things you love about Athena that you found in yourself before—they're still in you. I promise. They just seem lost to you right now. Okay?"

I nod. I know Mom wants to say the right thing to me. I can see how hard she's trying. Going slowly, measuring her words, her eyes brimming. I don't know if those things I found in Athena are still in me, but it does help to think she believes it. I want to tell her she doesn't have to say anything, that her hearing all this is what mat-ters. But then she says, "You deserve to love yourself." And it hits me suddenly how true that is.

"I love my girl," she says.

"I love you, too."

~ ~ ~

Standing in front of the elevators on our way back to the room, Mom pushes the up button. Beside the doors is an arrangement of lilies, their aroma maple-syrup sweet. I sink my face into it. Inside the elevator, we watch the floor numbers light up, stopping once to let on a ship employee pulling a cart of wineglasses. He glances at me with the slightest upturn of his lips, then looks at his feet for the rest of the ride.

In the cabin, I sit on the edge of the bed and take off my sandals. When I look around, Mom is staring at me with a look of perplexity.

"*What?*" I ask.

"Is that chocolate on your face?"

I run to the mirror.

My face is lined like a vampire—amber-brown streaks under my nose and around my mouth. *What is on me?* "I've been walking around the ship like this!"

In the mirror, I see Mom behind me, bent over at the waist, laughing. It becomes the moment I know I don't have to protect her from my feelings, that I can tell her the worst things and the world will not end.

Suddenly I remember the lilies. "It's pollen!" Now *I'm* bent over, laughing.

I scrub at the stains. "It's not coming off!"

"Use my astringent," Mom says, but she can hardly get the words out.

Our reaction is worse than when we started the cat-feeding frenzy in the Plaka, and it's probably as much from the catharsis of our talk as it is from my face.

"Did you see the way the guy looked at me in the elevator?" I cry. "Oh my god, how many people did we pass on the way to our room?"

"I don't know," Mom says. "About a hundred."

~ ~ ~

Before dinner we pass through the photo gallery to look for the picture the ship photographer took of us at dinner the night before.

Rows and rows of photos are arranged on the walls. We each take a side of the room and search. Mom spots it.

In the photo, we are sitting in the dimly lit dining room, small yellow chandelier bulbs blurred in the background and a tall window behind us splattered with light from the camera flash. We are shoulder to shoulder, smiling, and for the first time I see how true it is. Our faces are remarkably alike.

The clerk drops the photo into a transparent bag and hands it to us. "You share the same face," he says, and looking at me, adds, "But you have, how do you say . . ."

"Freckles," I answer.

Mom and I head for the double glass doors that lead outside to the Apollo deck. The sun is setting, the crisp light softening.

We rest our elbows on the rail and stare at the sea until I taste salt on my lips. As we stand there, the horizon turns blue, then violet. My ribs don't feel like a vise the way they have for most of the trip. I've admitted the worst to myself and to my mother: I don't feel worthy of blessings. I'm depressed. I'm lost. I don't know what to do with my life. Big, bleak issues I never thought I'd deal with.

We decide we'll do one lap around the deck before dinner, which should walk off about twenty of the five hundred cookie calories I ate earlier. Near the front of the ship, people have gathered along the rail and are pointing at the water. Dolphins, a hundred of them at least, are leaping and diving along the prow. They skim the surface like silver zippers, slicing open the water. Their breaths spew as loud as the roar of a fountain.

I don't know why, but I tear up. I press my hands to my eyes to keep the tears in. The dolphins swim beside the ship for several minutes, then turn out to sea. I watch till I can't see them anymore.

Staring at the swells of water, I'm able to tell myself: I will not go to graduate school. There will be no path that leads me back to Greece. These things are gone. But maybe there will still be something else out there. Something I can give my whole heart to.

Sue

———

Charleston, South Carolina

∽ Today—February 23, 1999—is moving day, and Charleston has turned crazily cold, sleeting just to the west of us, the sky knotted with dark, threatening clouds. Alone in the new house, waiting for Sandy and the moving truck, I stand at the windows in the upstairs room I've claimed for my study and frown at the sky, willing it not to rain. *Please.* Just then a drop splats on the pane.

The heat ticks and groans in the vent over my head, but beyond that, silence. I look out across the salt marsh. Browned grasses undulate like a field of wheat. The creek cuts through them, swollen with haze and wavy as a brushstroke. I decide I will put my desk where I am standing so I can see the little wetland of wildness and peace while I write.

Turning from the windows, I scrutinize the room. After more than a year in the teeny apartment, writing sporadically in a windowless cubicle otherwise known as the dining nook, the space seems outlandish, as if I am Alice in Wonderland shrunk to the size of a keyhole. I let my eyes drift to several boxes stacked along the far wall and my stomach does a strange, anxious flip. The boxes contain everything remotely related to the novel about the bees. After returning from Greece six months ago, I dove into writing it, but lately the whole novel has stalled. I haven't written anything since the new year.

~ ~ ~

When I got back from Greece, people were remarkably responsible about reminding me that I had come back to the *real* world, though it didn't seem that substantial to me. I'd returned to the four-room apartment, which was no more than a way station and which pressed around me, confining and cocoon-ish. What had I been thinking, moving into a place so windowless and dark? How deluded had I been to think we would be out of it in no time? As if the betwixt and between of the old life and the new one would be a finger snap.

That I felt migratory and displaced in my physical surroundings was hardly surprising, but I was a little shocked at how displaced I felt inside. So much of my sense of myself had been altered in Greece, far more than I realized. Old understandings of myself as a woman, a mother, a writer, and a person in search of the spiritual were unraveled by my experiences over there, by the places them-selves.

I cloistered myself during those months, struggling to sit in the cubicle and type on the keyboard. At one point the computer crashed and I lost every word I'd written. I wished for my desk, which was in storage along with everything else. I wished for some idea of what I was doing and whether it would amount to any-thing. A dozen times a day, on fire with a hot flash, I ran from the computer to the refrigerator where I stood with the doors thrown open, prickly with sweat, rubbing ice cubes on my arms, face, and neck. An acupuncturist brewed up a Chinese tea for me to drink that smelled like car oil, but it was a worse remedy than the ice cubes. I missed my estrogen.

It was the autumn of menopausal symptoms. Odd palpitations. Seizures of unexplained sadness. There was only one kind of sleep now: interrupted. I would steal out of bed to read and write, or situate myself by the lone window in the living room where I could see the moon. One night I calculated how many more full moons I could see if I lived to be eighty. Three hundred and fifty seven.

My memory began to nod off like a narcoleptic and I would be left with a thought curled up on the tip of my tongue—something like the name of the guy in the movie we'd just seen. (Half an hour later the answer would surface and I would blurt out the name— "Richard Gere"—to anyone standing next to me.)

My mother's generation summed up menopause in two words: the Change. As a little girl, I only heard the words whispered, as if they could not be spoken aloud in polite company, suggesting a slightly scary and shameful mutation of age. In the world of my grandmothers, menopause was often "diagnosed" as hysteria (from the Greek word for womb: *hystera*), referring to all kinds of hormonal maladies from night sweats to mood swings, and was treated as pathology and neurosis. As a baby boomer, I fantasized that it would be nice to come up with a new term for the word, like the Awakening or the Becoming. I wanted it to take into account the way every beautiful and dormant potential in you wants to wake up. How you get intimations of being untethered at long last, of power and audacity bubbling furiously on your two back burners. How you start thinking: *yes, I do believe women can save the world*. But, truth be told, that didn't tell the whole story either. There *was* a formidable Change bearing down, though I certainly didn't think of it as shameful. And I had my tiny bouts of so-called hysteria, or let us say "hormonal expressions," though I hardly thought they were pathological. That menopause is also an event of biology was never clearer than during that autumn of symptoms.

On the winter solstice, I became officially postmenopausal. Twelve months without menses. There seemed to be fluency in the timing, the solstice being the apex of darkness after which the light gradually returns. *It's done*, I thought. It seemed like I should mark the occasion. In what I thought would be a celebratory moment of closure, I read Lucille Clifton's poem "to my last period" aloud to myself and ended up crying my eyes out.

By Christmas, the need to examine my face for lines and sags left me. I recognized the growing permutations as more than the effects of time. They became a poignant history—tracings of my experience and character, the passionate individuality of my soul, the story of lived life written in the tenderness of skin. I began to find a worn beauty in all of that. I knew I could never cut it away.

Those six months between Greece and moving day—marinated as they were in hot flashes and pangs of loss—became a natural descent of body and soul *both*. I could only sit with it and let it happen. It was a time to molt.

~~~

When Ann drops by after work, Sandy and the movers are unloading furniture in the rain and I am cross-legged on the floor, unpacking the boxes that made my stomach do the funny flip-flop. Spread around me are books, files, scribbled notes, a three-ring notebook with my research, and the first fifty pages of the novel tied neatly with a piece of raffia. In my lap rests a collage the size of a small poster.

"So, where's *my* room?" Ann says as she plops beside me on the floor. It's the first house we've had without a room for her or Bob, a fact that has not quite sunk in until she asks this, asks it so matter-of-factly that I glance at her to be sure she's kidding. Her eyes give her away. "Yeah, about that . . . we still have the pup tent," I say. We laugh a little too long, as if to avoid the acknowledgment implied in all of this—that her leaving is now permanent and concrete. No coming back.

For one elongated minute we sit there and listen to rain pelt the roof. The closeness we discovered in Greece seemed to solidify during the fall. We talked endlessly about the experiences we'd had, pored over trip photographs, read passages aloud to each other from our journals, and picked up the conversations we started over there.

I smile at her. Her hair, pixie-short in Greece, is almost to her chin, her bangs wispy across her forehead. She looks thin to me and I stifle the urge to ask if she's eating enough. In two days she will be twenty-three.

I realize I'm still trying to work out the boundaries. How to love her without interfering. How to step back and let her have her private world and yet still be an intimate part of it. When she talks about her feelings, I have to consciously tell myself she wants me to receive them, not fix them.

Every woman needs to become self-mothering, I remind myself. To learn to take care of herself, to love herself. Ann has to find a mother in herself. She will replace me. That's the point now.

She peers at the collage in my lap. "What's that?" she says, and I'm glad for the diversion.

"It's a book outline."

"Very cool," she says and leans over it, studying the patchwork of pictures.

I started the collage soon after returning from Greece, searching through magazines, catalogs, postcards, photos, and prints, cutting out whatever inspired me. I was supposed to be writing an outline for the novel, and I was cutting out pictures. It didn't seem to matter whether I understood what the pictures meant or how they fit into the novel; it was enough to be drawn to them in some deep, evocative way. It was pretty much an unconscious process. I told myself I was being creative, turning my play instinct loose to roam around and find what fascinated it. Inside I was thinking: *This is nuts.*

I ended up culling the pictures to twenty images and randomly gluing them together. Among them: A white girl—fourteen maybe—a sassy smirk on her face, but a hint of something hurt and bruised there, too. A large African American woman, who looks like she could spit snuff and straighten you out at the same time. A bitter-looking white man in overalls. A pretty white woman with wistful eyes. A jail cell. A whirling cloud of bees. A black Madonna wrapped in chains. A shockingly pink house. A trio of African American women. A jar of honey. A banner that reads WALLS FOR WAILING.

I only know what the first half-dozen of these pictures mean and how they might be part of the story. The rest is an enigma.

Ann rests her finger on the girl I've placed dead center. "Who's this? The girl with the bees inside her wall?"

I nod. "Her name is Lily Melissa Owens. She accidently killed her mother when she was four."

She looks at me. "Killed her mother? *Man.*"

"Well, it makes things more interesting," I say.

Ann points to the large woman. "What about her?"

"That's Lily's stand-in mother, Rosaleen Daise."

"What's her story?"

"She gets into a fight with three racists and gets thrown in jail."

"Good Lord."

"Well, I don't leave her there. Lily breaks her out and the two of them run away together."

A jail break. By a fourteen-year-old. When the idea came, it felt inspired, but knowing how capable I was of doubt and how cold my feet would get, I wrote a note to myself: *Sue, this is a really good idea. Before you dismiss it, remember how you felt when it came to you.*

If it hadn't been for that note, the idea never would have survived. I still wasn't sure whether it was perfectly ridiculous or ridiculously perfect.

Ann does not laugh or roll her eyes. "So, where do they go?"

This is the part that makes me nervous, the part over which the novel has stalled. "I have no idea," I say.

~ ~ ~

That night I awaken in the new house sometime between 3:30 and 4:00 A.M. in a strange room flooded with light. Through the curtainless windows, I see the moon plugged into the black sky, shining on high beam, emphatic as a spotlight.

Sandy sleeps unfazed, but I lie in the lucent, white sheets, in the dazzling room, and think first about the house and what pieces of furniture go where, then slowly wind my way back to the problem of my two runaway characters.

Slipping out of bed, I wrap myself in the green chenille throw and pad up the stairs to my study, where the moon radiates with only slightly less wattage. I pick up the collage. My eyes wander back and forth between the picture of the three African American women and the uproariously pink house. I scan the cloud of bees and the black Madonna in chains.

And *boom*, it falls out of the night, landing in one unbroken piece in my head. My two runaways will escape to the home of three black sisters, who live in a pink house, keep bees, and revere a Black Madonna.

I consider writing a note to myself about it but decide no, this time I'm going to trust it.

~ ~ ~

The pink house and its inhabitants are all I think about. It distracts me from the fear that the idea is crazy. I unpack crystal and china, load it into the dishwasher, then stack it in the sideboard in the dining room, while my mind is a thousand miles away picturing shades of flamingo and Pepto-Bismol pink, cooking up ideas.

It is not until I whack two stems of crystal into the countertop and find myself standing in a pile of shards that I realize I'm not present to what I'm doing. I stop, make a cup of tea, and take it to the living room. I recline against the sofa pillows near the hearth and think of all the passages I've logged in my journal about hearth and Hestia—a Goddess who doesn't represent domesticity to me so much as the ability to dwell, to belong to one's place.

Journeying is the predominant means of developing one's self in this culture, not the habitation of place. It has been true of me. Always the seeker. Yet at this phase of my life, when I look at my house at the edge of a marsh, I want to learn how to *be* in it. I want to behave like a finder as much as a seeker. The irony is that I had to go on an elaborate journey to figure this out. So much of my growing older seems to be about paradoxes. The reconciliation of opposites. The bringing to balance.

For my fiftieth birthday, Sandy gave me a card with the moon on it. He handed it to me when I got home from Greece. It read: "I am not the same having seen the moon shine on the other side of the world." It's true, I wasn't. Yet the rest of the story is that it's just as possible not to be the same after seeing it over my backyard. At fifty, I want to be a finder of the commonplace moon.

Later, as I unpack a carton marked MISCELLANEOUS, I come across a photo of my seventy-seven-year-old mother. It was taken the month before at a workshop I co-led with my friend Terry titled "Maiden, Mother, Crone." It wasn't about chronological phases in a woman's life, but about an internal process of becoming. I'd invited my mother, wanting to spend time with her, and she'd jumped at the chance. The photo has captured her standing beneath a tree in a semicircle of women who are being led in a simple dance. Her arms, like the arms of all the women, are stretched out in front of her, palms up, as if she's waiting for something to be dropped into them. Her head is cocked slightly to the side in a gesture I recognize.

Someone snapped the picture and sent it to me. It arrived as I was packing up the contents of the apartment. I did not look at it closely then, but I do now. I study her arms stretched toward the camera in a gesture of beseeching and receptivity and I'm completely arrested by it. My mother, dancing. The closing line in her letter to me about *Dissident Daughter* comes to mind: *Oh, Sue. I don't want to miss the dance.*

Shortly after the photo was taken, Terry and I invited the group to call out the names of women who had made an impact on their lives or on history itself. The moment was designed to be a "dinner party" of female names. As we took turns around the circle, I started off the litany with the name Sojourner Truth. From around the circle came Georgia O'Keeffe, Virginia Woolf, Hildegard of Bingen, Elizabeth Blackwell, interspersed with the names of someone's mother, sister, grandmother. My mother, who had been quietly listening, suddenly spoke up. "My daughter, Sue," she said.

Still holding the photo, I go to the phone and dial her number. When we have finished all the small talk about moving, I say: "That day at the workshop when we called out the names, I never thanked you for what you said." Before she can respond, every bottled up thing comes out—how I have not valued her Hestian world, not been able to fully find that world for myself, how it has separated me from her in some internal way that has been almost too subtle to realize. "I know all the things you do at home, the way you're so content there, is your art, like writing is mine. I just want to find an experience of home now."

There's an awkward silence. Then I hear her laugh. "Sue," she says, "what you do, your writing—it opened me up to things I never would've thought about. So, I guess it goes both ways."

She has been the keeper of home for me, and I have been the keeper of journey for her. And now we look for the lost portion in each other.

~ ~ ~

When the contents of the house are in place and the pictures hung, I am tired and frazzled and get it in my head to visit Mepkin Abbey, a Trappist monastery near Charleston. Even though the spring equinox is still weeks away, I want to walk through the monastery gardens along the Cooper River and sit for a while in the church where the monks pray. I thought I was going because what goes on inside monasteries is a cultivation of being that I've come to associate with the metaphor of home, but it will turn out to be for another reason.

When I arrive at the abbey at 1:00 P.M. the day is warm. By the time I reach the gardens, however, the sun has barricaded itself behind the clouds and the wind picks up, flapping over the river and straight through my thin corduroy jacket. By 1:20, I am alone in the church, which is white-walled and without flourish, distilled to a Cistercian simplicity.

I walk between the choir stalls toward the statue of a woman around three feet tall. Drawing closer, I notice her figure blends into a block of wood near the hem of her skirt. The grayed wood is severely scarred; deep crevices on her face make her look elderly, if not ancient, and both of her arms are broken off at the elbows. Two unlit candles stand in front of her. *Is this Mary?*

It seems to be, but she wears a dress with a ruffled Peter Pan–ish collar, a string bow at the neck, and a nineteenth century–looking cape. Her hair is bobbed around her face and shoulders. And no baby Jesus.

There is no chair or pew, so I sit on the floor and begin to sketch her in my journal, gradually realizing that she's shaped like a figurehead from the prow of a ship.

Flop, squish, swish. The sounds come from the opposite end of the church. A young man, wearing sandals, sweatpants, and a black T-shirt with PHANTOM printed across the front, mops the floor, pushing around a yellow bucket on wheels. He seems not to notice me, and when I approach him from behind, he jumps.

"I'm sorry," I say. "I was just wondering about the statue over there. Who's it supposed to be?"

"It's Mary," he says, then qualifies his answer. "Well, she's not really Mary—at least she didn't start out that way. She became Mary when she got here."

I give him a puzzled look and he launches into the most extraordinary story. He's a postulant, it turns out, who tells me he was present four years ago when the monks debated whether or not to consecrate the statue as Mary.

"It's actually a ship's figurehead," he tells me, "that washed up somewhere, maybe the Caribbean, I can't recall. It wound up in Charleston and was purchased by some group for the monastery." I blink at him as if he has just told me the statue appeared miraculously in a tree like the dark *Panagia* had done at the convent in Greece.

"Some of the older monks really love her," he adds and slaps the mop back into the pail.

I return to the statue, thinking of the image of the Black Madonna in my collage. It's a postcard I brought back from Greece, picturing an icon of a dark-skinned Mary wrapped in chains. Legend says she was kidnapped several times by the Turks from a convent on the island of Crete but always escaped back to her homeland. Finally the Turks chained her up. Undeterred, Mary broke free and returned home, wearing the chains. The Greek nuns left them on the icon as a reminder of what Mary was capable of.

As I stand there, the Greek Mary in chains melds together in my imagination with the figurehead Mary in South Carolina. The fusion creates the Mary I want to inhabit my novel, the one who will live in the pink house with the sisters. She is a Black Madonna of the American South, an African American Mary. I close my eyes and I can see her—floating up on the shores of Charleston during the time of slavery. Not really Mary—at least she doesn't start out that way; she *becomes* Mary. A Mary who breaks chains.

I imagine her with a history of inspiring freedom and subversion among the slaves, of being handed down through the generations and coming finally to the sisters in my novel. I picture her in the pink house with her fist raised in authority, a heart painted on her breast full of consolation. I see a semicircle of women dancing around her. They wear hats with feathers and veils. They touch their hands to her faded heart. She is their mother.

I sit down again on the brick-colored squares of the floor and write it all down. When I read it back, I understand that the tale of the monastery's Mary is my story, too—that of a dark, older Mary lost for centuries, washing up on the shores of my consciousness, followed by the debate about whether to take her in.

I touch my hand to the figurehead, on the place I imagine a heart would be if anyone thought to paint one.

~ ~ ~

It is a balmy day in March when I imagine I see sprigs of green pushing up in the marsh grass. As the afternoon darkens, I walk out onto the dock with a handful of red camellia petals in my pocket. My intention is to make a ceremony with them, a home-coming ritual.

It's an impromptu idea spurred by a housewarming party I once attended in which guests tossed rose petals across the thresholds of each room as a blessing. Today, when I saw the camellia blossoms in a vase, I filled my pocket with petals. I picture myself tossing them onto the water in the creek. A blessing. Why not?

When I reach the end of the dock, the sky is pink and gold from the sunset and pelicans cut through the spatter of colors in long strands, flying home. The tide is almost all the way out, exposing the roots of the spartina grass and mudflats pocked with crab holes.

I stand out here and think of the Old Woman. I sense her in the brown grass and the hidden life teeming inside the pluff mud. Mostly, she is in the tide as it ebbs, stripping everything before it sweeps back full of generativity.

When I pull out the red petals, I see they have shriveled a little. I toss them onto the water and watch as they move with the tide toward its nadir.

Ann

Charleston, South Carolina

❧ "You haven't seen the gardens at Middleton Place?"

I've heard this six or seven times now from people who are unable to believe I've lived in the Lowcountry for an entire year and still haven't visited the oldest landscaped gardens in America. I try to tell them I've taken the ferry to Fort Sumter, walked the Battery, and seen Frankenstein at the Dock Street Theater on Church Street. "Oh, but you haven't seen the gardens at Middleton Place!" they say.

"Apparently, it's the holy grail of horticulture," I tell Scott. "We're going to have to go." We drive out there on a Saturday in May, starting early to avoid the afternoon heat. When we arrive, it is 9:30, cloudy, and overcast. I pick up a brochure at the gate and skim through a short history of the place: National Historic Landmark . . . Eighteenth-century plantation . . . Home to a signer of the Declaration of Independence . . . Rice Mill . . . Eliza's slave house . . .

I linger over the part about the gardens. Ornamental ponds . . . Classical sculpture.

We walk across an expansive lawn, which we share with grazing, dusty-colored sheep. I consult the map in the brochure, noting the reflection pool on the left and the ruins of the main house directly ahead.

"The house was destroyed in 1865 by Sherman's army," I inform Scott. "Then an earthquake toppled what was left of it in 1886."

"Earthquake? We have earthquakes *and* hurricanes here?"

"There hasn't been an earthquake since the one in 1886."

He looks at me from under the brim of his Braves baseball cap. "So, what you're saying is, we're due."

A shrill, *Wild Kingdom*–like noise breaks into the quietness of sheep chewing grass. "What was *that*?" I ask.

"I have no idea," Scott says, glancing around, vowing to find the source of it.

I go back to the map, matching the markers to their numbered descriptions, the same thing I did at Eleusis, the Acropolis, and all over Greece. It's been nine months since Mom and I returned. Nine months into my job at *Skirt!* magazine, nine months further into depression, nine months of being no closer to what I want to do with my life.

~ ~ ~

I savor weekends with Scott—Saturday morning doughnuts from Krispy Kreme, going to the movies, going to the beach. We share an apartment now, and most Sunday mornings I wake up to coconut-scented surf wax mixed with the smell of coffee brewing and find Scott waxing his surfboard on top of the kitchen table. All week he works hard managing real estate properties for his company, but on surf days he's like a kid out there, floating in the waves, unaware of an entire afternoon passing. Sometimes, sitting on the beach, I'll gaze up from my book and watch him and wish I could know about the rest of my life the same way I know about Scott. Yes, he leaves wet bath towels on the bed and shakes his electric razor out in the sink, but these annoying habits are not a big deal in light of the love I feel when I'm with him.

My depression is sort of like a miserable allergy, in that some days are better than others but it never quite leaves me. I function all right until something comes along to rile it up. Like a TV show on ancient Greece, in which professors wax on about the Golden Age of Athens and about Pericles like he is their close cousin. At moments like these, I withdraw to my desk where I keep a collection of mementos by the computer monitor: the red pomegranate charm, a small replica of Athena's helmet, and an owl feather—a reminder of Athena's mythic companion. I sit there and stare at them because I don't know what else to do.

Being in Greece did not resolve the big questions for me, but I *did* discover some things. I learned how easy it is to give up and become draperies while everyone else is dancing. I learned there is a name for how I feel—depression—and I had to face up to that. I learned that Persephone does eventually come back from the underworld and that maybe I would, too. That I could talk to my mother. That while I have no idea what to do with my life, I am not a total loser.

When I'm sitting there like that, an awful desperation gets going in me. It's like a balloon expanding in my chest until it pops, and out pours nothing but sadness. Then the next day, I get up and go to work. Maybe Scott and I meet my parents for supper. I swing by the grocery store for coffee filters. Take a day trip to Middleton Place. Life goes on while I try to figure out what to do next. In all of this, I am glad for my mother and the talks we have. And for Scott, who seems to ride through life the way he takes the waves— with a steady, even keel. I worry sometimes he may grow tired of my sadness and confusion . . . disappointed that I'm not the girl he first met.

~ ~ ~

As a full-time assistant at the magazine, I answer the phone as instructed—"*Skirt!*, this is Ann"—but I can't quite spit it out without the words running together.

"*Skirt!*, thisisZan."

"Who?" people ask.

"Ann. I'm new here."

"New to *Skirt!* or new to Charleston?"

"Both."

("Have you seen the gardens at Middleton Place?")

Then there are the calls that begin with me telling an advertiser the amount of his or her overdue bill, which elicits a variety of responses: "The check is in the mail," or "Sorry, it has been tough lately, what with the business going under and all," or "Don't ever call me again and tell me I owe you money! I'm well aware of it!" To the latter I want to reply, "Perhaps, however, you are *not* aware that rudeness is a misdemeanor in Charleston." Instead, I say, "Yes, I understand. Have a nice day."

A few months ago, I began to read article submissions. After the editor's initial reading, she will hand me the manuscript and say, "Read this and tell me what you think." Afterward, I always get the impulse to write something myself. It fizzles out quickly, though, almost like I never had the thought. *What do I have to say? How could it possibly be any good?* Impulse going . . . going . . . gone.

Lately, the editor has been encouraging me to submit an article. Does she think I inherited my mother's writing genes? Does she know that the last essay I wrote was an academic paper about the Peloponnesian War? I tell her I'll think about it, which is a polite way of saying no.

I grew up thinking I wanted to be a writer. My writing experience amounts to a batch of stories, comic strips, family newspapers, and embarrassing poetry I began in elementary school, plus two writing competitions. The first was a seventh-grade fiction contest, in which I won first place in my school. My prize was a trip to

Columbia, South Carolina, to attend seminars by local authors. Whatever happened to trophies? I didn't want to go. My mother, who didn't really have a history of insisting I do anything extracurricular, insisted. She drove me there herself and in the end I was glad I went. Then, in the tenth grade I placed third in a Halloween story contest sponsored by the local newspaper. This time I won a white beach towel with the newspaper's weather mascot on it—the Weather Hound, a gangly dog, standing on two legs and wearing a cape. My brother, Bob, teased me about it. "Are you going to hang it on your wall?" he'd say. I don't think the editor at *Skirt!* would be impressed by my grade-school contests or my cutting-edge poems about teddy bears and skyscrapers.

~ ~ ~

Scott and I hear the *Wild Kingdom* sound again. This time we track it to the stable yard and find a peacock draped on top of a fence, its iridescent plumage folded up like a Chinese fan. We look at each other and laugh. Mystery solved. I will discover later that the peacock is associated with Hera, Goddess of marriage, the way the owl belongs to Athena.

Behind the plantation house, we walk down wide grassy terraces onto a straight, manicured path that cuts between two lakes, which are shaped like the open wings of a butterfly. "We're on the butterfly's back," I say, suddenly realizing the layout. From here we have a clear view of the Ashley River, the marshes and rice fields. It took one hundred slaves close to ten years to build this butterfly and just about everything we've seen.

Strolling into the gardens, I see hydrangeas bloom everywhere, violet-blue and pink. We stop before a giant live oak, estimated to be five hundred years old. Rooted on the banks of the Ashley River, it is massive—eighty-five feet tall and thirty feet around the trunk. The limbs spread out one hundred and forty-five feet in twisting tangles. Moss hangs from the branches like old Christmas tinsel that has been slung on impatiently.

Dwarfed beneath the branches, Scott and I cannot resist the urge to touch the trunk. We stand there for a few moments with our hands pressed against the bark, as if to say, *Yep, it's a tree, all right*, though this could never be perceived as an ordinary tree. I think about all the things that must have gone on around it in five hundred years, all the terrible history—slavery, Sherman's army, earthquakes, and hurricanes—but mostly I just feel the enduring beauty of the tree. I actually feel peaceful in its presence. The feeling hits me like the kerplunk of a stone splashing into the river and sending out its ripples.

Scott says, "This tree is amazing, isn't it?"

"It is," I say. I love that he gets this tree.

~ ~ ~

After I returned from Greece, I wrote Demetri a letter. I told him I hoped he could forgive me for not seeing him in Athens. I did not mention the part about purposely not answering his phone call. How could I? I had not even attempted to explain it further to my mother. In the letter, I merely said I'd missed his call and that we'd left Athens the next day.

No letter came in return.

Then one afternoon when I was alone in the apartment, folding laundry, the phone rang.

"Ann?"

I saw the Acropolis over his shoulder—a world away.

"Demetri?"

"Ann, how are you?"

"Fine. I'm fine. How are you?"

"Good. I just got your letter. I'm sorry, too, that I did not see you."

"Oh." I paused.

"I'm not mad at you."

"Good," I said. "I was worried you might be."

"Maybe there will be a next time."

"Yeah, maybe," I said, because I didn't know what else to say.

He said, "I will write to you and you write to me, okay?"

"Okay."

He let out a breath.

"Well . . . it is nice to hear your voice."

"It's good to hear your voice, too."

After we hung up, I sat on the floor beside the laundry basket. He was on another continent, but his voice was still in my ears. I picked up a hanger and draped Scott's dress shirt over it, unnecessarily fastening every single button until I reached the collar.

Demetri and I continued to write letters. Sometimes Scott picked up the mail and hand-delivered them to me. "You've got a letter from your pen pal," he'd say, jokingly. And I would tell him, "It was thousands of miles from here, a long time ago. We're just friends."

Once, when he dropped the envelope with the Greek stamps into my lap, I remembered the movie *Shirley Valentine,* which I'd watched at least twice now. Shirley goes to Greece and meets a handsome Greek man. She sums up her experience by saying, "I didn't fall in love with him, I fell in love with life."

I wondered if that was what had happened to me.

~ ~ ~

Scott and I decide to end our day at Middleton Place in what the map refers to as "The Secret Gardens." When I see them, I understand how they got their name. Two large, square-shaped enclosures are surrounded by tall, English hedges, thick as walls.

In one of the gardens, a marble statue of a woman stands in each corner. Scott sits on a wooden bench while I take a closer look at them.

"I think they represent the four seasons," I tell him, "because this one has flowers, and this one is holding wheat. Spring and fall, right?"

I sit down beside him and rub my arms to settle the chill bumps. I had dressed for heat, but the sun never came out. We sit there without talking. Scott reaches into his pocket. When he pulls his hand out, he's holding a tiny box.

Inside is a diamond ring. It gleams in the light while I stare at it.

"Will you marry me?" he says.

I had expected we would get engaged in the future—*future* being the operative word. I assumed I would know about it before-hand, as if the proposal was something we would plan together, then enact, preferably in a garden setting like this with all the seasons of life looking on. I hadn't expected to be surprised.

My brain is sending signals to my mouth, informing it what to say, but astonishment has created some sort of interference. I can only look at him. In those paralytic moments, I don't wonder if I'm too young or if I should wait till I figure out my career. Instead, what goes through my mind is that I've always been sure about him.

I nod.

"Is that a yes?" he asks.

"Yes!" I say, laughing, finally able to talk.

Scott breaks into a smile and reaches for my left hand, and there's my Athena ring on the finger that's reserved for engagement rings.

"I know what she means to you," Scott says. "We're not replacing her."

I work the Athena ring over my knuckle, then move it to my right hand, and Scott slides the engagement ring onto my finger.

"It's beautiful," I say.

~~~

When I get home, I call my mother. "Guess what? Scott and I are engaged!"

There are about three seconds of stunned silence and then: "Ann, I'm so happy for you! Congratulations! Oh my God." Now I hear sniffles. "You must be so excited."

"Yeah, I am," I say.

"Did you talk about when the wedding might be?"

"Next June, I think."

"Are you thinking of a church wedding?"

"I'm wondering about getting married under the oak tree at Middleton Place."

SEARCH

France / South Carolina

1999–2000

Sue

Jardin des Tuileries, St.-Germain-des-Prés, Louvre–Paris

ᔕ The Tuileries Garden in Paris seems filled with old women. Or is it just that I notice them more these days? Three of them sit in green metal chairs beside a fountain and talk with their hands waving around in the air. Another sips coffee beneath the red umbrellas. Two more stroll arm-in-arm through the corridors of tall, skinny trees. It's as if I've only now developed the rods and cones in my retina that allow me to see them.

It is October 15, 1999, our first afternoon in France, one filled with glinting light that glazes the hedges and the marble statues and the helium balloons tied to the baby strollers. Ann and I are here with eighteen other women who make up a small tour I am co-leading with my friends Trisha and Terry. I have arrived in France, fifty-one, soon to be mother of the bride, a woman who has spent a great deal of her time over the last six months sitting out in the marsh with the birds and the tides, writing a novel about a girl's search for her mother, and cooking up this trip to France with my two cohorts. The three of us conspired to create a way for women to travel together in quest of sacred feminine images in art and history, and I'm sure in the back of my mind I was also thinking it would be a way for Ann and I to go on traveling together, too. It's been over a year now since our trip to Greece.

At the moment, the group is cutting through the vastness of the Tuileries, sixty-two acres which run from the Carrousel du Louvre all the way to the Arc de Triomphe. We are on our way to St.-Germain-des-Prés, the oldest church in Paris. Ann and I trail the others mainly because I am trying to walk and write at the same time, a ridiculous enterprise that does justice to neither. My observations in the seventeenth-century gardens move in squiggly, uneven lines across the page of my journal, shorthand notes about this and that old woman.

I nudge Ann and point to one old woman with a little white dog and a black beret yanked over her stubby gray hair. The openings of her high-top maroon shoes are trimmed in yellow fur. They bring to mind the ruby slippers that Dorothy clicked together in Oz in order to get home, and I wonder if the elderly woman wears them as her own special conveyance to freedom. Or, maybe they are the shoes her daughter left behind in the closet, which the woman forces onto her feet like a stepsister in "Cinderella" in a desperate act of clinging to her youth. Or—and this is the scenario I prefer—they are her cunning way of not being invisible. It is also possible they are just shoes.

One of the women has spectacular white hair that reminds me of my paternal grandmother, Ruth. I think of how she wore it swept back and pinned with rhinestone combs, of her red lipstick and the indulgent ways she loved me.

When I was eight, she caved in to my pleas for a puny, violet-dyed chick which was in the window of the Golden Seed and Feed store, and which she then allowed me to set loose in her very grand parlor. I spread a carton of Quaker Oats across the handwoven rug, upon which the chick left the stain of its lavender droppings for all eternity. After the fracas, she would say to my shocked father, "But Sue *wanted* to play with the chick in the parlor."

The last time I saw her, she was propped in bed, eighty-nine years old, tiny as a sparrow in a pale blue bed jacket, and, looking at her, I got a searing flash of that pastel chick. Her hair, which she'd let me brush when I was a child into every sort of concoction, was all askew. I took her brush with the worn, lopsided bristles and combed it. I said, "Do you remember when you let me play with the chick in the parlor?" After a long pause, she nodded, but I was never quite sure if she did, or if she only wanted to please me. She died a week later.

My maternal grandmother, Sue, died at ninety-nine. During her last years, she told me about a time in 1918 when my grandfather, a World War I flight instructor, took her on a flying spree in a two-seat open-cockpit biplane. "He wasn't supposed to take civilians up," she said, and turned to gaze out the window, where the sky was lapis blue. "I really wanted to go up there, though, and see what it was like, so I dressed up in his roommate's leather jacket, goggles, and the cap—the funny one with the flaps on the side—and we took off. We were up there doing loop-de-loops and all kinds of things."

All I could think was that Wilbur and Orville Wright had only invented the airplane a few years before this. I couldn't decide what astonished me more—her subterfuge or the aerial acrobatics.

"You weren't scared?" I asked.

"Well, sure I was," she said, looking at me like I was daft.

It surprises me that my grandmothers have turned up like this, and even more that the elderly women in the garden occupy me so. I am trying to work out my fears and hopes about the Old Woman—who she is, what's she like, what's she's capable of.

These days when I walk into a public place with Ann—like the brasserie today at lunch—eyes gravitate to her and I get a taste of being invisible. I've waved away such moments, uncomfortable that

I've even noticed them, but today I paused to see exactly what it was I felt. It wasn't envy, I realized. Rather, it felt like I'd just handed off my youth baton and now I get to go sit on the bench.

On the bus, driving to the hotel, I missed untold French wonders sweeping by while I wrote about it in my journal. "Does it bother me or relieve me?" I asked myself. Truth be told, I've found freedom in these little tastes of being unseen; it's a relief not to be compelled so much by how I look, to have that part of my life become more or less passé. It reminds me a little of getting down-sized out of a high-profile job and discovering it's a blessing in disguise—now you can go do the thing you *really* want to do. But I also feel an unease about it, as if the invisibility of my appearance might extend to my work, my voice, my relevance. Am I afraid of disappearing, of shrinking into my bed jacket? Will I have to buy yellow-furred shoes?

My mind goes to the classic moment in the tale of Snow White, when the mother is eclipsed by the daughter. The queen consults her magic mirror: "Mirror, mirror, on the wall, who's the fairest of them all?" She expects to hear her own name called as usual, but her stepdaughter has recently become a young woman and the queen is getting crow's feet. "Snow White," the mirror blurts, and *zap!* the queen is dealt her first shock of age.

Perhaps all mothers of daughters possess a secret talking mirror that announces when their young womanhood begins to fade and their daughters' begin to blossom. As in the fairy tale, the experience can unleash a lacerating jealousy in some mothers, which turns up like poison apples on the daughter's doorstep. It can also usher in fears that I would've sworn I'd never have. Of invisibility, anonymity, irrelevance. And deeper down, fears of decline and death.

I watched a television piece not long ago about an art gallery featuring paintings and drawings of women. "Here you will see every variety of the female form," the male reporter said, "from the young woman to the old hag."

"Did he say *hag?* Did he?" I ranted to Sandy. "When did the opposite of young female become old *hag?* For God's sake!"

A year and a half before this trip, I got my first intimations that the young "variety of the female form" was beginning to pack up to leave me. I'd felt it through the dramatic changes in my body, the onset of thoughts about my mortality, the spiritual vacuity that set in, the way the sap leaked from my writing. It was evident, too, in the way the word *hag* set me off, betraying my fear that I would not find the potency to generate the third act I wished for. Now and then a dread rose in me—this irrational and passing *thing*— and I would succumb for a moment to the illusion that it was all diminishing now, the best of my life.

As Ann and I hurry along the Avenue du Général Lemonnier, trying to catch up to the others, I realize what a strange in-between place I am in. The Young Woman inside has turned to go, but the Old Woman has not shown up.

My new journal is green. When I purchased it, expressly for this trip, I thought of the quote I inscribed at the front of the red journal I took to Greece—"Pilgrims are poets who create by taking journeys"—and I wondered if there were words that belonged at the beginning of this one. It was Ann who gave them to me. Her e-mail popped into my in-box not long before we left: "Have you seen this quote by George Sand? 'The old woman I shall become will be quite different from the woman I am now. Another I is beginning.'"

I copied the quotation on page one of the green journal. The fact that it came from a French writer born here in Paris and a subversive woman of courage was mere gravy.

Another I is beginning.

~ ~ ~

We cross to the Left Bank at Pont Royal and walk along the Quai Voltaire, winding to Rue Bonaparte and coming finally to the church. Our group stands in a cluster on the sidewalk with our necks hinged back and our mouths parted, staring at the eleventh-century tower of St.-Germain-des-Prés. From the corner of my eye, I notice someone taking a photograph, not of the thousand-year-old belfry, but of us gaping up at it.

Trisha, our religious art scholar who lived for a time in Paris, informs us that the church was founded in 542 and was part of a flourishing abbey built on the site of a former temple to Isis. Supposedly a statue of black Isis was worshipped here as the Virgin Mary until 1514, when it was destroyed by the abbot.

My guidebook emphasizes the church's Romanesque architecture, several sixth-century marble columns, the fire during the French Revolution, along with the bewildering detail that a king of Poland is buried inside. Nothing about a mysterious Black Madonna who descended from Isis.

Since returning from Greece, I've read everything I could about dark Madonnas. Only several hundred still exist in Europe, the majority here in France, where they call her *Vierge Noire*, the Black Virgin. Sometimes she's referred to as the other Mary, a tantalizing reference to her pagan family tree.

Ann and I move along the ambulatory until we come to the small, circular chapel of St. Anne. I've been drawn to her since I discovered the prolific image of her holding her grown daughter Mary in her lap. There's a legend that St. Anne's body was brought to France by Mary Magdalene fifty years after her death and her bones were revered at Apt in Provence, but I can't imagine anyone takes it seriously anymore.

We stare at the exquisite marble altar in her chapel. Someone has left a creased photograph on it of a dark-haired girl around three years old. I point it out to Ann, sure it's someone's granddaughter. Anne is the patron saint of grandmothers. For an instant I try to imagine myself as a grandmother, a woman called Grandma, or Nana or Granny, but it feels foreign and other, like trying to imagine myself as an astronaut.

I look around for an image of St. Anne in the chapel, but there isn't any. When painted as an older woman, she was often given a green cloak, like the mantle of spring, which is somehow unexpected. Her emblem is a door. Probably because she was the doorway for Mary, but my mind fidgets with the idea that she could represent other thresholds, too. A Grandmother door . . . the Old Woman door . . . some passage to the other side.

Ann photographs the picture of the little girl left here for St. Anne's safekeeping, while I plop down on a bench and pull out the postcard I tucked inside the back cover of my journal. It depicts Picasso's *Girl Before a Mirror.* I first saw the painting in the Museum of Modern Art in New York many years ago and was affected by it, though I couldn't have told you then why that was. I bought the postcard in the museum gift shop, but eventually lost track of it. It surfaced again when we moved, and since then I've kept it out on my desk.

It portrays a young woman, haloed in light, gazing into an oval mirror. Her pink, unblemished profile merges with a frontal view of her face that's painted in bright yellow and shaped like a crescent moon. But the mirror is a wrinkle in time, and the image staring back at her reveals the young woman not as she is, but how she will one day be. The woman in the glass appears old and dark, her face shaded in violet and red, her eyes grown hollow, her body beginning to shrink.

What touches me is how the younger woman's arms reach out

for her older self, as if trying to embrace the rather formidable mystery she has glimpsed. And curiously, her older self reaches back to her. Whatever Picasso may have had in mind when he painted this (at the age of fifty, for what it's worth), I see an aspect of the Demeter and Persephone reunion in it—the reunion of the Young Woman and the Old Woman *within*.

I show the postcard to Ann, who studies it and says, "What is it—two sides of one woman?"

"That's what I think," I say and go on for a moment about the young woman with her vitality, fertility, and sense of beginning and the old woman with her wisdom and creative and spiritual powers.

"Don't you love how they're both reaching for each other?" As I say this, I understand for the first time that I'm looking at the *I* I want to find. It is not captured solely in the dark older woman or in the bright younger one. It is composed of both of them, conjoined and integrated. It happens in the embrace.

I listen for a moment to voices, females voices, somersaulting along the Gothic vaults. "I have a photograph back home of my mother on her wedding day," I tell Ann, excited that I've suddenly remembered it. "I don't know if you've seen it. She's sitting at a dressing table in her white gown, looking into a mirror. My grandmother is standing at her shoulder."

Ann shakes her head.

"It's Mother's face the camera catches in the mirror."

"Like the painting," Ann says.

Except it's reversed—the old woman is looking into the mirror and seeing the young woman's face.

~ ~ ~

That night in the hotel bathroom, I stand at the sink, exhausted. Tired from the flight and the walking. I just want to go to bed.

I squirt toothpaste onto my toothbrush, and when Ann appears in the doorway with her cosmetic bag, I step over to make room for her at the sink. As we stand side by side and brush our teeth before the mirror, I gradually become aware that despite my fatigue, I am watching her face.

Mirror, mirror.

She is so beautiful.

~ ~ ~

We spend the next morning in the Louvre, gazing at paintings of Mary. There are more paintings of her in the world than of any other woman, and a preponderance of them seems to be right here. They flow along the walls like a moving picture of her life—of both the human Mary and the divine Mary.

What I notice, almost as much as the paintings themselves, is the way certain incidents in her life are repeated over and over: annunciations, nativities, flights into Egypt, pietàs, assumptions to heaven. . . . Each event feels like a universal story, offering points of entry into my own experience.

When I visited Mary's House in Ephesus, during Ann's and my first trip, the theological polarization I felt about how to relate to Mary began to be resolved. Over the past year, I have been slowly coming to understand her not only within a biblical and human context, but also as a living symbol of the Divine Feminine, a spiritual presence able to hold large archetypal mysteries. Why then shouldn't the paramount occasions in her life create a guiding story for women?

As I move through the Louvre, I begin to record notes about the paintings and what they might be suggesting:

Annunciation—the summons from within to bring forth something new, particularly one's own spiritual and creative life.

Pregnancy—the season of waiting, incubation, holding the tensions of the process.

Visitation with Elizabeth—seeking community and support from other women; telling the story.

Nativity—the labor to bring forth what has been conceived from within.

Flight into Egypt—protecting the new life from threat, within and without.

Nurturing the Child—reordering everything in order to feed and tend the new life.

At the Cross/Pietà—descent, embracing necessary loss, surrender, and grief.

Mary's Death—dying of an old self or way of being; the dark night.

Assumption into Heaven—ascent; rising of new self; crossing threshold into new realm.

Coronation—the realization of new life; its fruition and impact on others.

My speculations click with me. Each event possesses a core of generic feminine meaning along with the possibility of interpreting it personally.

In the Louvre gift store, I scour the racks for postcards portraying each of these pivotal dramas. I spread them along the counter in the right biographical sequence, compelled by the idea that each one could be a window into my own experience, allowing me to glimpse it through the lens of a grand maternal matrix. Even in the busy shop, I can see that it's no longer the annunciation image that defines where I am right now with my creativity or with my spiritual life. Nor is it the picture of the pregnant Mary who waits, who incubates and bears the tensions. It's the nativity image that grabs me—the necessity of labor, the lonely beauty of birthing.

~ ~ ~

"Don't let me wear a pink dress to your wedding," I say. Ann and I sit at a table in the café below the Louvre's glass pyramid and talk

not about all the sublime art we've just seen but about wedding
outfits. "Not powder-blue either. And no jacket with shoulder
pads."

"I promise," says Ann.

The wedding date is set—June 3. Seven months away, but we've
already spent a lot of Sunday afternoons making wedding plans.
As I tell my friends, I have rented the tree. I love that she picked
out a five-hundred-year-old moss-laden oak to be her "church." We
have a guest list of a hundred and twenty, which is about all the
people we can fit beside it. She will walk to the tree down a path
that cuts through a rose garden. Floral arrangements would be
redundant.

I am sincerely happy about the wedding and I adore Scott, but
several times since Ann called me with the news, I've felt a small
wrench at the back of my heart when I think about it. I know it
isn't about her, it's about me, but I don't know precisely what the
feeling is—a longing? a sadness? the baton passing again?

I'm eating some sort of sandwich that I fear could be spread
with goose liver. I push it aside and drink my *demi pression*. Last
summer when I brought up *her* dress, she announced she wanted
to wear my wedding gown. "No kidding?" I said, taken by surprise. "Are you sure?"

She nodded. "I'm sure."

I should have guessed this. When Ann was a girl, every time
we visited her grandparents, she would beg my mother to take my
wedding dress from its storage bag in the back of my old bedroom
closet so she could put it on. It did not take a lot of begging; my
mother was her willing accomplice in most everything. I have a
memory of Ann at five with the skirt billowing out around her on
the floor like a melting vanilla cone.

It was the first wedding dress I tried on. I fell in love with it at first sight, but when I noticed the price, my heart sank. Six hundred dollars, a fortune. I tried to be stoic about it, and Mother and I kept looking, trudging from shop to shop, until finally she proclaimed she didn't care what the dress cost, we were going back to get it. "It's only money," she said, as if steeling herself.

When I walked down the aisle in it, it was August 1968 and I was barely twenty years old. My "church" was an actual church. It was packed with everybody from our small town. I had seven bridesmaids, who wore white dresses and wreaths of blue flowers in their hair. Wired to my bouquet was the small white Bible I carried to Sunday school as a child. In my shoe was the 1947 dime my mother wore in her shoe when she got married. There were years and years stretched ahead of me.

I close my eyes and try to picture myself as I was on that day, to be that girl again, to be at the beginning. Across the table, Ann is talking about the so-called "acid treatment" we will have to subject the wedding gown to in order to remove the yellow tint.

~ ~ ~

Before we leave the museum, I wander back to Leonardo da Vinci's *The Virgin and Child with St. Anne.* When I stood before it earlier, I found myself looking at it from Anne's perspective, not Mary's. I was unsure if and how it belonged with the other, more paradigmatic events in Mary's life that I had recorded.

I inspect it again—Mary sitting in her mother's lap reaching for Jesus, who plays beside her skirt. Behind them are craggy hills and a lone tree. There is an easy intimacy between the two barefoot women. Mary gazes down at Jesus, but Anne stares at her daughter with an enigmatic smile reminiscent of Leonardo's *Mona Lisa*—the same smile, only better. I try to read Anne's expression. Wistful, bittersweet, knowing. She seems moved by the thought of her daughter as an adult and a mother herself.

I wonder if, perhaps like Picasso's *Girl Before a Mirror*, it captures the reunion. What I know is that, for me, it is the most personal of all the paintings in the Louvre. The aging mother reaching for her grown daughter. The way she tries to make a lap for her younger self.

Ann

___

Seine River, Notre Dame Cathedral—Paris

❧ I've only been in Paris long enough to glimpse the cityscape and order onion soup. I'm sitting on the bus with the Fun Girls again, only this time they are my mother's age and much more uninhibited. We've just had lunch at a brasserie and are headed into the heart of Paris when Trisha picks up the bus microphone and introduces us to St. Genevieve, the patron saint of Paris.

"Jon-vi-ev," she says, with a French pronunciation. It sounds musical. I like the name. To me, it suggests a self-assured woman. If I had a name like Genevieve, I would know exactly who I am and what I'm supposed to do. A Genevieve, it seems to me, could paint a self-portrait, would know how to say: this is who I am.

The bus chugs along Rue de Rivoli. "Coming up, you'll see an entirely gold statue of Joan of Arc," Trisha tells the group. "It's situated not far from where she was wounded during an attack she led against the English in 1429. She was only seventeen. Can you imagine?"

No, I can't.

I turn toward the window and see the gilded statue come into view in the middle of a large intersection known as Place des Pyramides. Joan sits on her horse, clasping the reins in one hand and holding a flagpole with the other. Seeing her reminds me of when

I was twelve and took horseback riding lessons, trotting and cantering on a horse named Harry. The fact that Joan and I both sat on saddles is about as far as the similarity goes. Before those lessons I'd never been on a horse, and I would discover there's a reason truck engines are measured in *horse*power. Riding back to the stables one day, Harry was spooked by a tractor and took off. At first I was terrified, but then it became thrilling. Something came over me—a small rush of bravery. I held on with my knees and got control of the reins, gradually slowing him to a trot. A picture of me on Harry that my mother snapped afterward was tacked to my bulletin board for a long time.

As we leave the Joan statue behind, I write a reminder in my journal to find this picture when I get home.

"Joan was burned at the stake in Rouen and became a saint in 1920," Trisha is saying.

Somehow Joan's sainthood had escaped me. *Saint* Joan. *That* we do not share.

Trisha goes on to tell us that Joan heard voices. St. Margaret, St. Catherine, and St. Michael all conversed with her about her mission to save the French from the invading English. Joan also thought God spoke directly to her about it and declared she wasn't afraid of her mission because she was born for it.

That is what I want—to know what I was born to do. What I wouldn't give to hear voices about now.

Just before we came to France, I read a poem by David Whyte with four lines that nearly stopped my heart:

> *You must learn one thing.*
> *The world was made to be free in.*
> *Give up all the other worlds*
> *except the one to which you belong.*

Tonight, when I climb into bed in our hotel room, I will realize those lines are my "St. Michael" voice, spelling out my mission: find the world to which I belong.

~ ~ ~

After a quick stop at the hotel to unload luggage, our group is off again on a long walk to St.-Germain-des-Prés, followed by a boat ride on the Seine River.

At the Pont de l'Alma, we board the *Bateau-Mouche*, an open-air boat which literally translates as "fly-boat." I find a place next to my mother among the bright orange seats. My point-and-click camera inexplicably broke back at the hotel, so I fiddle with my manual 35mm and practice taking some pictures: dozens of boats floating like cork lures; the BATEAUX-MOUCHES sign in tall, white letters; Mom and Terry gripping the scarves around their necks.

The Seine divides Paris into two banks, and the boat cruises right down the middle of the city, past some of the most famous monuments. We pass the Place de la Concorde, the Egyptian obelisk, the Tuileries, and move toward Pont Neuf and Notre Dame. The wind and sun make me forget my jet lag. The light creates soft strobes on the river, so different from the light on the Aegean, which had a way of blazing against everything it touched.

As Terry leans toward Mom to discuss the afternoon schedule, a woman in our group, whom I met just hours ago, asks a question—*the* question, really: "So, Ann, what do you do?"

I search my memory for her name among the many introductions from earlier but can't place it.

"I work for a magazine back in Charleston."

"Oh, a magazine—what kind?"

"A women's magazine. I work on both sides—advertising and editorial."

"So, do you write like your mom?"

A few months ago, I finally decided to take my editor up on her offer and wrote a couple of articles. As a member of the staff, I felt like I ought to contribute something. But write like my mom?

"No, hardly," I tell her. "I mean, yeah, I do some writing for them. A few articles and profiles. But I wouldn't say I'm a writer. You know, I should probably stick to answering the phones."

The woman, whose name I still cannot remember, squints at me. "What were your articles about?"

Really? We're going to talk about this some more?

"They were just personal experience pieces. I wrote one about my dad and one about Earth Day."

"Well, I bet you've got your mom's talent."

She obviously suffers from delusions. "Oh, I don't know about that," I say. And laugh.

If I went into writing, I would inevitably be compared to my mother. Even this woman is thinking I have talent like her. I realize there are a million subjects to write about and writing can take so many forms—fiction, playwriting, journalism, essays, poetry, TV commercials—but still I fear comparisons are inevitable. I imagine the silent indictments if I failed. "Wow," people would say, "the apple fell way, way, *way* far from the tree."

Mom has been writing since I was a year old. Throughout my youth her presence as a writer grew in my mind—from those first book signings she did in the greeting card section at Belk department store while I sat beside her reading my Judy Blume books, all the way to the crowds that lined up more recently with their copies of *Dissident Daughter*. When she spoke at my college, I overheard the amazing things my professors said to her about her book. Her career makes me proud.

When I search myself honestly, I know my mom's success as a

writer isn't really the deterrent to my own attempts at writing. No, my hesitation comes down to this: writing is what my mother does; I need to find what is mine. I've just assumed that what is mine would be different from hers.

As the boat circles the Île Saint-Louis and heads toward the Eiffel Tower, I recall that I *liked* writing those articles. Sitting at my desk after dinner, typing out a tangled mess of thoughts around an idea, an image, or a line of poetry, then shaping and tinkering until I had a draft—there had been a particular satisfaction in it, like I was in some sort of "flow," content and challenged at the same time. I would lose all track of time. It would grow late as I worked. Scott would fall asleep. The soft-watt bulb in the lamp on my desk would be the only light on in the apartment. Just me alone with the words. I didn't have the slightest idea what I was doing, but I felt more connected to myself when I finished.

It reminded me of the feeling I had writing my prize-winning story in seventh grade, back when I was sure I would end up a writer. My story was about a girl and a horse. It was very *National Velvet*-y in theme, though I'd never read the book. I even worked on my story through recesses. When my English teacher called me into the hall, I thought I was in trouble, but she informed me I'd won the writing competition. I didn't belong in the Science Club, Pep Squad, chorus, or modern dance class, but writing stories . . . that had felt like mine.

The problem, I discovered, is that it isn't enough just to *like* writing. I stare at the water of the Seine and run through all the reasons a writing career is a bad idea for me. For one thing, it's not practical. I'm not thirteen anymore. What twenty-three-year-old says: I'm going for job security and a steady income—I'll become a writer? The truth is I need to pay the bills. There's a point at which you have to be realistic.

Not to mention the matter of talent. If I was cut out to be a writer, wouldn't I be better at it? Wouldn't it come easier? Wouldn't I have majored in English instead of history and applied for a graduate program in creative writing? I've heard Mom say that a person can learn the craft, but that's only half of it; a writer needs some innate capacity that can't be taught. Did I have it?

After the solitary writing process at my desk was over, I would feel reasonably satisfied with my articles, at least until the realization dawned that people would actually read them. Then, feeling exposed and self-conscious, I would regret they ever saw print. I could not read my newly published articles without hearing trumpets go off in my head announcing how bad they were.

Which brings me to what may be the most serious of all reasons a writing career for me would be plain ludicrous: it requires far too much confidence. Why would I choose a career that's notorious for its *rejection letters*? I don't want to lose faith in the words I wrote on the scroll of paper that I left in the cave at Eleusis ("I will return"), but another big rejection and I don't know if I would get back.

As we approach the Eiffel Tower, I read the digital numbers on the countdown clock, which tracks the days until the year 2000. Seventy-nine. The sight of it calls up the forecasted chaos of Y2K. Computers crashing, warnings of failing airline traffic control, Conan O'Brien's "In the Year 2000" skits.

Propping my elbows on the boat rail, I focus and click on the countdown clock.

~ ~ ~

On our second day in Paris, after half a day in the Louvre, Mom and I walk to Notre Dame. Along the riverbank, we pass vendors selling books, art prints, and vintage postcards. We linger at patisserie windows displaying raspberry tarts, *pain au chocolat,* petits fours, and madeleines. When we cross the Pont Neuf, I can still see the desserts in my head.

At the cathedral square, I pull my Fodor's guidebook from my backpack and scan the pages devoted to the cathedral: *Construction began in 1163 . . . completed in 1345 . . . walls are lined with chapels . . . don't miss the three rose windows.*

"This says there are three portals that lead into the church," I say to Mom. "One represents the Virgin Mary, one, the Last Judgment, and one, St. Anne."

"A St. Anne portal?" Mom asks.

"Yeah."

She walks through that one while I go through the Virgin Mary entrance. Looking up, I see a depiction of the Coronation of the Virgin and remember the fresco on the wall in the monastery in Greece, where I first discovered Mary, Queen of Heaven. Up until yesterday, I would've guessed Mom would choose the Mary portal, too, but then she spent all that time in St. Anne's chapel at St.-Germain-des-Prés, and today she seemed transfixed by Leonardo's painting of St. Anne in the Louvre. I know that she sees herself in Anne all of a sudden and that it has to do with "the Old Woman," as Mom fondly calls her. I've always thought of my mother as ageless. It's hard to think of her growing older, to watch *her* thinking about it. *I won't have her forever,* I think, and the sight of her walking off toward the Anne portal nearly levels me.

This morning, I woke to the buzzing of Mom's blood pressure machine as the cuff tightened around her arm. Even before we left home, she was having a problem with her blood pressure. "What's the reading today?" I asked, and she said, "Oh, it's up a little, but I'm okay." But I wonder silently—how okay can it be if she's *traveling with the machine?*

I meet up with her at the ambulatory, and we walk past the first of thirty-seven chapels that line the interior of the cathedral, looking up at the vaulted ceiling and lit chandeliers. I smell candle wax and stone. Some chapels glow with more votive candles than others. You can easily tell the popular saints from the unpopular ones. All the visitors to Notre Dame seem to be on the same path, circling the church like bobbing toys caught in a swirl of bathwater. Now and then I see strips of pastel-colored light from the stained glass float above their heads.

I stop at the chapel of Joan of Arc. She's one of the popular saints. Her chapel is ablaze. I hadn't expected her to be here, though I don't know why not. Of course she would be here. Her statue stands on a tall stone pedestal. She wears a long skirt, armor across her shoulders, and a helmet opened to reveal the face of a nineteen-year-old girl. My eyes are drawn to her hands, folded around a spear, the tip of which is sculpted into a fleur-de-lis. The helmet and spear remind me of the *Mourning Athena* relief at the Acropolis Museum that I had not gotten to see. I try to imagine this warrior-girl charging through Paris on horseback, commanding an army. I love her youth, her boldness, her clear vision, her whole wild story. She is like Athena, but a real girl.

Sensing I want to stay here awhile, Mom says she'll meet me at the Madonna statue near the choir screen. I drop a few francs into the offering box, light a votive candle, and set it in the stand in front of the statue. I look at Joan's face and entreat her silently: *Help me listen to my own voice. Help me find what I'm born to do. Help me find the courage to do it.*

The yellow flame of my candle burns in a steady flicker. My prayer is reflexive. I do not pause to wonder if I deserve an answer, but I do ask, which is progress, I suppose. I don't know what will come from something as simple as asking. Prayer and faith are enigmas—but I feel alive, like the girl on the horse. Maybe this is hope.

~~~

Outside the cathedral, our eyes adjust to the daylight. On our trek back to the hotel, we stop in a patisserie and I buy a chocolate éclair. I walk, and eat, and think. I hear that poem in my head. My St. Michael "voice."

Give up all the other worlds / except the one to which you belong.

Sue

Island of Gavrinis

🙠 On a ferry in the Gulf of Morbihan, along the coast of Brittany, I begin to think morbidly about my blood pressure. I took it last night and again this morning with the battery-operated machine I brought from home, and it was alarmingly high, stirring up the familiar panic I've felt lately about my hypertension. It started out mildly a few years ago—as something to *watch*. In the months leading up to the trip, however, it erupted into uncontrolled episodes like this one, so many that my doctor looked uneasily at me, ordered an electrocardiogram, and upped the dosage of my medication. One minute I had a little pile of leaves burning in a corner of my backyard, and the next, a wildfire was whipping across the grass. I did not see it coming.

I have responded with yoga, aerobics, diet, acupuncture—a sort of holistic bucket brigade—but so far without effect. I'm probably working too hard at them, turning them into hypertense activities, but I don't know how to relax about something referred to as a "silent killer." The words are emblazoned across a big poster about hypertension in my doctor's exam room. During my last visit, while waiting for the nurse to take my blood pressure, I refused to look at it, but my body reacted anyway and I was soused with adrenaline by the time she got there. My blood pressure soared off into the stratosphere like the starship *Enterprise*, going where no reading of mine had ever gone before.

I don't like to talk about my hypertension. As if it has a stigma attached to it. As if it reveals too much about me, some glimpse into myself I cannot allow, cannot bear. It feels ridiculously like a failure, a revelation of my inability to rest, a reflection on the paucity of my stillness, serenity, and centeredness—all those contemplative graces I value. The whole matter leaves me embarrassed, helpless, afraid, and amplifies my already touchy thoughts about my mortality.

By the time we board the small, white ferry, the panic I felt earlier this morning about the readings has blunted into a dull percussion along my breastbone, enough to send me outside to the rail, wanting to be alone. It doesn't help that we are on our way to the tiny island of Gavrinis to see a five-thousand-year-old burial chamber, known as a "tumulus."

Not discovered until 1865, it is thought by many to be the finest tumulus in the world. In the tourist pamphlet, it's described as "the Sistine Chapel of Prehistory," though it's hard to imagine what could lead to such hyperbole. A tumulus is a piece of stone-age architecture, after all, earth and stones and that's about it. What intrigues me most is that archaeological evidence suggests the tumulus was not just a grave site, but that it had a ceremonial purpose. What that purpose may have been, however, has turned into one of those Stonehenge-like mysteries.

~ ~ ~

When we decided to visit Gavrinis, I wondered if my time at the tumulus could become a private ceremony for me as well, a way to have an overdue conversation with myself about the fact that for the first time in my life I think about death. It always comes unbidden, suddenly there in front of me like someone unsavory stepping out from an alley into my path, startling me and taking my breath, and then a tiny burst of anguish occurs in my chest—*yes, it will end, it will all end.* For several moments, the feeling will ricochet inside, then it's gone.

The intimations have come more and more frequently and at times bring on a slightly frantic litany—*I am fifty-one, so young. Dying is far in the future. Cross that bridge when you come to it. Focus on today. Don't be morose.*

I first read Eavan Boland's poem "Ceres Looks at the Morning" after I returned home from Greece. Sometimes, like now, entire lines of it come back:

Already / my body is a twilight: Solid. Gold / At the edge of a larger darkness.

The words offer some kind of latitude-longitude reading of my soul, positioning me in interior time and place—*at the edge of a larger darkness.* At the strange, uncompromising border with my finitude. Deep down, those bearings seem right to me. The growing recognition of my mortality seems part of the threshold I'm crossing, and I know my soul is asking me to come to terms with it, to develop the ability to look at death, to find my way into its secrecy and wisdom, its stunning ordinariness.

Over the preceding summer, Sandy and I vacationed in Bermuda at a place called Ariel Sands, so named for the water sprite Ariel in Shakespeare's *The Tempest.* The hotel desk clerk handed me a copy of the play when we checked in. Having never read it before, I opened it one afternoon sitting beside the waves and found a story about a man, Prospero, making a rite of passage into his older years, though I'm sure I was reading it through the lens of my own life. At the end of the play, Prospero announces that every third thought he has from then on will be of his death. *Oh, great.* I closed the book with a sinking feeling.

Back home, I searched for spiritual commentary on the play and discovered Helen M. Luke's essay *"The Tempest."* By allowing death to come often into his thoughts, Prospero is *preparing* himself for it, she wrote. The conscious and meditative attention to death becomes a spiritual task during the last part of life, she insists, and contrary to what we might suppose, it creates the opposite of despair; it creates *release* and *meaning.*

But now, on the ferry, with this intensifying blood pressure crisis, knowing there's something physically wrong with me that neither I nor medication has been able to fix, the subject of death seems too visceral, too lacerating. I'm not sure if I have the stomach for a meditation on it.

~ ~ ~

I glance at my watch—only 2:00 P.M. but it looks like early evening. I watch the city of Larmor-Baden recede into the distance and shiver inside my raincoat despite the red shawl I've draped over it and the floppy wool hat pulled low on my forehead. Yesterday, when we left Mont-St.-Michel and arrived in Brittany, the weather was spectacular. We roamed the fields and woods, exploring prehistoric stone alignments around the village of Carnac, the sun glazing the megaliths. But today is bitterly cold. Grayness lacquers the sky and weighs down the air.

The water along the bow churns the same slate color as the sky, and I think fleetingly of the River Styx, the mythological river between life and death over which souls are ferried to the other side. It is a ludicrously grim association, but then I *am* crossing a body of water, on a ferry, to what the pamphlet calls "a sanctuary of dying." Ann taps on the glass window from inside. Turning, I smile at her, ignoring her querulous expression—*what are you doing out there in the cold?*

Really, what *was* I doing?

She had listened this morning to the whir of the blood pressure cuff inflating on my arm and then the steady *beep, beep, beep.*

"Is it high?" she said.

She's aware of my recent hypertension, but I've said nothing about the elevated readings I'm getting here in France.

"Just a bit," I told her, as if it's no big deal. I didn't want to lie to her, but neither did I want to fill her with a lot of unnecessary anxiety. I tried to pick something in the middle.

My body is a twilight . . . I turn the fragment of poetry over in my mind, considering that the first tint of it has come to *my* body. I can only share so much of that with Ann. She is a young woman; how much of my truth should she take on? I struggle for intimacy with her, and then I struggle with the reality of boundaries, that there are places between us that intimacy cannot, perhaps should not, happen: the twilight, the larger darkness. I can barely handle them myself.

Since being in the Louvre, I've returned often to the idea that pivotal events in Mary's life reveal windows into our own. I've sorted through the annunciation paintings—all those angels summoning all those Marys to bring forth new life—and wondered if there's an "annunciation" embedded in my hypertension.

While in the thick of doctor visits before the trip, I dreamed about a strange woman who shows up to tell me my "true problem." She diagnoses it as "Excel-eration and Acceleration." She is annoying in the way all-knowing people usually are. I treat her like a quack and belittle the way she has apparently repeated my so-called true problem twice. Unfazed, she sits me down and speaks to me like I'm in kindergarten: "The words sound alike, but they're spelled differently," she explains, then writes the pair of words in big block letters on a school chalkboard. *My true problem.*

Does the dream suggest that my drive to excel and the hurriedness it breeds—these old, implacable daemons of mine—are at the root of my hypertension? It does take me back to the need I've uncovered to cultivate being and find the contemplative writer in myself. I decide the woman in the dream is a "knowing" part of myself and that she has sent me back to repeat grades, to relearn basic truths I supposedly already know.

After disembarking the ferry, we follow a path to an igloo-shaped mound of earth, one hundred and sixty feet in diameter and twenty feet high. The tumulus. I hadn't expected anything so mammoth. It looks like a vast pregnant belly. One side is covered with small stones laid on top of each other like fish scales. In the middle of them, a low doorway.

~ ~ ~

I pause at the tumulus opening and peer into the feeble light, feeling the slightest hesitation. The tunnel is straight and narrow, leading forty-five feet into an interior chamber. It's lined with twenty-three massive stones, joined together to form what our thickly accented French guide earlier called "Pel-VEEC wallzzz."

"Did he say *pelvic walls?*" I whispered to Ann.

"I do believe he did," she replied.

I watch the other women threading into the tight space. The stones tower over them in colors of russet brown and bleached gray. While the birth canal design is unmistakable, what registers in me is *bones*—earth bones, Old Woman bones, that bone I dug up in my dream last year in Greece. I get a fanciful, if not eerie, picture of the group strolling along a column of vertebrae.

Stepping inside, I feel a lurch of dread that starts tiny, then fans through my chest and arms before fading. As my sight adjusts to the gloom, lavish carvings appear on the stones. Their surfaces are covered with finely balanced designs associated with the ancient Goddess: spirals, chevrons, crescents, egg-shaped ovals, and serpentine lines.

The most prolific motif by far is clusters of concentric arches nested one inside the other. They mushroom out in every direction, creating a complex and magnificent unity. Stepping close and studying the pattern, I notice a small navel protrusion on top of each set of arches and realize I am looking at birth canals. Not only am I standing in what is apparently a replica of a birth canal, they are all over the walls.

As I move deeper into the passage, the birth images repeat on the stones in new, unexpected ways, inducing the odd feeling in me of moving inward, traveling to what matters, down to the marrow. They possess a free and primitive beauty, the power to make me cry. I want to take back every condescending thought I had about this being the "Sistine Chapel of Prehistory."

My only personal encounters with death have been with those of my grandparents, who were ripe with old age and the fullness of their lives, and with that of my father-in-law, who died abruptly of a heart attack at sixty. When his death occurred, I was nine months pregnant with my son. I sat on the church pew during the funeral, so great with child I was down to my one last pathetic maternity dress. Somewhere during the service, it hit me how sharply birth and death were intersecting in my family's life. The words *womb* and *tomb* began to reiterate in my thoughts. I don't know now if the minister uttered them and I picked them up like a refrain, or if they just materialized from a place in my own head.

Now here I am, in a burial chamber awash in the metaphor of feminine birth, when *whack!*—my foot strikes against something hard on the stone floor and I trip. I feel myself going down and reach out for one of the stone masterpieces, which we are, of course, forbidden to touch. I catch myself, but my bag lands with a thud and the French guide scurries over, more worried about the Pel-VEEC wallzzz, I suspect, than about me. He is kind and very gallant, however, taking my elbow and guiding me over the hurdle, which turns out to be an oblong rock stretched across the corridor like a door sill.

"Do not worry, you are not the first to trip here," he says in his rich accent, trying to make me feel less clumsy. "It is possible the rock was even placed here deliberately—as a stumbling block. Such things were done, you know, in initiation ceremonies . . . to make people think about the obstacles."

He points to an even larger sill stone ahead. "See, there is another one. You do *see* it, Madame?"

"Yes," I assure him, aware that I've literally tripped over a piece of the ceremony that may have gone on here.

I notice Ann making her way back to see what the commotion is about, and I wave her on. "It's nothing," I call and walk along more alert, but thinking about the symbolic stumbling blocks. Mine, perhaps, being the reflex to look away from death, to shield myself. What am I afraid of? Oblivion? Of losing self and identity? Of the grief it would cause those who love me? Of my own despair at leaving them? Of physical suffering? Of regrets?

~ ~ ~

The passage ends in a room eight feet square—a small mausoleum lined with six more of the huge, sumptuously carved stones. Approaching it, I have the feeling of peeling away insulation, coming to an exposed wire. I halt at the entrance and stare up at the stone lintel over the door, noting the labyrinthine carvings. As I step inside, I take one of those long yoga breaths I've learned.

The inner chamber seems intended as a symbolic womb and carries the aura of a Holy of Holies. The layout suggests that one's dying is a return to the womb and conjures up an astonishing image of birth waiting in death, of the dead buried like seeds in a Great Mother's womb. I circle the chamber, inspecting the stones. The feast of sensuous lines appears as watery as fingerpaint on canvas, though each has been painstakingly etched with tiny quartz pebbles.

The memory of the rite of death and rebirth called the Eleusinian Mysteries that Ann and I had learned about in Greece fourteen months ago flits through my mind. But the context was different then, wasn't it? I was focused on the death of my womb, the death of a former self, not death itself. My God, how much easier was it to think about death as letting go of some part of life: leaving behind a job, a relationship, a self, a pattern, a way of being, a hundred different things? Now I realize: they are all practice. Each a rehearsal for death, challenging my clinging and resistance, developing my soul's facility to turn loose and open to what is new and unknown.

I stand in a corner of the inner chamber. Close my eyes and try to let the Larger Darkness in. Acknowledge that it will come and take me and then I will not exist. Disappearing like an exhaled breath, like that breath I let out a minute ago.

I don't know if the meditation lasts a full minute. The truth grieves me and, opening my eyes, I feel quietly split, like the shell on the blue crab when the time comes for the creature to slough it off and grow. I've seen the shells lying broken on the creek bottom and the crabs scurrying, as raw and unprotected as newborns.

One day I will have to forgive life for ending, I tell myself. I will have to learn how to let life be life with its unbearable finality . . . just be what it is.

Already / my body is a twilight: Solid. Gold / At the edge of a larger darkness.

I cannot remember the next few lines of the poem, only that they contain a radiant assertion about death flowing into life. When I am back home, I will look them up. . . .

But outside / my window / a summer day is beginning. Apple trees / appear, one by one. Light is pouring / into the promise of fruit.

~ ~ ~

As I leave the chamber and move back through the tunnel of stones, I start to think about a winter visit I made to Thomas Merton's monastery in Kentucky, the Abbey of Gethsemani, when I was in my thirties. A wife, mother, and writer caught in a profusion of busyness, I was full of excel-erating and accelerating, but still hopelessly drawn to Merton's writings and the contemplative life. Merton had introduced me to what he called the True Self, referring to the God spark or divine nature in the human soul that's described by practically every mystical tradition in the world. If we could glimpse it, he wrote, "we would see these billions of points of light coming together . . ." At the time, I had no idea what he was talking about.

During that visit, I walked for miles in the cold woods, considering the notion that beneath my ordinary self dwells a deep transcendent Self, a timeless and eternal part of me. Then, standing idly beside a woodpile, having given up on figuring it out, something at the core of me flared up. I recognized the truth of that eternal Self, as if I were remembering what had always existed in me, though that hardly seems to make sense. I was left with a new feeling about myself, about life: neither were quite what I thought. There was something immense going on.

My problem, as I would soon find out—and really *the* problem, as Merton pointed out—is that I was deeply attached to my "external self," to my beloved and tenacious *I.* Even now, as I revisit all this, I want to retreat into an internal argument about what a necessary thing the ego is, how I need a well-developed sense of myself to bring forth my work in the world. And all that's true, but why do I belabor the point to myself? Is it because I hate to think of the ways my *I* has grown entitled, selfish, and wounded, how sometimes it runs my personality like it's the CEO of Everything, how prone I am to imagining that this external self is who I really am and all that I am?

In my fifties, I feel too enclosed within the walls of my small self.

As this awareness comes to me, here in Gavrinis, I realize that the truest approach to death is, in fact, the gradual shift within from the external self to the True Self, loosening the hold of my ego and coming to identify with the billion lights within and all around—with what is larger than *I.* The thought brings me a deep, uncanny relief.

~~~

Outside, on the path to the ferry, I hurry to catch up with Ann. I stare at the back of her short black raincoat, her brimmed indigo hat, her profile as she turns her head. One day she will be in the world and I will not, and for a second the thought catches me off guard, but then fills me with such extravagant love I abruptly stop walking.

A tiny, green fern grows close to my feet, its tendrils fluttering in the air, and I am caught by a sensation close to joy, but not quite joy—what I feel is more powerful, more inflamed, that exultant wildness in the heart that comes with the dilation of life. It's not the fern that stirs these sudden, expansive feelings, though I have never been more sure in my life that the plant, like everything on this earth, is a singular glory in its own right—rather, it's that I am seeing the fern at all, seeing it as it should be seen.

How peculiar, yet obvious, that I would be invaded by the presence of *aliveness.*

On the ferry, I sit beside Ann, letting my hand rest on her gloved fingers. The wind slices sideways, making gashes on the water. The grayness comes down in sheets of brightness.

~ ~ ~

After dinner, in the hotel room, we are tucked in our twin beds, journals open on our laps. We nearly always end the day like this, revisiting our experiences, holding them up like prisms, writing them down, telling them to one another. I love this part of traveling with Ann as much as anything—the quiet pajama party.

Tonight, though, she is subdued. I think she's worried about me. Practically every morning since we arrived in Paris, she has hovered nearby as I took my blood pressure, then quizzed me about the reading. Twice today she asked me if I was okay. And why wouldn't she ask? I spent most of the afternoon aloof, preoccupied, noticeably glum.

My heaviness, though, has given way to a feeling of lightness. The aliveness, that sense of inhabiting the moment that invaded me after being inside the burial chamber, has not entirely faded. Common moments still have all this poignancy about them. I am not sad. I am—*what?* I read the last two lines I wrote in my journal: *I feel tender. Life feels tender.* I struggle to express what I sense: the way to leave my small self is through a simple return to love. . . . Readiness for dying arrives by attending the smallest moment and finding the eternal inside of it.

"You're so quiet," I say.

She stops writing. Her eyes drift to the blood pressure machine on the bedside table. A miffed-looking frown gathers on her face. "Is there something you're not telling me?"

"What? Oh, no, it's not like that."

"But you seem *really* worried about yourself. I just wondered . . ." She drops back against the pillows as her voice trails off.

"Look, I'm okay, I promise. I'm not hiding anything. Sometimes when I get a high reading, I get anxious about it. I start to obsess that I won't be able to get it under control. But, honestly, I believe it'll be fine."

She regards me for a moment. "You were freaked out by Gavrinis, weren't you?"

"Freaked out? No—" I protest, then stop. "Okay, a little . . . The thing is—I'm moving into the last third or fourth of my life, and I've started thinking I won't be here forever. It comes with getting to this place in life, I guess."

I take in her face, the hot, bright look in her eyes.

"What happened in the tumulus," I say, "was that I tried to come to terms with it—accept that death is part of life. It sounds grim, but it was actually a good thing."

I try to explain to her that I re-found my faith in the part of us that goes on, and maybe even more in the part that is right here.

She comes over, curls up beside me on the bed, and lays her head in my lap. "I like you being right here," she says, her voice drifting into sleep.

Ann

Garden of Venus de Quinipily,
Font-de-Gaume Cave

❧ The caretaker at the Garden of Venus de Quinipily, near Baud, is an elderly Frenchwoman with cinnamon-colored hair. She greets us at the garden entrance, jubilantly waving brochures as if we're the first tour group to come through here in ages.

On the bus, driving through rural Brittany, it took me ten entire minutes to locate Baud on my Michelin map. Out-of-the-way is not the word for this garden. Obscure, maybe. Secluded. Unheard-of. But there's a Venus inside, a Goddess statue with a history.

"Bonjour, mesdames," the caretaker cries, then her eyes light on me, and she adds, "Bonjour, mademoiselle."

I rub my thumb over my engagement ring and think, *Not for long.* In eight months, I'll be a Mrs., a madame. People will call me *Mrs.* Taylor. I think of Scott back home. We haven't really been apart since we were engaged.

On the bus, I wrote him a postcard, then practiced writing my soon-to-be new name on a page in the back of my travel journal, experimenting with different possibilities:

Ann Taylor (drop the Kidd)
Ann Kidd Taylor (no hyphen)
Ann Kidd-Taylor (hyphen)
Ann Kidd (leave off the Taylor)

I felt ten years old doing this, as if I were writing my first name in imperfect cursive and attaching the last name of my fourth-grade crush. Except back then there was only one imaginable choice, the one in which you drop Kidd completely and become Ann Whatever-His-Name-Is.

The name issue has weighed on me. For weeks I've gone back and forth about it. But not until the caretaker called me mademoiselle did it dawn on me that the way I'm addressed will change, too.

Scott will go on being Mr., while I'll go from Miss to Mrs.—a new classification. How is it that he is addressed according to his gender and I am addressed according to my marital status? Well, that's unfair, and now that I'm looking at becoming Mrs. Taylor, it feels personal. Which, of course, is why Ms. came into practice, to give a woman an alternative to being recognized by her marital status, and thereby known as herself. How do I want to be known?

I wish it didn't matter so much to me. I tell myself I'm being nitpicky. It's just another technical hoop women jump through when they marry. I should just accept that this is the way the world is. Except . . . that's not how I feel. It's not a small thing to give up your name, change it, hyphenate it.

"Ann." Hearing my name, I look up to see Mom gazing back at me from the end of the pebble walkway. Even the caretaker is over her excitement and walking back to her little house.

~ ~ ~

The garden is bordered with rose hedges and old stone walls tangled in ivy. It's not unkempt; it's natural, and profuse, and slightly untidy, like a manicure that's starting to wear off. Pink and yellow flowers bloom in uneven spurts, and here and there a flowerpot sits on a rock with a mix of plants, some alive and some dead. The opposite end of the garden slopes up a steep hill covered in lavender.

The fragrance is strong, and suddenly I remember digging through my mother's slip drawer when I was a child, finding a sachet of lavender buds. The way it smelled—like her, like this garden. I had secreted it away to my room, hiding it in my own drawer.

The Venus stands on a pedestal atop a massive fountain, which is built into a wall that skirts the hill. Her arms are wrapped around her column-like figure, and her eyes are huge and egg-shaped. Solid granite, she must weigh a few tons and looks it, appearing taller than her seven feet. She's named for the Roman Goddess of love, as so many statues from antiquity are, but archaeologists debate whether she's an Egyptian Isis statue, a Celtic deity, or the Roman Mother Goddess, Cybele. I tell Mom, if she's Cybele, then her Greek counterpart is Rhea, mother of Demeter and grandmother of Persephone.

Her age is a mystery, too. Originally she was located on a hill at Castennec in the Roman settlement of Bieuzy-les-Eaux, where she was revered by peasants. In 1661, the bishop became so outraged about the pagan veneration, he ordered her thrown into the Blavet River. Three years later, her devotees defiantly dredged her up and revived their worship of her, but in 1670, the Venus, who would also come to be known as the Iron Lady, was mutilated and thrown into the river *again*. This time it took twenty-five years to recover her. She was resurrected from the river bottom and eventually came to be here in the gardens, presiding from the pedestal above the fountain. There's some question about this statue's authenticity, whether it's the same one that was resurrected, but, replica or not, she was revered as a Goddess.

"She looks so heavy," I say to Mom. "I wonder how they managed to toss her into the river?" The bishop must have been desperate.

"Think of the poor people that pulled her out," she says.

They must have been desperate, too.

As we listen to the water spill into the trough below the fountain, I notice the stone wall behind it is lined with hydrangea bushes. I walk over and examine the blossoms. Their colors range from faint pink, to ivory, to bright blue. Middleton Place had been swamped with blue hydrangeas the day Scott and I became engaged.

~ ~ ~

Before coming to France, I had the same dream *twice*. In it, I sit in my college English class, reading Charlotte Perkins Gilman's novella *The Yellow Wallpaper*, aware there is some elusive facet of the story I need to discover, a key piece of information.

That's the entire dream—just that one brief scene.

I had, in fact, read the book in English class. It's a haunting story about a woman suffocating from the stifling social conventions and restrictions of marriage in the late nineteenth century. Losing not just autonomy but her whole sense of herself, she is diagnosed with "a nervous depression," confined to the nursery, and forbidden to write, which had been a kind of lifeline for her. This was the so-called "rest cure" often used for women with this condition.

In the novella, the character sees no recourse but to comply with her husband, saying: "If a physician of high standing, and one's own husband, assures friends and relatives that there is really nothing the matter with one but temporary nervous depression—a slight hysterical tendency—what is one to do?"

Prohibited from writing, the character goes mad. Soon, she is "creeping" along the floor, scraping the yellow wallpaper off the walls of her room.

What a thing to dream, considering I was about to be married.

Dreams have always been part of the conversation in the Kidd household—a kind of unique, and weirdly wonderful, family trait. Growing up, I watched Mom write down her nightly dreams. She

and my dad, a marriage and family counselor, would get into long
Jungian discussions at the dinner table about dream symbols, bor-
ing Bob and me out of our minds. We would heckle them—Look,
sometimes a cigar is just a cigar. But later on, the whole mysterious
landscape began to intrigue me. I started to throw my dreams into
the pot and to get a feel for my own personal symbols. From time
to time I would write my own dreams down. I didn't have an
inkling what they meant, but I felt like there was wisdom in them,
whether I could divine it or not. Mom has had some truly
life-changing dreams. Me, I'm in the Dreams for Dummies
stage.

When I told Mom about my yellow wallpaper dream last
August, she said, "Why don't you read the story again? A recurring
dream really wants to be heard." I took her suggestion.

By the time September came, I'd reread it. Mom and I were
consumed by wedding plans then. I didn't mention the dream to
her again, but I came to believe that the missing piece of the story
I was trying to discover in my dream was my own simmering fear
about losing myself in the marriage.

I started thinking maybe I wouldn't change my name. But then,
what about any children we had? They would share Scott's last
name, not mine. And what about the fact that, technically, my last
name is my father's, and my mother's maiden name is her father's?
It began to feel like taking the lid off a box, only to find a box inside
another box. Maybe it was too complicated. Maybe I should leave
it alone.

I explained to Scott my jumbled feelings about changing my
name. I didn't want him to confuse that with how I feel about him;
I just needed him to understand my perspective. "I mean, do you
want to become Scott Kidd?" I asked.

"No," he said.

"But, it doesn't mean you don't love me."

He smiled a little. "You won't get any pressure from me about changing your name. I'll be okay with whatever you do, but yeah, if I'm being honest, I would like it if you took my name."

~ ~ ~

Mom and I walk up the hill and easily step over the stone wall right onto the roof of the fountain. Walking around the base of the pedestal, we stare up at the Venus, still dwarfed by her size. She's covered in dark splotches from her age and possibly all those years in the river, but here she is—untamed and uncompromised. I photograph her from below, unable to get all of her in the frame, then flip on the telephoto, sweeping the lens across the French countryside: rolling hillsides, cedars rising like green parapets, sharp, pointy light, and then, on a distant rise, a tiny wooden stable with a white horse peering through the open half of the door. Thinking of Harry, the horse from my girlhood, I take the picture.

Later, sitting on the grass near the crest of the hill, Mom and I stare down at the garden, and I think about the conversation I had with Scott, the names I've written in the back of my journal. I can't deny that I'm afraid the independent girl I'm trying to find inside will end up on the river bottom. I just want to be me *and* married, and I wonder if that's possible.

"Remember when I had that yellow wallpaper dream?" I say to Mom.

"Yeah, of course."

"I went back and read the story. Why would I dream about a woman losing herself in her marriage if I'm not worried about it happening to me?"

"I'm not too worried about that happening to you as long as you're asking the question. When I got married, I didn't even think about this," she says. "It wasn't until much later." Then she tells me about a comic strip she kept for a long time, an old *Hagar the Horrible* that she cut out of the paper. A bride chirps to Hagar's wife, Helga, that "marriage is when two become one." Helga, wearing her horned Viking helmet and pigtails, gives her a knowing look and asks, "Which one?"

"For you, it's about love and freedom both," Mom says. "It eventually was for me, too. It's not easy to balance them, and I'm not sure it ever really comes out perfectly."

We talk about the question of wanting love and freedom, how even on the verge of a new millennium women are still dealing with it. Not like the woman in *The Yellow Wallpaper*, obviously, but in more complex ways—like the matter of names, the pursuit of career, the division of chores, the care of children, the making of time for oneself, the intricacies of choosing and deferring. I think of Athena for a second. How she has come to represent freedom to me. The part of myself that belongs to me alone.

Once, after one of our wedding planning sessions at the table in Mom's kitchen, I looked through her wedding album to see what choices she had made for her wedding day. I'd seen the photographs before but couldn't recall the details. I stared at Mom in her wedding dress (now, *our* wedding dress). Her arm was linked through my father's. She had on hardly any makeup, just a little mascara and a rosy color on her lips.

Pointing to her bouquet in the picture, she told me her very first Bible was attached to it and that my grandmother's dime was in her shoe. The dime was a custom that started with the Victorian rhyme: "Something old, something new, something borrowed, something blue, and a sixpence in her shoe . . ."

I liked the idea of carrying on the tradition of the Bible and the dime, but now, sitting here among the tufts of lavender on the hillside, I decide I also want to add something of my own.

"I think I'll take my Athena ring and the pomegranate charm down the aisle with me," I tell Mom.

"And I'm not taking any vow of obedience," I joke. "If I did, I would end up peeling wallpaper for real."

"Believe it or not, I took the vow," she says.

She has got to be kidding. "You?"

"Well, in my defense, it *was* 1968," she says. "The vow was part of the wedding ceremony—it never occurred to me to change it. The women's movement hadn't made a dent in small Southern towns like mine."

I joke that her writing *Dissident Daughter* left no doubt now about where she stood on the obedience vow. The memoir about my mother's feminist spiritual search had prompted a few angry letters to the newspaper in the town where we'd lived then. Even now, over two years after the book was published, letters still showed up in her mailbox with personal attacks on Mom. I always remember the one that began, "Dear Whore of Babylon." It made Mom laugh—I think it was the "Dear" part. She'd been pretty unflappable, but I knew dealing with all that hadn't been easy.

My mother's experience had prompted me to examine my own religious experience. Not long after I arrived at Columbia College, I called her and said, "Guess what—the chaplain is a *woman*." In my whole Baptist childhood, and later as an Episcopalian, I'd never seen a female priest or minister. What did I think about church doctrines that marginalize and exclude women? Could I live with them? What did I believe? I didn't question God so much as how God had been defined. When I was growing up, God was a "he," but I came to understand that was only one picture. I remember my religion teacher saying, "God is he, she, neither, and both," and that still seems right to me.

When I read the wedding service that we planned to use from

the Book of Common Prayer, though, it was all God-he. I want our marriage to be blessed by God our Father *and* God our Mother. Again, I want both.

I wonder how Scott will feel about altering the ceremony to be more inclusive. I'm sure he will be fine with it—he's the guy who told me we were not replacing my Athena ring. Then it actually crosses my mind that it would be easier for me if he objects; then I'd have an excuse to ditch the idea. Honestly, inserting God our Mother makes me nervous. I would be revealing a lot about myself. There will be wedding guests—family and friends—who hold traditional views. The minute feminism and God are paired, people tend to get worked up, offended, and appalled. And to think Mom wrote an entire book on the subject.

Since I was in Greece the first time, I've thought a million times about that Isadora Duncan line: dance is a manifestation of the soul. It was hard to get up there and dance on a tabletop in Greece, harder to risk my articles being published, and now this whole thing about changing the ceremony—tampering with tradition, God-*she*—felt like another one of those moments. It provokes the terrifying feeling of visibility, of exposure, my soul out there talking.

Over the last year, I've thought a lot about what makes revealing myself so scary. I realize I hide my real self because I'm afraid of being rejected. Lately I've tried to confront the fear by asking myself: so what if I am rejected? I can't count how many times I've gone back to the moment when Mom and I were on the ship near Patmos and everything spilled out. All my self-hatred and fear. And I hear her gently say, "You deserve to love yourself." I remember how that hit me right between the eyes, right in the chest. I know it all goes back to that—loving myself. Believing I deserve to.

We notice the other women starting to trickle out of the garden, making their way back to the bus. Mom and I get up and walk down the hill. At the bottom, I focus the camera for one final picture of the Venus, getting her all in, head to toe. There are still so many decisions to make for the wedding, but what goes through my head as I stare through the camera at the seven-foot Venus is a series of decisions that had been gathering in me while we sat up there in the sachets of lavender. I'm going to ask my college chaplain to perform the ceremony. I want my father *and* my mother to walk me down the aisle. I don't want the minister to ask, "Who gives this woman?" because I don't want to be *given* away. I don't want to be announced at the reception as Mr. and Mrs. Scott Taylor. Ann and Scott will be fine. Mom and I will write the ceremony ourselves and include God, the Mother. As for my name, I will be Ann Kidd Taylor. No hyphen.

I sling the strap of the camera over my shoulder and start to leave the garden, hoping that when I'm back home and the Venus is only a memory, I won't lose my conviction about these decisions.

I am almost to the exit when I turn around and sprint back to the hydrangea bushes. I break off a sprig. Blue petals with a violet center. It is going in my bouquet.

~ ~ ~

On the bus, riding through the Périgord region of France, Mom and I sit next to each other and share a bag of roasted almonds. In my lap is the blue hydrangea I picked two days ago at Quinipily, wrapped carefully in tissue paper and tucked inside a ziplock bag. My mission is to get through the rest of the trip without squashing it.

It is raining, the cold, wet pellets hitting hard against the windows, and the road is slick and black. We are on our way to Font-de-Gaume to visit a fifteen-thousand-year-old cave. The thought of being underground inside a cave makes me uneasy, even though I'm not claustrophobic. At least the cave is dry. Or so I hope. Apparently, it has a gallery of art inside—wall paintings by late-prehistoric people. I imagine them in there drawing by torchlight while woolly mammoths roam around outside.

We stop for lunch in Montignac and find a café, where three brown dogs are curled up in a single clump of fur just inside the front door. Sitting at a table with Terry and Trisha, Mom and I warm our hands around mugs of hot tea. Mom and Trisha order *croques-monsieurs,* toasted, open-faced ham and cheese sandwiches, but in what must be a bad case of American nostalgia, Terry and I order the hamburgers. *"Hamburger, s'il vous plaît,"* I tell our waitress and feel ridiculous saying those words together.

Mom and Trisha's sandwiches arrive like something from the Cordon Bleu, cheesy and golden. The hamburgers are the size of biscuits and sizzle inside the plastic bag in which they were microwaved.

When I cut the plastic open, a puff of steam escapes. *"Bon appétit,"* Mom says, and we all burst out laughing.

Terry and I order two *croques-monsieurs.* The waitress smiles. On the way out we feed the microwave hamburgers to the dogs, who wag their tails as if to say, Oh good, the Americans have ordered the hamburger again, our lucky day.

Back on the bus I write the most obvious thing ever in my journal: when in France, order French.

By the time we arrive at Font-de-Gaume, the rain has stopped. It is only one of a vast number of prehistoric caves that dot the region, shaped by cliffs, rock overhangs, and valleys. I remember being in an art history class and seeing several slides of paintings from the Lascaux cave, which is not far from here. The horses in the slides had looked flat and primitive, stirring nothing in me like the images of ancient Greek sculpture had. I understand the paintings in Font-de-Gaume are renowned, but unless one of them depicts Wilma Flintstone vacuuming with an elephant trunk, I don't expect to be blown away.

After a short climb from the bottom of the valley up a rock-crusted hill, we reach the cave opening. Our French guide, who has a red bandana tied around her hair, turns on her flashlight and leads us inside.

"Watch your step," she calls.

Ground lighting projects low, shadowy beams up the cave walls, but it is still too dark, and I flip on my flashlight, too. Soon a lot more circles of light are bouncing along the cave floor.

"There's enough oxygen down here, isn't there?" I ask Mom.

"I guess," she says.

She guesses? I was kind of joking around, and she *guesses*?

We inch along one hundred and thirty yards into the main gallery in silence except for shoes shuffling on the walkway and an unusual amount of throat clearing. The walls are covered with paintings of bison, horses, mammoths, reindeer, oxen, goats, felines, rhinoceros, a bear, a wolf, a man, and four human hands.

As we stop beside a painting of horses half-hidden beneath a layer of calcite, I think of Harry yet again. As if the scene depicts his great-great-great-great (and on) grandparents. In the picture Mom took of me sitting in the saddle after Harry's runaway episode, my blue jeans are hiked above my ankles, revealing thick, red socks, and my smile is full of braces. I appear to be a pleased and happy twelve-year-old. It was such a geeky, awkward phase, but I wish for that girl's bold spirit, red socks, and all.

The group gathers around a frieze where five well-preserved bison are painted on vanilla-colored limestone. The guide asks us to turn off our flashlights, then flicks on two cigarette lighters beside the painting. As the flames wave, the animals seem to come alive. Shadows cut back and forth, creating an uncanny image of running bison.

"The artists who created this would have painted by fire and they would have seen the bison just like this," the guide says. "Look at how the natural relief of the wall was used to give volume to their bodies. The animals were drawn firmly and without the slightest hint of hesitation."

As I listen to her wax on about the confidence of the cave painters, I consider my own lack of it. I stare at the bison. Whatever it is I'm born to do, my fear of failing at it has almost become greater than my desire to figure out what it is.

I make out Mom's silhouette five people ahead and think about the bee novel she's writing. She has fears that it won't be published, but she's writing it anyway. Over the last few months, she has handed me chapter after chapter to read. The most recent is about a wooden statue of Mary that the women in the story dance around, touching her heart. Mary fills them with fearlessness, and if they ever grow weak, they have only to touch her heart again. I love this passage.

Every time I read a new chapter, I tell Mom, "This is *really* good." And she says, "Well, I don't know." It isn't false modesty; she actually doesn't know. She thinks I'm biased, and okay, I'm biased, but still I see it. Why can't she?

I'm crazy about Mom's main character, fourteen-year-old Lily, who is wounded but brave and funny. She takes control of her life and goes searching for her mother, but really, it seems, she is looking for love, trying to find out if she's worth loving. Lily ends up in a pink house with the sisters, which turns into a kind of mothering refuge. I'm always telling Mom to hurry and write the next chapter; I need to find out what happens.

Once Mom told me, "I don't know if this novel will ever see the light of day, but I'm doing it." All I can think as I see her in the cave is how determined she is to do it in spite of herself.

I remember my prayer to Joan of Arc in the chapel at Notre Dame—*I want to know what I was born for. I want the courage to do it.* I feel like I've been spinning my wheels, stuck between the need I have to blaze my own path, doing something that doesn't resemble my mother's work, and the inclination I have toward writing. Earlier, on the bus, I was thinking about those dreams I had about *The Yellow Wallpaper*, but it isn't until right now, standing in the damp darkness with all these women, that it hits me finally: the character in the story was cut off from her *writing*.

I'd been so concentrated on the character's loss of herself in her marriage that I'd glossed over the colossal detail that she'd lost her writing.

Nearby, the guide is talking and the group is horseshoed around her, but I don't hear a word. I'm asking myself: was the prohibition against writing part of the reason I dreamed about the story? Twice? Later I would wonder why Mom didn't point this out. She has a remarkable acuity when it comes to dreams. There's no way she didn't notice it.

Could Gilman's cooped-up wife represent *both* my worry about my independence and my fear that I have cut myself off from a genuine desire to write? As I ask myself this, I recognize the truth and well up with tears. Yes, it's both.

Ever since I began working on my articles for *Skirt!*, I've treated writing a little like the Rebound Boyfriend, a fling not to be taken seriously, considering how it followed my breakup with ancient Greece. I've resisted writing because I thought there had to be more to it than these intimations and impulses I keep having, or the fact that I enjoy doing it, or even the belief I might become reasonably good at it. But now I'm wondering if all these things are the very ways my true self speaks—signs that they come from a real place inside of me.

How many times have I heard Mom refer to writing as her "necessary fire"? The first time I heard her use those two words was during a talk she gave at my college. She was standing behind the pulpit in the chapel and I sat in the front row. I don't recall her exact words, but the message has stayed with me: look within and find your "necessary fire," a phrase she attributed to the novelist John Gardner. To me, this idea meant finding work with which I had a deep compatibility, a true affinity, yet work that also held the possibility to bring me alive.

A fire was ignited in me on that first trip to Greece, but I can't say now that it was the necessary one. Groping along with the others in the cave, I admit to myself that if the university called me today and said, Oh, about that letter of rejection, it was a big mistake, we want you after all, I doubt I would go. Graduate school has lost most of its combustion, and it's not just the disappointment that dampened it. I'm beginning to see it differently. When I separated the romance of teaching ancient Greek history from the daily demands of the job, I realized it was never teaching I wanted; it was Greece. I did not have a deep compatibility with teaching, and chances were it would not bring me alive.

Writing. Growing up, it's all I wanted to do. Now I feel the way it pulls at me. Not like a dramatic allurement, but like I've been away from home and have returned to the quiet things I love.

~~~

Our hotel, Le Relais de Moussidière, turns out to be a country manor house surrounded by woods, ponds, and old-looking sundials. Inside, we are greeted by the manager and his two sleek

Afghan hounds, who prop their front paws on the desk and wag their tails like we have microwaved hamburgers in our pockets.

Rolling my luggage along the corridor to our room, I notice Mom and I both are covered in dust from the cave. It could be moon dust for how far away that subterranean world seems now.

Suddenly I feel exhausted. Like I may have to lie down in the hallway. Right now, I can't tell whether my speculations about writing made it out of the cave with me. It's funny how different things seem aboveground. When we clambered out of the cave into the blinding daylight, to the guide broadcasting that the gift shop was down the hill to the left, I felt yanked back to a more pragmatic reality. The *Aha!* about writing and the feelings that flared up in me underground are faint and untraceable, like those paintings on the cave wall after the light is extinguished.

In the room, I drop my clothes in a pile on the bathroom floor and step into the shower. Mom still has the light on when I fall asleep and dream what I will come to call The Dream.

I take a home pregnancy test. A positive sign emerges on the white plastic test stick. It can't be. I take two more tests. There are two more positive signs. I'm happy beyond belief. I'm going to have a baby! Then the scenery changes. I'm in the woods and it's very dark. I walk until I come to a clearing encircled with tall stones. A bright yellow fire burns in the center of it, and someone is standing in the flames, though she's not getting burned. Amazed, I go a little closer and see that it's me in the fire. It blazes all around me, but I'm not hurt. Then I realize this is how I conceived.

When I open my eyes the room is filled with morning light. The awed feeling from the dream lingers in me, along with the picture of myself in the fire. I sit up slowly, afraid if I move too fast, the image will dissolve.

Mom's alarm clock repeats four rapid beeps. I want to tell her about my dream, but before I pounce on her like our beagle used to do, waking her with his nose an inch from her face, I give her time to get up and find her glasses.

"I had a dream," I tell her.

"Yeah?" She looks at my face and sits back down on the bed.

"When I was in Joan of Arc's chapel in Notre Dame, I asked her to help me know what I was born to do."

"Is that part of the dream?" Mom asks.

"No, that's real. I'm just mentioning that first because . . . well, just because."

Then I tell her the dream: the pregnancy tests, the walk in the woods, the fire in the stone circle, the realization that I conceived in the flames.

"I know it's not an actual baby I'm having," I tell her, and laugh.

Mom jokes, "That's a relief."

"So, help me understand it," I say.

She takes off her glasses and cleans them on her nightshirt, which is a thing she does when she needs to think. "I guess if I dreamed that, I'd say the baby is some potential inside that wants to be born."

"Um-hmm," I say, and feel how that falls into place. I call up the image of the fire again. I associate it with the "necessary fire" that Mom had talked about. In the dream, the fire consumed me, but unlike the fire that consumed Joan, it wasn't the end of me, but maybe the beginning. More like the emerging phoenix than the immolated girl-warrior.

My heart starts to beat very fast. "I think I know what the baby might be," I tell her.

"Really? What?"

"Well, what if it's . . . I'm not sure, but I think it might be writing." Admitting this out loud for the first time makes me nervous, but also relieved.

Mom looks at me, surprised but not-surprised, her mouth parting and her eyes blinking wide, but that fades and she smiles at me like maybe she knew this already.

"By the way," I say, "when I had that dream about the woman in *The Yellow Wallpaper,* did you make the connection between me and the character both being cut off from writing?" Once I finally noticed it, it seemed so obvious. I couldn't imagine she missed it, too.

"I guess it did cross my mind."

"Why didn't you say something?"

"I didn't know for sure. But even if I did, you needed to discover writing for yourself. You didn't need me to tell you."

I agreed. That seemed right. If she'd pointed it out, I might never have thought becoming a writer was coming from myself. Or felt like it was conceived in a necessary fire.

Mom hops off the bed, gives me a quick hug, and disappears into the bathroom. I walk to the window and stare out toward the woods, at the trees well into their long, autumn shedding, their orange and yellow leaves bunched around their trunks, the early morning mist already burning away.

Sue

_____

Chapel of the Black Virgin of Rocamadour

༄ Along the eastbound road from Sarlat to Rocamadour, our French driver pulls the bus to the side of the road. Standing in the aisle, he sweeps his arm toward the view in the distance—a gesture he accompanies with a little bow, as if he's unveiling a European landscape he has personally painted.

Yesterday we had to call the bus company about him. Not because he fancies himself a tour guide, but because after lunch we noticed he was driving us around while smelling like a bottle of Cabernet Sauvignon. It came to our attention when he tried to pinch the rear end of a nun who was traveling with us.

Trisha, Terry, and I took him aside for a stern talk, but in the excitement, Trisha's remedial French failed her. She ended up rubbing her finger under her nose and sniffing at him, while Terry and I backed her up with vigorous nodding. The company threatened to fire him, and he vowed no more imbibing on the road.

Now, however, I notice Trisha, in the front row, lean in close to him and sniff.

Not again.

Trisha glances back at me, smiles, and shakes her head, visibly relieved. "Okay, don't worry," I whisper to Ann, "he's sober." Like my two co-leaders and me, Ann has barely recovered from yester-day's scare. Apparently he is only being a slightly flamboyant tour guide.

Ann and I migrate across the bus aisle and peer out at the vista. The medieval city of Rocamadour is clamped against a rugged four-hundred-ninety-foot cliff that rises out of the valley like some mystical province in the clouds. The Alzou River surrounds it like an old moat, the gorge floats in thin, austere haze, and the churches and houses appear to be bolted directly to the rock face. Crowning the summit is an actual fourteenth-century castle complete with ramparts.

Somewhere up there is the nine-hundred-year-old Black Virgin of Rocamadour—one of the venerable old Black Madonnas of Europe. She has secretly become the focus of the trip for me.

After breakfast this morning, in a meeting room in the hotel, I gave a little orientation talk to the group about why Black Madon-nas are black or shades of brown. I'd discovered it's not all about candle smoke, which was the automatic answer for a time. Sum-marizing months of research, I explained that most scholars believe the Black Madonnas' darkness derives from their connections to dark-skinned, pre-Christian Goddesses once worshipped widely in Europe—Goddesses with African, Eastern, and Mediterranean roots.

"People weren't so willing to give up their old Goddesses," I told the group. "In some rural areas worship went on into the fourth and fifth centuries, and the church often responded by placing a Mary shrine right on top of a Goddess shrine. In some cases, they seem to have simply renamed the Goddess statue Mary."

As the bus takes the U-shaped curve up the escarpment, I think about the way the Black Madonna has taken on a big role in my novel, in the lives of my characters, and in my own life, too—a little like the queen bee in a hive, I've started to realize. I know some of my fascination comes from her kinship with these powerful Goddesses and how that might have shaped her image. Official stories about the Black Virgin of Rocamadour include miraculous healings, calming storms, saving drowning sailors, and freeing captives, but also famously receiving and forgiving heretics during a period of history when they were more often burned. I like her slightly subversive tendency. It puts her in league with other Black Madonnas who stood in for wayward, runaway nuns so they wouldn't get into trouble; resuscitated unbaptized dead babies long enough for them to escape Limbo; and eased the pain of childbirth, which was not always looked upon favorably since it was considered God's punishment upon women for Eve eating the forbidden fruit.

We arrive at the forecourt outside the Black Virgin's chapel by elevator, bypassing two hundred and sixteen steps known as the Sacred Way. Arduously steep, the staircase was considered torturous enough for Ecclesiastical Tribunes to assign it as penance for heretics and prisoners, who then climbed it on their knees and in shackles. At the top, the Black Virgin freed them and a priest removed their chains. I've read that some of the chains still hang on the back wall of her chapel.

Trisha and Terry gave me the task of coming up with a simple ritual that would honor the tradition of the pilgrimages here, yet also evoke a way for each woman to have her own individual experience with the Black Virgin. I kept thinking about *chain*. I bought a heavy strand of it at the hardware store and had it cut into twenty separate links, which took up a precious amount of space in my suitcase, each one being roughly the size of a big, chunky hoop earring.

As we gather under the overhang of the cliff near the door to the chapel, I hand them out, recounting the role of chain in Roca-madour's past. "If you're inclined, you can let the chain symbolize something inside yourself you'd like to be free of—some conflict, or fear, or old pain, whatever chains you, so to speak—and like the pilgrims that came here, you can leave it with the Black Virgin."

Saying this, I wonder if the idea is as simplistic as it sounds, too innocent-minded for the complex knotting that tethers us to old patterns and struggles. Well . . . yes, of course it is. But trying to unlace them starts somewhere, I reason. Usually with a very simple intention. And if setting the intention feels sacred and memorable, perhaps it really could start a shift of some sort.

"Should we literally leave the chain in the chapel?" someone asks.

"Sure, if you want," I say, then consider that I have no idea whether it's okay or not, whether a guard will wag his finger at us, whether there's a place to even put twenty fat links of chain.

I press one of the two remaining links into Ann's hand, then let the other drop into my coat pocket.

"I bet you've already figured out what yours is going to repre-sent," she says.

"Nope, not yet. I'm going to let it pop into my head when I get in there."

"Wow," she says. "Who *are* you?"

I laugh, then shrug. "So what's your chain going to be?"

She opens her palm and stares at it. "Well, I have to *think* about it," she says, and wanders to an iron bench in a nearby archway and sits down to deliberate.

Eager to go inside, but also wanting to wait for her, I walk to the edge of the balcony and peer down at the maze of steps and passageways, then up at a twelfth-century fresco high on the back of a Romanesque apse. It depicts an annunciation scene which, as the saying goes, I could not make up if I tried. In it, the Holy Spirit in the form of a dove pecks at Mary's forehead in order to impregnate her.

My thoughts overflow suddenly with Ann's annunciation, so freshly dreamed, and inventive in its own way—a conception by fire. I am not that surprised by the dream or the intuition it stirs in her about writing.

Seeing her over on the bench, journal on her lap, shoulders hunched, her hand moving furiously across the page, I am reminded almost painfully of myself. I think of her growing up with the same abiding need to write that I had, always with a diary or a notebook, penning poems and stories (where does all that come from?) as if some seed inside her simply started to sprout one day. Is there DNA involved? My grandmother, the one who sacrificed her parlor for the lavender chick, had the writing seed, though it never really grew into anything. Her poems were published in her college literary magazine and then she got married and that was that. It's reminiscent of *The Yellow Wallpaper*, a story that has recently captured Ann about a woman's loss of selfhood after marriage. My grandmother seemed happy with her choices, though, but I suspect the inclination to write dogged her all her life.

I have a flash of Ann's seventh-grade English teacher taking me aside and saying, "Ann wants to be a writer, and I'm encouraging her—I really think she could be one." I saw that in Ann, too. I praised her writings, but I did not encourage her to be a writer. Wouldn't that sway her *too* much? Wouldn't it come off like the overbearing father pushing his impressionable son to follow in his footsteps? She had to arrive at it on her own. Standing there on the terrace, though, I realize I may have bent the other way by my silence.

Ann looks up and finds me staring at her. "No rush," I call, and walk over to the empty tomb of St. Amadour and stare at the plaque without reading it. Thinking back on it, I'm pretty sure Ann believed, as I did in early adolescence, that she'd found the small, true light in herself. Then, like me, she lost it.

Perhaps she fought any urge to be a writer out of a need to separate herself from me and my path, the same way I separated myself from my mother and her path. When Ann went to college, I felt the invisible way she broke from me, in that way mothers feel barely discernible things. Even now, as we weave this new closeness, I do not mistake the separate core in her, her own nascent true self, and I watch how she protects it, even as she struggles to unfold it. Do her intuitions about writing come now because she has finally found enough of her separate self to entertain them?

In my case, losing the small, true light was more like turning my back on it and finding something manageable. Becoming a nurse seemed more doable and sensible. You graduated and took a board exam. When you said, "I'm a nurse," you knew what you were talking about. You had *proof.* Nobody would register me as a writer. Would I be a writer if I never published anything? Would I be one even if I did? And the real question: how likely was it to happen? At eighteen, I couldn't find the courage. I took all that passion and sublimated it into nursing. Until, at twenty-nine, it simply refused to go there anymore.

I wonder if that's the perennial story of writers: you find the true light, you lose the true light, you find it again. And maybe again.

As Ann puts away her journal and pen, I recognize that what I've witnessed in her over the last year is the same restlessness and hunger that I felt at twenty-nine. The same sense of exile, the homesickness for one's place in the world. Oddly, the desire to be a writer seems to be coming back to her not unlike the way it returned to me: gradually insinuating itself into her thoughts; her desire, once gone cold, heating again by degrees like popcorn in the microwave, with the slow *rat ta tat* and then the bombardment. Finally, at the bursting point, the desire must be said out loud. Like she did to me this morning as she sat on the bed. Like I did to Sandy at the breakfast table on the morning I turned thirty—"I want to be a writer."

I watch Ann cross the terrace, stopping to look up at the fresco, and I think: *I have always sensed the writer in her.*

Now her dreams talk to her about it, seeming to say what I never did.

~ ~ ~

High atop a gilded bronze altar, the statue of the Black Virgin of Rocamadour is just over two feet tall. As I step into the semidarkness of the chapel, she's the first thing I see: small, thin, her facial features strangely hawkish. She looks like a dark, old bird that has flown in from an open window and perches up there, watching me watch her.

Every chair is taken. Ann and I move along the side wall toward the altar rail, edging as close to the Black Virgin as we can. She is covered with blackly tarnished plates of silver, now cracked and peeling. Her hands are worn to mitts, her feet are mostly missing, and her walnut-wood face is split and splotched.

"She *looks* nine hundred," Ann whispers.

The Christ child sits on the Virgin's lap like a miniature adult. She rests her arms regally on the sides of her chair. Her back is erect and her chin lifted. She wears a crown, not a veil. She looks utterly self-possessed. Old. Bony. Authoritative. Powerful. A much fiercer version of Mary than I expected.

As I look at her, my throat tightens and I dig through my bag for the travel-size Kleenex. Just in case. I'm not sure what moves me about her, only that she's beautiful to me.

Someone vacates a chair, and I sit down, staring at the flinty old Virgin until the tears really do start to leak. I rub them away and focus on the back of Ann's brown hair. Ann's fingers, I notice, are curled around the stubby piece of chain, and I wonder what she has decided about it. What I will decide about mine.

I look up at the vaulted ceiling, locating the iron bell that legend says rings on its own when the Black Virgin performs one of her miracles. Then, twisting around to inspect the back of the sanctuary, I find myself staring at a wall of bare rock and realize the tiny chapel has been built right against the cliff. The surface of the rock gleams here and there from the candles in front of it. As my eyes adjust, I distinguish fragments of chain and shackles dangling from the wall on iron hooks.

When I turn back to the Black Virgin's peeling face, the teary impulse has gone. I gaze at her unguarded for a long while, aware mostly of how fearless she looks. Her boldness and strength break through, as does her aged wisdom. She is without any need to please, any need to act, or look, or be a certain way. It's as if she's done with that, and rests now in the solid center of herself, having arrived at her own condensed truth. She is herself. And that is all.

I know suddenly what moves me about the Black Virgin of Rocamadour: *She's the Old Woman*. It comes with some surprise, as if the bird on the altar has just pecked me on the forehead.

Old Woman I meet you deep inside myself. May Sarton's line. That had started it all, the whole inquest, giving words and an image to my first inexpressible urge to become a new self after fifty. I've been searching for the Old Woman ever since reading the line. Now, I cannot help but feel that I'm looking at her.

~ ~ ~

The chain links I handed out form a winding trail along the marble altar rail. Most of the group has left the chapel, headed for the small Museum of Sacred Art nearby. In front of me, Ann rises from her chair and, after a quick nod over her shoulder at me, disappears into the back of the chapel, I suppose to light a candle.

My thoughts wander to the Black Madonna in my novel—the figurehead with her fist in the air, a heart on her chest, a moon at her feet. Of course, it would come back to her. The chapel is like a quarry, inviting those who wander into it to mine their own Black Virgin. I wonder if that's part of what I've been trying to do in the novel. To dig her up for myself. The last scene I wrote before leaving home was one in which Lily creeps through the pink house late at night, slipping into the parlor to see the Black Madonna. She presses her hand against the Black Madonna's painted heart. She says: "I live in a hive of darkness and you are my mother."

Sitting in the shadowy stillness, I could almost laugh at how the Black Madonna has gotten herself such a prominent role in my pages, how she has been curiously mixed up with the novel from the beginning, from the moment I stood before the icon of the dark-skinned Mary in the myrtle tree in Greece and spilled out my prayer . . . my admission: I want to be a novelist. In a way that I'm only beginning to understand, the Black Madonna is slowly becoming like a muse to me—the personification of the dark, old voice of the soul.

Yet I've been slow to trust what is inside me—this new well of images, story, characters, and language. I haven't wanted to confess to myself how plagued I am with skepticism. I've finished seven chapters of the novel, roughly half of it—believing in the work while simultaneously doubting the whole thing. Some of that is simply part of writing, but too much of it comes from enfeebling notions I have inside about my creative abilities, remnants of inadequacy that go back to my childhood, with its commanding old fear that I would not live up to expectations, that I would disappoint. How humbling to sit here, wanting to believe the fear has been unplugged and find it sputtering determinedly on like a rundown generator in a back room.

A couple of times since arriving in France, I've entertained the unreasonable thought that when I get home, I should just print out the half-novel, package it up, and send it off to the literary agent I met three years ago—the only agent I've ever met—who has probably forgotten she ever met me. The thought comes to me again now, but who sends off half of something? And the idea of someone besides Ann reading it, of it being out there, in the world, makes me squeamish.

I get up and deposit my piece of chain on the altar rail, knowing what I would like to be free of: the part of me that dares too little and fears too much. The terrible voice that pipes up: you *can't*, and the next minute, *don't*.

As I leave the chapel, I glimpse Ann lingering still in the back, and it is only because I pause to wait for her that I see the nun striding in in her big black shoes, heading straight for the altar rail, toting a handbasket. Ann and I watch from near the doorway as she gathers the pieces of chain the group has littered all over the place. I cannot see her face, but I envision her lips pressed together making the *tsk, tsk* sound. This is her job. Keeper of the Chapel. Custodian of Offerings. Cleaning up after the messy pilgrims. Another day, another basket.

She scoops up every last loop of chain, letting them drop noisily into her confiscated stockpile. *Clink. Clink. Clink.*

Just before she carries them away, though, she lifts the basket up toward the Black Virgin with a hasty genuflection. As if to say, here they are. Do what you can.

Ann

————

Cathedral of Notre Dame–Le Puy

❧ The Cathedral of Notre Dame in Le Puy sits on a large volcanic pinnacle. To reach the door on the western side, we trudge up a cobblestone street angled like a ski slope, then mount a stairway with so many steps I'm inspired to count them. These are the same steps that launched the First Crusade. We arrive at the top of them, huffing and puffing.

"My guidebook says there are one hundred and thirty-four steps," I say to Mom. "I counted one hundred and one." I look down the slope, able to see red-tiled rooftops *below* us. "How did we miss thirty-three steps?"

Perspiration has beaded across Mom's forehead. She unwinds her black scarf from around her neck, revealing a light pink turtleneck.

"Hot flash?" I say.

"No. Steps," she replies, stuffing the scarf into her bag.

It's hard to tell whether the red flush she gets is from a hot flash or a cardio workout. Yesterday, when she began fanning herself at breakfast, I asked, "Is this what I have to look forward to?"

"Yes, it is," she answered, without the sugar coat.

The steps have made me considerably warmer, too, and on this autumn day, I peel off my overcoat and sling it over my arm, anticipating what awaits us inside. Another Black Virgin.

France is Black Madonna country. There are hundreds of them. Just yesterday, we visited the most famous one, the Black Virgin of Rocamadour, nearly seven hours from here.

My visit to her had turned into something memorable. Before going into the chapel to see her, I sat on a bench outside the door and thought about the question Mom had posed to the whole group: *What do you want to be free of?*

Mom had even handed out pieces of chain that were supposed to symbolize the answer. I placed my piece in my lap and flipped through my journal until I found where I'd recorded the dream I'd had a couple of nights earlier. Beneath it was a stream of thoughts.

I believe my dream is about my potential to do what I'm meant to do. I'm taking a series of home pregnancy tests, as if trying to figure out whether my speculations about becoming a writer might actually be true. Naturally, it takes not one, not two, but three positive test sticks to convince me, but despite that, the idea that I possess the possibility of being a writer resonates with me. And the fire. Creative fire? Baptism by fire? A hint of Joan in the fire? My "necessary fire"? Whatever it is, I conceived something in it. I'm hesitant to say it's writing even though my soul seems to be suggesting it, even though I said as much to my mother. If I go that route and fail, then what? I need to believe I can do this, but I'm only halfway there.

Closing my journal, I looked down at my piece of chain and knew it represented anything that would keep me from realizing the potential revealed in the dream.

Inside Our Lady of Rocamadour's chapel, I began a silent conversation with the Black Virgin. She was the first black Mary I'd ever seen. She looked ancient, and seemed to say: Don't bother with easing into your scalding bath—just tell me. So I jumped right in and told her that since my dream, I'd felt excitement welling up, but I'd tried to temper it. I told her that I was reluctant, afraid, already worried about the disasters that would strike if I failed. Slipping to the back of the chapel, I placed my piece of chain on a rusted eye hook on the wall. By leaving it there, I was trying to move on from the self-doubt, the fear of rejection—and yes, sometimes even self-hate. I thought: why can't this be the place I start to love myself?

~ ~ ~

Now, stepping into the cathedral at Le Puy, I'm anxious to see if the Black Virgin here is similar to the one we saw yesterday. Inside, a woman is singing, accompanied by a violin, practicing, perhaps, for a concert. Her voice echoes through the nave as Mom and I walk toward the high altar where the Madonna reigns.

The stone walls, arches, and cupolas overhead are the colors of flour and cocoa, an alternating brown and white pattern similar to the design in Spanish mosques, a welcome sight to the countless Spanish pilgrims that passed through on their way to St. James of Compostela, or so the guidebook says.

I read the Who's Who list of visitors aloud to Mom. "King Louis IX, better known as St. Louis, Charlemagne, King Louis XI." I stop when I come to this name: *Isabelle Romée.*

Six hundred years ago, she came here at the request of her daughter, Joan of Arc, who was on the brink of her mission. Joan had asked her mother to say prayers for her to the Black Virgin of Le Puy.

I lower the book, mindful of the coincidence: my prayer to Joan, the dream with the fire, then coming here with my mother only to find out Joan's mother had been here, too.

"You won't believe this," I tell Mom. "Joan of Arc's mother came here and prayed for her."

As we move down the main aisle, I notice the violinist has placed his instrument in its case, and the singer has gathered her sheet music. It is quiet as Mom and I slide into a pew.

In front of us, three steps lead to a kneeler. The Madonna sits behind it on a raised white marble altar lit with six brass candlesticks. She is coal-faced, wearing a gold crown inlaid with jewels and topped with a cross. Cloaked in a richly embroidered white robe, her face is the only part of her that shows. Jesus peeks out from his mother's robe like a joey in a kangaroo pouch.

Known as the spiritual heart of Le Puy, she seems softer, more maternal, and younger than the wizened old Black Virgin of Rocamadour. As I stare at her alluring black face, I remember the scene in Mom's novel in which the women go up to the statue of Mary and touch her heart, and I wish we could do the same thing here. I tell Mom it's my favorite part of the novel so far, and she smiles and admits it's one of her favorites, too. "I wanted Mary to empower Lily and the women and be like a loving mother to them," she says.

I look at the Madonna. My feeling for her doesn't surprise me as much as it might have, at least not after yesterday when I poured out my soul to the Black Virgin of Rocamadour. Something about her *did* empower me, maybe the boldness that shone through her, or the faith I found inside myself by hanging my piece of chain on her wall. I actually felt like some loving presence in the universe was bent over my life, tending it.

Sitting here before *this* Mary, the "spiritual heart" of the cathedral, I have that same feeling—the sense of being loved, the desire to love myself.

It does not escape my notice that Mary is becoming important to me. I tell myself that if Athena represents independence and self-belonging, and Joan of Arc a passionate sense of mission, then

Mary represents the spiritual heart—my ability to love and be loved. Athena, Joan, Mary. It's an unlikely combination, but I realize they've become my female triptych.

There are other people sitting nearby staring at the Black Virgin, too. I imagine them composing their prayers, all the urgent questions that must weigh on them.

I turn to Mom and whisper, "Is it crazy? Me being a writer?"

She scoots closer to me and says, "No, it's not crazy; I think it's great. It's kinda always been there, hasn't it? When you were a child, it's what you wanted to be."

I remember the headlines I broke in the family newspaper I wrote: *Brother Rips Wiring from Dollhouse. Pound Cake Falls. Spaniel Eats Baby Robin.*

"Yeah, but is it too late?" I ask. "I never studied writing in college. I dropped my grammar class."

"I didn't study it in college either, remember?"

I ponder this for a second. "A few articles and one dream doesn't make me a writer. Maybe I should take a class."

"A class is good. You can start to learn the craft. I think you have the instinct—you've given me good feedback on my novel." She pauses. "Now, I can be *your* reader."

"Okay, but be prepared—the stuff I write now is pretty bad."

"I think that about my stuff, too, sometimes. I've been writing twenty years, and I never expect to get it right the first time. If you sit down at the piano, you can't expect to play like Beethoven right off the bat."

This makes sense, but I wonder about the Beethoven analogy. I think maybe Beethoven *did* sit down and play a masterpiece the first time. I don't know if Mom senses how overwhelmed I am at the thought of beginning.

For a few moments, Mom and I are silent, gazing at the Black

Virgin, at the people kneeling before her with their collections of questions and prayers.

"Are people going to think I'm becoming a writer because you're a writer?" I say.

"Why would people think that?"

"I don't know. Because that's what can happen when kids don't know what else to do. They join the family business."

Mom says, "It's not like you're defaulting to writing. Look at the dream you had—that was all you."

I know. It *was* all me. It came from the inside. Yet I remember the rule I set for myself—that I do something different from my mother. When I put the Athena ring on my finger in Greece, I promised to forge my own way and be autonomous. I started to believe I couldn't really do that if I was following in the path of either of my parents. My love of Greek history, of all things Greek, felt like mine alone. That so-called rule helped me separate more fully from my mother and father, I realize, but maybe it also kept me from seeing what was right in front of me.

~ ~ ~

We gather our coats and walk to the kneeling bench where we settle onto our knees side by side. It's not anything we planned or talked about, but here we are, and I'm positive this is a first. We've never knelt and prayed together before. I fold my hands, a motion so involuntary that in a flash I glimpse the child in me who learned how to pray. My eyes fall on the hem of the Black Virgin's robe. Her feet are hidden beneath it, but I imagine they are dainty and black, shod in ballet slippers.

I glance over at my mother. Her eyes are closed, her fingers interlocked. I wonder what her prayers are about. Her novel? Her blood pressure? Peace on earth? The two of us praying like this to the Black Madonna suddenly washes over me, and I'm filled with love for my mother. The best gift she has given me is the constancy of her belief. Whatever I become, she loves me. To her, I am enough.

I look up at Mary and concede what I am coming to know. I will become a writer.

~ ~ ~

Wandering through the cathedral, gazing at the elaborately carved capitals, I consider asking Mom what she prayed for, but I'm distracted when I spot a sculpture in the nave. Joan of Arc. An inscription says the statue commemorates her mother's visit to the cathedral to say prayers for Joan at the feet of the Black Virgin. There's no place for offerings or I would light a candle.

~ ~ ~

In the gift shop, Mom and I buy books about the Black Virgin of Le Puy in English and in French, which, of course, we'll never be able to translate. We buy small pewter medals bearing her image, the same one the pilgrims once stitched onto their hats and clothes. I decide in the moment that I'll wear mine on my wedding day along with the one I bought at Rocamadour.

As we descend the stairway, I tell Mom that since we only have two more nights in France, we should go all out on the meals. No hamburgers. Bring on the baguettes. The cheese plate. Steak au poivre. Champagne.

Then, after a few moments of wondering, I come out and ask her, "What did you pray for back there on the kneeler?"

"You," she answers, and peels off her coat again.

Sue

———

Charleston, South Carolina

Given in marriage by her father, the bride wore a gown of white French organza over peau de soie. The hemline of her A-line skirt was trimmed with Alençon lace. The Empire bodice was enhanced by a sheer bertha cape, accented with seed pearls. Her cathedral-length train was adorned with lace appliques.

I read the paragraph in the yellowed newspaper clipping while waiting for Ann to come out of the alterations fitting room where she's trying on the gown. The article, from my hometown weekly newspaper, has been tucked away in a box for the last thirty-one years, and I'm sure I have not looked at it for the last twenty-five. I've forgotten how earnest the wedding coverage could get in 1968 in my hometown. It goes on for half a page and even includes a passage about my "going-away" outfit: a white, knit two-piece suit (*knit!*) with a navy-and-white-striped jacket, a navy straw hat, and white gloves with navy "monogramed" initials (monogrammed, I notice, is misspelled).

This morning I pulled out the article, reasoning that if the seamstress needed to remake any part of the dress, such details would be useful. It barely survived the "acid treatment," which has left the organza white as snowflakes but nearly as fragile. A tiny tear has appeared in the skirt like a run in a pair of hose.

With my reading glasses perched on the end of my nose—a new and necessary nuisance these days—I smooth the clipping out a bit further across my knees and stare at my bridal photo. The bertha cape dipping to my elbows, the endless train, the bouffant veil, the single strand of pearls, the young woman with the beaming face.

Across the room, Ann's bare feet are visible below the curtain drawn across the dressing room cubicle. I watch as she stands on one leg to slip on her panty hose and does the wobble-hop-hop as she loses her balance, then tries again. I fold up the article and slip it back into my purse.

It is a warm, bright day in early February, three and a half months since Ann and I returned from France. The matter of my blood pressure goes on unresolved like a small, daily trauma. Each morning after breakfast, I wrap the cuff around my arm and stare disconsolate at the readout. "That can't be right," I'll say to Sandy, then take it again, only to find it's worse and becoming a self-perpetuating stress all its own. I am in the midst of yet another medication change. I exercise, visualize, watch my diet, take my supplements, and excise all sorts of things from my schedule, trying to *do* less, but nothing seems to lower it for long.

Now wedding plans have begun in earnest—invitations, florist, musicians, caterer, wedding cake, a morass of details—though quite honestly I am delighting in them, savoring this time with Ann. Lately, we've been writing her marriage ceremony together, using the beautiful old liturgy in the Book of Common Prayer as a guide, but adding inclusive language and touches of feminine sacredness. Last Saturday we sat in the wicker chairs on the screen porch and penned the opening prayer:

Eternal Spirit, Mother, and Father who art in earth and heaven:

We acknowledge your presence on this holy occasion.
 Like the oak branch that reaches into heaven,
And the roots that travel into the earth,
You are above us and below us, and everywhere around us.
 May we know You in the beauty of the green earth,
In the music of the flowing river, and
In the hearts that rejoice together at the wedding of Ann and
 Scott.
Amen

I read the finished version of the prayer out loud, then we sat and stared at the oak beside the marsh.

When I can, I work on the novel. Instead of launching the second half of it, I rewrite and polish the first seven chapters, telling myself I should send them off like I envisioned in France. Not only have I not done so, I notice that when I finish sprucing up chapter 7, I start over again at chapter 1. As if I cannot see through what I am doing.

A sewing machine starts to hum just outside the fitting room, a sound I cannot hear without thinking of my mother and the music she made with her Singer. It played all through the house as she sewed clothes for herself, for me, and even for my dolls, who had fur-trimmed ice skating suits, poodle skirts, lounging pajamas, and dozens of other creations she dreamed up. She gave me my own Singer sewing machine when I got married. I eagerly sewed three pairs of overalls for Bob when he was an infant, an enterprise that involved so many tortured, ripped-out little seams I retired the machine to the closet, along with any desires I may have had to follow in her accomplished footsteps.

"You must be the mother of the bride," a voice says, breaking into my thoughts, and I look up to find the seamstress beside me with a pincushion on her wrist like a bracelet.

"And what are *you* wearing to the wedding?" she says after we've dispensed with every other wedding-related topic and Ann is still in the dressing room.

"A black dress," I answer. "Floor-length, silk—it's very simple with a sheer matching jacket."

I sound like the newspaper clipping.

"Black?" she says.

Which is exactly what the salesclerk said when I tried on the dress last week in a shop on King Street. It was just the opposite of now: *I* was in the fitting room while Ann sat outside waiting for *me* to emerge. I paraded out in mint green, aquamarine, persimmon, lavender, champagne—perfect colors for the mother of the bride at a garden wedding in Charleston in June. I disliked every one of them with an intensity I could not account for.

In the yellowed article, the preposterous fashion coverage had extended to my mother's dress, which was "blue crepe with a jeweled and lace yoke," and to my mother-in-law's, "rose pink with a scalloped neckline."

"The black dress fit perfectly," I tell the seamstress, "which isn't the easiest accomplishment anymore." I wonder why I am explaining myself to her. The truth is the dress simply felt right the moment I put it on, and it wasn't because of the fit; it was because of the color.

"You don't think it's too . . . somber?" I asked Ann. "Because that's the last thing I feel."

"It's great," she said. "And it's the one you like; you should get it."

Now, stepping from behind the curtain in the wedding gown, Ann holds the billowing sides of the skirt under her arms like two small, white barrels, dropping them around her as she steps onto the platform in front of the mirror.

I watch as the seamstress fusses with the bodice—aware of how I force away the image of myself in the wedding dress. The way my daughter takes me back, against the ferocity of my will, to what was.

~~~

On February 14, as the sun sets over the marsh behind the house, the creek turns dark magenta and the egrets lift out of the tall grass and fly home. I watch this familiar circadian rhythm from the windows in my study. Sometimes I think I should never have faced my desk toward the creek. The view is a constant distraction from work, but with the birds moving like flares of white in the gathering dark, I know the desk is exactly where it should be. There is wisdom in this sort of loitering. I watch until the egrets are gone, until the light becomes a piece of fringe on the horizon.

Downstairs in the kitchen, I hear Sandy beating a wooden spoon in a mixing bowl, cooking Chicken Biryani—my Valentine's Day present—which has spiced up the whole house with turmeric, cumin, and minced gingerroot. "Dinner in half an hour," he shouts up the stairs, used to me tarrying at my desk.

I've been tampering with the novel all afternoon, changing words and changing them back. I glance at the picture of the Black Virgin of Rocamadour that I keep propped on a stand atop my desk—the beautiful old black Mary face—and I think about the piece of chain I left in her chapel.

Send the novel off already.

My mind winds back to that time, years ago, when I unveiled the first chapter at the writer's conference and got the tepid reception, the teacher saying its potential as a novel was small. For a long time I believed the teacher was right. Now I think he was right *and* wrong. He saw a truth, regardless of how he interpreted it—my work wasn't ready then; I wasn't ready.

But sitting at my desk with the windows glazed dark and black Mary staring at me with her bold, impenetrable look, I know the first half of the novel is probably as ready now as it will ever be and maybe I am, too, because nothing is perfect and I should lay down my ego and let happen what will happen. It is just life. It's time to settle more fully into my own condensed truth and find my strength and boldness in *that*.

I print out the pages, stick them into a big padded envelope, and address it to Virginia Barber, the literary agent I met three years earlier.

The next morning I hand the envelope to Sandy as he leaves for his office. "Could you mail this for me today? Overnight express."

He tucks it under his arm and steps through the door.

"If I call you before you get to the post office, don't answer."

"Right."

"I mean it."

"Consider it mailed," he says.

Several days later, the phone rings and Virginia Barber is on the other end, asking if she can represent me. She wants to send my half-novel to several publishers. I say yes, while simultaneously having a silent talk with myself about not getting my hopes up.

After two weeks of vacillating between hoping and not hoping, I am in the waiting room of my optometrist's office, poking through a pile of magazines, when I receive a second call from the agent. She has found a publisher.

"Congratulations," she says.

I impersonate a woman who seems to know more or less what to say—*How exciting . . . I never imagined . . . I'm thrilled . . . Thank you so much . . . I really appreciate it*—but in reality, I am walking deliriously around the empty waiting room silently mouthing the words *holy shit*.

She concludes the conversation by saying, "The publisher wants the rest of the novel by September first."

I count on my fingers. *Six months.*

A few minutes later in the examination room, I stare through the lens while the eye chart letters float into the circle of light on the far wall. E D F C Z P.

"Which is better?" the optometrist says, flicking back and forth between the settings. "This . . . or this?"

~ ~ ~

Getting the novel published is "better," yes, definitely. The dazed sensation I had in the optometrist's office gives way to joy and wonder, which will always be the most pervasive feelings I have about it, but I also possess a modicum of mild terror at the prospect of pulling it off.

As spring flies by, I lie in bed too many nights and flip back and forth about whether I should have waited until life was calmer before sending my work out there. But when is there any guarantee of that? Anyway, it's irrelevant. I leaped, and now I have to put my head down and *do it*.

To compound the matter, Terry and Trisha and I decided to put together another trip. Next October in Greece. When I asked Ann if she wanted to go, considering she would be a newly-wed then of only four months, she said, "Of course I want to go!"

I'm excited to have at least one more trip with her, but there is work involved—itineraries, travel arrangements, research, lectures.

There's no time for egret watching or other sorts of wise loitering. No time for contemplative thoughts about anything, much less about Ann getting married and what that might mean as an event in my own soul.

Each day I sit at my desk and plug away on the book. The work moves with painful slowness. When the agent mentions that the publisher would like to see my outline for the final half, I have to explain there is not one, that I have no idea from day to day what will happen in the story. Worse, an old voice is back, popping up every time a new idea emerges, explaining to me why it is stupid. I regress to a place I've passed through before. I do not trust what comes to me.

By mid-May I am not on any sort of reasonable pace to complete the book on time, and I'm too much of a novice to imagine I can miss the deadline, as if at midnight on September 1 everything goes back to pumpkins, mice, and cinder rags.

The one leniency I allow myself is long, weekly phone conversations with my mother. More than nice respites, they become moments to weave our lives together. We talk about the wedding—the junior bridesmaid dress she's sewing, her progress hand-tying white bows on two hundred small bells for the guests to ring instead of throwing rice, whether we should have crab cakes at the reception—but our discussions inevitably drift to other topics. She tells me about her osteoporosis, which she has reversed with weightlifting. I disclose worries about my blood pressure, how it sweeps up and down and up, which I can't seem to reverse at all. She asks me about Ann's and my travels, about Mary and the Black Madonna. I ask her about her fifties: "Did you have hot flashes?" "Did you gain seven and a half pounds the first year after menopause?"

She jokes, "I didn't have a lot of time to think about it. When I was fifty, I still had an eleven-year-old!"

"Good point," I tell her. And it *is* a good point. Who has time to think about this stuff?

One day Mother says, "It must be special for you that Ann is wearing your wedding dress."

"Yes. Yes, it is," I say, and change the subject, but not before I realize the words have made a tear in the dike.

~ ~ ~

Then one morning, two weeks before the wedding, I wake at day-break with a feeling of overwhelming sadness. In those first, amorphous seconds, the grief overtaking me is so strange and dislocating I wonder if I have forgotten some terrible happening. It takes a moment to understand that life is the same, but I have somehow awakened into a depression.

My body feels weighed down on the bed. I have little will to get up. I force myself into the bathroom. Close the door. Sit on the stool before the mirror. I try to get my bearings, shake myself out of it, but it is like something inside of me has dropped anchor.

On the surface, the sudden melancholy shocks me, but deeper down, I've almost been expecting it. I'm guessing that what commandeered my soul during the night has to do with me, Ann, and the dress.

At times like this, I feel the small curse of my introspective nature and its obstinate demands, how it wants to be allowed, wants my unhurried and undivided attention, how the moments of life insist on being metabolized and given expression. As usual, having failed to stop and tend to this unmitigated part of myself, it has stopped me.

My eyes fall upon the cup beside the sink, and my dream from last night instantly replays. . . .

I'm in a boat on a river somewhere. Am I piloting it? Yes, I seem to be. I seem to be the only one on the boat. The water is choppy and dark, the wind picking up. I notice that women are wandering to the edge of the river, tearful, holding out their hands. I go by, curious about them. Why all the crying? What do they want? Suddenly, I feel cut to the bone, as I realize—I am driving the boat that dispenses water to dying mothers. I have to stop for them.

Tears come. The anguish I felt in the dream sticks to me as though I've walked through a cobweb.

Everything ceases. Sunday, Monday, Tuesday, the sadness is unremitting. I sit for hours on the dock beside the marsh, watching the tides migrate. I try to come to terms with what Ann's marriage means for me inside. I let myself feel what I feel. I write it down, trying to understand and give it form, acquiescing to the inner transaction I seem to need. These acts quench the thirsty places inside I've neglected. They are a small mercy I bestow on myself. Like dispensing water.

It feels like I am finishing the process I started in Eleusis, Greece, when I sat by the well where Demeter grieved and first confronted the dying of my motherhood and my younger womanhood. As much as I would like to believe that confrontation is over and done, it's clear that remnants of longing for those aspects of myself are vividly present in the Persephone-like image of Ann in my wedding dress. The image takes me back to the time I was young and setting out into a new life, and at the same time it thrusts me forward toward the life ahead. I am stuck somewhere between clinging and fear.

There is nothing to do but stay with the whole miserable process, believing that if I hold the feelings, tensions, and conflicts as fully as I can, a shift of some sort will happen.

And so it is that a week before the wedding, I have a dream:

It is Ann's wedding day and I am walking with her down the aisle, arm in arm. I notice a woman standing at the end of the aisle and realize she is waiting for me. Drawing closer, I see that she's old and dressed in black. When we reach the altar, I turn loose of Ann's arm and walk over to see what she wants. She smiles at me and reaches out her arms as if she wants to dance. I resist, thinking this is not on the program, but she keeps on standing there with her arms out. I agree, finally, and we dance through the church while the wedding goes on. I am surprised at the beautiful and improvisational moves she makes, by how energetic and powerful she is, how completely free. She leads, I follow. It is exhilarating. Then it hits me: this is the Old Woman.

When I wake, I am flooded with lightness, like a fever breaking. I open my eyes, aware of how still the room is, the wood blinds drawn open on the window, a pale sky, and an awed, numinous feeling spreading through me. The movements and feelings in the dream seem astonishingly real, as if they've actually happened. They linger in my body like memories—my arm linked in Ann's, walking, dancing, trying to keep up with the Old Woman as she leads, the whole mystery of her alive and regenerating.

Lying there, I remember that the well I sat beside in Eleusis is called the Well of the Beautiful Dances, and suddenly, the dream feels like a consummation, like a coalescing of the last two years. The walk with Ann toward the altar seems like a final acknowledgment and letting go of my old self, while the encounter with the Old Woman feels like an integration, the commencement of a new dance inside.

I met the Old Woman, I think. This time, in myself.

~ ~ ~

On June 3, at six o'clock, I am at the rear of the rose garden, gazing at the wedding aisle—a dirt path that leads to the mammoth oak beside the Ashley River.

The guests are congregated under the branches, the sun hangs behind the clouds, and three musicians, with oboe, cello, and flute, sit in chairs on the riverbank and play *Ave Maria*. It is perfect, and for a moment the sight of the soft light coming across the river and the strains of music pierce me with such happiness, such beatitude, I think I might cry. But as Bob has already pointed out to me, I cannot walk down the aisle dressed in black and my eyes running with mascara. I suppress a laugh.

"What's so funny?" Ann asks. She stands between Sandy and me, radiant in her white gown with crimson roses popped open all around her.

"Bob," I say. "He told me if I cried at your wedding, I would look like Morticia in *The Addams Family*."

This cracks her up, but then everything he says cracks her up, his sense of humor being even more acerbic than hers.

I smile at her. "You look beautiful."

"You, too," she says.

There are a few seconds of quietness, then Pachelbel's *Canon* floats across the garden. I watch the groomsmen move along the aisle, focusing on Bob as he takes his place in the lineup near an urn of flowers. I smile at him, aware that the letting go between mother and son is every bit as important, and yet different.

When the "Bridal Chorus" starts, Sandy leans over and kisses Ann's cheek. I kiss the other one. The three of us start down the aisle, arm in arm toward the minister. I give myself admonitions: *don't trip, breathe, smile.* I gaze at my bouquet of calla lilies, where

I've tucked the sprig of wheat that Ann found at Eleusis and presented to me as we left the cave where Persephone returned. Demeter's wheat.

Then those thoughts are gone, and I see the tree and the river and feel Ann beside me. I hear the slight jingle of what I think might be the medals of Mary from Rocamadour and Le Puy pinned beneath the bodice of her gown.

Ann

Charleston, South Carolina

❧ At five minutes after six, the chamber trio plays "Here Comes the Bride." Standing in the garden, about to walk down the aisle, I decide I'm no longer worried about the 20 percent chance of thunderstorms the Weather Channel has called for all day.

It's a typical hot day in June. As my father wipes his forehead with his handkerchief one last time, I am aware of his presence, not only beside me now, but throughout the whole of my life. He's the one who taught me to whistle, tie my shoes, ride a bike, love baseball, and make basil pesto. The one who built my *stuffed* puppy an actual wooden doghouse, who came to my rescue when my kindergarden teacher critized my penchant for coloring outside the lines, who labored patiently with me over math homework, and who drove me to weekend slumber parties. Dad bestowed on me not just freckles, but an exorbitance of love. I put my arm through his, careful not to jostle loose the hydrangea blossom from France that I've stuck into my bouquet. Faded to lavender, the dried petals are easy to distinguish among the roses and other plump, blue hydrangeas. Mom rests her hand on my elbow, and I feel her fingers pat my long cotton glove.

I try not to step on my hem, stare at my feet, or worry about dragging the long train through the dirt. As we walk, I focus on the tree with its canopy of shade and on Scott in his morning suit, standing in front of a dipping oak limb, smiling at me, and looking as relaxed as I've ever seen him.

On a big safety pin attached to my bra are the small medals of the Black Virgins from Le Puy and Rocamadour, my Athena ring, and the little glass pomegranate. I slipped them on and fastened the pin over my breastbone where it wouldn't cause a lump beneath the bertha cape. The sum of my objects has become a comical topic among my immediate family.

When I told Mom I had medals of French Mary but no Greek Mary, she offered me her small icon of the Virgin Mary from Tinos, which had come to her so mysteriously. I took it to the florist along with Mom's childhood Bible so they could both be attached to my bouquet. The florist joked that maybe I needed a wagon for all my "stuff." I thought: *Lady, you don't even want to know what's going into my bra.* Despite that, when I left the shop, I realized I'd left out Joan of Arc. All I had was a postcard of her. I figured she would understand me omitting the card. I had to stop or else I'd end up hauling that Radio Flyer down the aisle.

My eyes scan the guests standing on either side of the walkway. The ceremony is such an intimate and private undertaking that it strikes me as weird that Scott and I have assembled one hundred and twenty people to watch. *Don't overthink*, I tell myself. I see faces. They click like slides in a carousel. Dr. Gergel, the professor who led my college tour to Greece. My close friend Marla. Trisha, from our trip to France. My three grandparents.

Certain memories have returned to me lately, a flow of mental snapshots. My grandmother at the stove, stirring a beat-up pan of sugar, butter, and milk while dictating to me the secrets of her caramel icing like the host of a cooking show. My "Biggie" (as we call my dad's mother), allowing me to paint her fingernails various shades of pink—watermelon, raspberry, tutti-frutti. That time my grandfather (not my mother, or my grandmother, but my *grandfather*) took me shopping at the mall. How we scoured the racks for the special outfit he insisted on buying for my tenth-grade class trip to President Clinton's inauguration. That houndstooth blazer with a suede collar we chose.

Halfway down the aisle, I see Bob lined up with the groomsmen, watching me and our parents coming down the aisle. On his face is an expression of pure affection, a look I would have killed for when I was eleven and he fourteen. Last night I stayed at my parents' house, adhering to the tradition of not seeing the groom, which seemed kind of silly, considering that Scott and I live together. Bob and I stayed up late, in a magnificent regression, watching old MGM cartoons on television. During a cartoon of monkeys singing "Hear no evil, see no evil, speak no evil," Bob fell asleep.

I turned off the TV and wondered if this was the last time we would act like kids in our parents' house. Childhood seemed far away, like a country I would not return to. And I sat there a moment with the clicker in my hand and the screen gone dark, with a wash of images born of nostalgia, but also from a recognition—I think maybe my first real one—that everything ends, life passes, it is all changing. Getting married tomorrow would take me across the border, into a new country, one that seemed beautiful, and unmapped.

Right then, I felt perfectly positioned between two worlds. I tried to say to myself what they were—old and new, childhood and grown-up-hood, going solo and going duet, *madame* and *mademoiselle*. I wasn't sure, but the in-between-ness swept over me with wonder and sadness and excited anticipation.

Last week, my parents took Scott and me to a Spanish

restaurant in the Old City Market downtown. Mom handed me a small box. Our wedding gift, she said. Inside lay three linked pieces of chain. I remember Rocamadour: *what's with Mom and the chain?*

I read the card:

Years ago, your father and I adopted this piece of chain as a symbol for our marriage. The two outer links represent each of our lives and the center link, our marriage. It reminds us that we have independent lives, dreams, and journeys, but at the same time, we are joined in a center space where our lives are one.

We toasted our upcoming wedding and sipped sangria. I joked to Scott that his link was the surfer. Mine, he said, was the traveler who would go off to Greece in four months.

Now, as the flute sings its last notes, my parents and I reach the tree. Quietness drifts up. I hear the insects hum. Two egrets are gliding down to the grasses at the river's edge in slow motion. I smile at Scott as Cathy, the minister, reads the prayer.

Eternal Spirit, Mother, and Father who art in earth and heaven . . .

~ ~ ~

Before the ceremony, we dress in an upstairs room of the Rice Mill House near the Butterfly Lake. Mom follows me inside with the veil draped over her outstretched arms like she's bearing the queen's jewels. Trailing behind her is my grandmother, then Laura, my maid of honor, followed by my three other bridesmaids, carrying their sea-foam-green dresses.

I turn the knob of the window air-conditioning unit to a promising shade of blue and hang my wedding dress on the back of the bathroom door. Settling into a chair in front of the blast of cold air, I pin the assortment of sacred objects onto my bra, which is more like an unforgiving corset contraption.

Everyone is busy. Ironing, applying mascara, plugging in curlers, unboxing bouquets. I sit still a moment, watching the flurry.

Spotting my dress across the room, I try to picture the nineteen-year-old my mother was when she wore it, a girl I never knew. Wearing the dress honors the bond between us—that's how I've thought of it—but what I think about when I look at it now is the essence of my mother's life, from the nineteen-year-old to the fifty-two-year-old, all that she has lived and become, and that makes me eager for the possibilities in my own life.

I finish dressing by the air conditioner, stepping into the gown and standing in front of the mirror while Mom crisscrosses four bobby pins in my hair to hold my veil. It is wired with white rosebuds and blue delphinium. I've never worn flowers in my hair before, and gazing at them with the white tulle falling down my back, I feel like a real bride. Mom stands behind me and smiles. Later, this configuration will make me think of the photo she has kept on her desk since France, of her mother and grandmother in this same pose.

~ ~ ~

The wedding ceremony took a year to pull off and lasts twenty-five minutes.

As Scott and I walk into the reception, one of the band members heralds us in a booming Barry White voice—"Ladies and Gentlemen, the newly married couple . . . Scott . . . and . . . Ann," and "It Had to Be You" starts to play. The spotlight dance is the only part of the wedding I've dreaded. I set my bouquet on the cake table and follow Scott to the center of the dance floor, which suddenly seems like a stage with the curtain going up, the audience hushed, lights dimming, and one big spotlight in the center. But in fact, the whole room is ablaze with light. We are in a large glass-walled pavilion on the grounds, not too far from the tree. It is filled with candle flame and palm trees strung with tiny white lights, all of which reflect in the glass.

I do not know if I will ever make my peace with The Spotlight.

But I'm out here. As we dance, I have a soundtrack in my head: *Tune everyone out. Focus on Scott. We're the only ones here. We're the only ones here.*

When it's over, I sit down, take off my shoes, and eat chocolate wedding cake, followed by a plate of Charleston food—shrimp, crab cakes, sweet-potato biscuits, country ham, mango chutney, and benne wafers, eating like I do not have on the corset contraption. When Scott and I chose the songs from the band's list, we had crossed off "Play That Funky Music," but there it goes, pulsing through the speakers. I look up and see Bob dancing to it with our grandmother.

A guest drops by the table to ask, "Did you know an alligator swam by in the river during the wedding?" She has a concerned look, as if this is an omen.

"No," I tell her, thinking, if it's an omen, it's a good one.

We leave to the sound of ringing minibells. Slipping outside, the two of us alone now, moving across the lawn in the darkness, the night sounds rise up: tree frogs and crickets and the rhythmic call of a whip-poor-will. When I turn and look back, I see the glass pavilion gleaming with light. I see Bob talking to Mom, making her laugh. My dad channeling James Brown on the dance floor to the muffled sounds of "I Feel Good."

Scott and I climb into the car and drive off with my wedding gift to him strapped onto the top of the Honda. A new surfboard.

~ ~ ~

The thunderstorms begin sometime after midnight on the first day of my married life. I'm not implying any sort of sign or portent. It simply rained. It is, however, a deluge. We are staying in one of those impeccable five-star inns around Charleston before departing for our honeymoon destination, and I wake to the crash of rain and the wind howling in the oaks and pines. Lightning from far away fills the room with faint, vibrating light. The Carolina Lowcountry has its quick summer storm bursts, but this one sounds apocalyptic. I lie in the four-poster rice bed, which is so tall it has its own set of steps to get to the mattress, and I listen to the thunder.

There is the saying—a favorite of my grandmother's—"Into every life a little rain must fall," and while I don't think the barrage outside means anything particular, I allow it now to have meaning in general. Something about the way life is. Taking the severities as part of it. About the weather patterns in the new country.

~ ~ ~

After the honeymoon, I begin my second writing class. I read books about becoming a writer by authors like Brenda Ueland, Natalie Goldberg, Anne Lamott, and Julia Cameron—sensible advice that sounds good in theory. For example, "Write every day." I cannot argue with this, except I'm working at the *Skirt!* offices every day. Once home in our new apartment, there's dinner to worry about, which is not so bad because I actually like to cook. By 7:30 the joy I found trying out the marinara sauce turns to fatigue, and I don't want to sequester myself in the second bedroom that I've turned into my writing room. What I want is to stretch out on the sofa and watch *The West Wing*.

Tonight I forgo the sofa. I sit at my desk, staring at the images I've placed around the room. Beside the computer is the red pomegranate charm, a postcard of the Black Virgin from Le Puy, and the little Athena helmet with the owl feather. The fragment of the David Whyte poem is thumbtacked to a bulletin board—*Give up all the other worlds except the one to which you belong*. Next to it, the photograph of me with Harry the horse, a reminder that when circumstances appear beyond me, it's possible to rise to the occasion.

I need all the inspiration my collection of sacred objects and incantations can provide, since becoming a writer seems like it could take a hundred years. When I got back from France, I assumed that doing what one is meant to do would come more easily. During the first writing class, I wanted near-perfect drafts from the start. When that didn't happen, I felt myself retreating. I would want to quit, even when Mom's logical example about Beethoven came back to me. But quitting wasn't an option.

One day I thought: *what if I approached learning the craft of writing as if it were an apprenticeship?* Just do myself a favor and accept that it's going to be a *process*, a slow, laborious process. In the Middle Ages, an apprenticeship lasted seven years. That was believed to be the minimum amount of time it took to learn a craft. I started to think of myself as an apprentice. I would tell myself, *Relax, you've got seven years.*

Even so, it doesn't stop my critical voice from droning on, but it does give me a way to go on working whether or not I like what I write, whether or not I think I have anything important to say, and whether or not my words sound like they come from someone I don't know. Which is often. I've only written one story I felt slightly comfortable reading aloud in class, and afterward, I wished I hadn't read it. In this respect, Mom says, I sound like a writer to her. She continues to hand me chapters of her bee novel, asking me to read with an editorial eye. I read them when I get into bed at night, unaware how my editorial eye is being trained. Mom reads drafts of my articles for *Skirt!* and even my class homework, then we talk about the works' strengths and problems and how to fix them. She marks them with a red pen. "It's bleeding," I told her the first time she handed back one of my papers.

"It's the best way to learn," she said. I suppose I would rather hear criticism from her than anyone, and who else could I ask to use a different color pen? Purple. Green. Anything but red. From my desk, I hear the TV in the den. Sounds like *Iron Chef* night. I love the show, but I'm trying to go at my writing determinedly, à la Joan of Arc.

"Can you turn that down a little?" I yell to Scott. I hear "Chef Morimoto" and "abalone battle," then the sound fades, and the silence of being alone envelopes me.

I pick up one of the writing books and turn to a page I've flagged. It suggests that I see the value in composing one short paragraph no matter what it is. At the end of my six lines, I wonder if there is any value in a paragraph about why I don't want to write the paragraph.

"Did Morimoto win?" I holler.

"It's not over."

I stare at the blinking cursor on the monitor and remember a writing exercise my second-grade teacher taught us. I don't know how it has come back to me, but I take it as payoff for sitting in the chair. It was St. Patrick's Day and Mrs. Seaborn gave us five words and asked the class to create a story with them: Leprechaun, pot-of-gold, rainbow, hat, sky.

I type five words: Parthenon, Athena, girl, dancing, moon. I have a way to begin. My story opens at the Acropolis in Athens. The Caryatid porch on the Temple to Poseidon, the olive tree nearby, tourists milling around the Parthenon. I decide abruptly that Athena is telling the story. I write without worrying about the words, the structure of my sentences, or who's winning *Iron Chef.* In the story, the moon comes out, and Athena, who sees everything that goes on in the city named for her, watches a girl learn to dance in the Plaka. When I look at the clock, it is one in the morning.

Sue

Charleston, South Carolina

꿈 When rain falls on the tin roof over the dock, it sounds like thousands of those windup monkeys beating drums and clapping cymbals over my head. Weirdly enough, the effect is calming. I sit in the Adirondack rocker, facing the creek, and listen to the clatter.

The month of July is nearly over. In the eight weeks since the wedding, I have been in some sort of flow. I've spent my days moving back and forth between my desk and the dock, alternatively writing for a couple of hours, then sitting out here, doing nothing. Back and forth. The rhythm has suited me.

A tiny barge of reeds floats by, swept on the tides, and behind it, the dorsal fin of a dolphin breaks the surface, its shiny body curving up, followed by the spew of wet air. I recognize the fin, which is partially missing from an old wound. This dolphin comes like clockwork to feed. I time my visits to be here.

Surprisingly, my blood pressure has normalized. No elevated readings all summer. I cannot say I understand this or that I expect it will stay this way. The stabilization seems like a beginning, but I know there is a shift going on inside of me. A deceleration. I can feel the striving leaking out of my work. It's like I'm just figuring out how to lean back into the simplicities of being. It reminds me of the first time you try to learn to float, the way you have to keep letting go and rest in the moment, believing the water will hold you, that it is enough, that it is *everything*. And then you sink and you have to sputter back and start again. I can trace much of this straight back to Gavrinis. Since my experience at the tumulus, I am tending time differently.

More startling to me than the blood pressure drop is the simultaneous surge of creativity I've felt. The writing has poured out. I try not to think too much about why I'm having this fertility spurt, I've just let it happen. Sometimes, though, I revisit my dream of dancing with the Old Woman and wonder if the spurt is not a fluke, as I fear, but the continuation of that dance in my waking life. Where does the improvisation, the freedom, the hint of new authority and potency come from? Images well up in me more spontaneously, trailing along a stream of ideas, memories, feelings, and symbols, and I feel connected to a sourcelike place in myself.

It seems to me now and then that the dance in my dream was the beginning of a new center inside myself—the feminine matrix that the Old Woman seems to represent—but it's hard to know. I can only watch the rain fall into the creek and repeat the line in Sarton's poem that has been the most enigmatic to me: *Old Woman . . . Under the words you are my silence.*

Out in the creek, in the blur, the dolphin with the deformed fin goes about her unhurried moments.

~ ~ ~

I stand in line at Kinko's, holding a white box containing the manuscript of my novel. Four hundred and three printed pages. I took the liberty of typing THE END on the last page, which is probably the mark of a neophyte, but it gave me so much pleasure I didn't care.

It is the day before the appointed deadline, the last pickup for Federal Express is twenty minutes away, and five people are ahead of me in line. I glance incessantly at my watch, recalling that at one point in my novel, the main character, Lily, quips that Rosaleen is moving with the speed of a bank vault door. That seems fast compared to this.

I know I'm imposing an artificial and ridiculous sense of urgency upon the situation, but I keep thinking *Surely I have not written through the summer, composing the last line a slim hour ago, and arrived here only to miss the deadline.* I am flush with nervousness, which, truth be told, is more about how the publisher will react to what's in the box. I haven't let myself think about that for twelve weeks.

Dawdling in line, feeling the weight of the manuscript in my arms, I'm hit full in the chest with the realization I've completed it. A sensation washes over me, some odd combination of elation, relief, and stunned incredulity.

My mind sweeps back to October 1993, to the convent at Palianis in Crete—me, slipping beneath the low, twisted branches of the myrtle tree, standing before the icon of the dark-faced Mary. *Panagia Myrtidiotisa*, the Virgin of the Myrtle. I hear the Greek nun: "You ask her for the thing at the bottom of your heart, yes? The Virgin will give it. Then you give to her something."

I felt a little cynical about the nun's words that day, at least at first. Then I thought, why not give up the attitude, the arrogance; there are, after all, mysteries in the world. *I would like to be a novelist.* The words were unexpected, but so incisively true. So much of prayer is like that—an encounter with a truth that has sunk to the bottom of the heart, that wants to be found, wants to be spoken, wants to be elevated into the realm of sacredness.

Only one person is in front of me in the Kinko's line now. The Federal Express driver has pulled up out front, and there's no way he's getting out of here without my package. And it's about now that it occurs to me: the prayer—*it was answered*.

Was it a coincidence? Was it a matter of coming to terms with what I really wanted and giving over to it? Is there something to the saying by Joseph Campbell that when you follow your bliss, unseen forces come to your aid? Was the nun right about Mary working wonders? Could a surrender of self, mingled with a little faith, will, and self-honesty, account for it? Are there just mysteries in the world?

I don't know. It seems like all of these things could be true. *Then you give to her something.* The last part of the nun's entreaty comes back again—reminding me of the custom of returning to the *Panagia Myrtidiotisa* with a gift after she answers a prayer.

Seven years spin full circle. I have a tiny thunderstruck feeling as I realize I am about to go back to Greece. We leave in October, only six weeks from now, and a brief part of the trip will be spent in Crete.

How is it that life has arranged itself this way?

There's no question—I have to return to Palianis convent and leave a gift. I don't remember where on Crete the place is located, whether it is remotely close to anything on our tight itinerary, but I will call Trisha and Terry and explain why I need to reroute the trip. They will *love* this, I think ruefully—then realize, no, they *will*. They will actually love this.

When I reach the counter, I watch the manuscript disappear into the envelope, trying to imagine what gift I will take to the dark Madonna, what Ann will think when she lays eyes on Mary propped in the tree.

RETURN

Greece

2000

Ann

———

Palianis Nunnery–Crete

❧ I'm thinking, *these are the planes that always crash, the prop planes, the island hoppers, the ones that shudder on takeoff like the screws and bolts are shooting out of the wings.* Sitting in a window seat over the left wing, I try to calm myself, but the captain has come on the speaker with an announcement about turbulence. My fear of flying shows up only when the cabin lurches, when the unidentified noises start, all the strange thudding and creaking.

I close my eyes and do the visualization I use when I'm sure my plane is going down. I'm on the Flying Dumbo ride with Bob at Disney World and he has control of the little knob, swooping us up and down in a herky-jerky, but harmless, motion.

The propellers make a muffled roar, as if we're at a deafening rock concert with cotton in our ears. I elbow Mom. "I'm starting to get nauseous."

"What?" she yells.

"I'M GETTING SICK."

She digs out the Dramamine, then points at her watch, a gesture that says it won't be long till we land in Crete.

Popping the yellow pill into my mouth, I lean my head back against the vibrating seat and close my eyes again.

It's Greece. It's worth it.

~ ~ ~

On the first day of the trip, the bus drops off our group of twenty-five women in the countryside of Crete beside a blue street sign that reads PALIANIS NUNNERY in both Greek and English. The convent is just up the hill, the same one Mom visited on her trip here in 1993. According to her, a myrtle tree grows inside the walls with an icon of the Virgin Mary in the branches. She, Terry, and Trisha revamped the tour schedule to get us here. I pull my camcorder from my shoulder bag and zoom in on the blue sign, then pan the surrounding hillsides terraced with olive groves and grape orchards.

As we walk toward the convent gate, I film a whitewashed chapel alongside the road, its fluted terra-cotta roof tiles and prayer bell, then turn the camera on the women in the group, who tromp up the hill in clumps of twos and threes.

When I hit the stop button, one of them asks, "How's married life treating you?" The question I got most in France was "What do you do?" Now, it's the one about married life.

"Fine," I say. "It's great."

Four months into our marriage, the one thing that has plagued me is just what I anticipated: that question of love and freedom. It crops up in the negotiation of daily stuff. Who grocery shops and who cooks? Who does the laundry and who folds it? Will we clean the apartment first thing Saturday morning or will Scott go surfing? On Sunday, will we spend time together or will I write? We work it out, though at times it takes a little doing.

I don't tell the woman any of this, of course. Instead, I go into a rendition about Scott giving me surfing lessons this past summer. No reflection on his teaching, I say, but I spent most of the time lying on the board, floating, worrying a shark would mistake me for a seal. He was good about it, I add. He kept me company by floating, too.

My story prompts her to divulge memories of her own newly-wed days. "But just wait till you have kids," she says, smiling like she possesses a secret I don't.

Her comment about children brings back the conversation Scott and I had on the Saturday before I left. I'd attempted a Greek feast in our tiny kitchen, billing it as the official farewell dinner and set-ting the table with candles and the good wedding china. Between the *horyatiki* (Greek salad) and the *kotosoupa avgolemono* (chicken lemon soup), Scott turned to me and said, "Let's get a puppy."

I went through all the reasons this was a bad idea just to keep us from flying out the door right then to get one. The apartment is too tiny; a dog needs a backyard with a fence; puppies equaled house training, vet bills, chewed-up stuff—but it was too late. In my head I was already trying out dog names.

"Get thee to a nunnery," the woman quips as she catches up with her friends. It was the joke that got passed around the bus on the way here.

"Is that from *Monty Python?*" I ask Mom in all seriousness.

She tries not to laugh, but her voice cracks apart when she tells me, "It's *Shakespeare.*"

It takes us all the way to the top of the hill to get the Monty Python comment out of our systems.

The entrance to the convent is four tall, wooden doors with an arched mosaic tympanum of the Virgin wearing an indigo-blue robe. It is flanked, weirdly, by two blue and white striped poles that remind me of pictures of the candy-cane mooring poles in Venice. They have small crosses on the ends. I stare at them while Trisha knocks.

Mom has told me her story of being here, about asking the Virgin for the thing at the bottom of her heart. Every time I think of doing that myself, I get an expectant feeling inside, a chemical reaction bubbling over a beaker in the pit of my stomach. What lies in my heart. It seems like I've spent two years trying to solve that puzzle. What's really in there and what does it mean? Everybody deserves to ask those questions. I finally came to a conclusion about what to do with my life while kneeling before the Black Virgin of Le Puy, and it only seems to have solidified since then. This time, returning to Greece has not stirred up any of the old yearnings for a career in ancient Greek history. No ambivalence, no self-doubt. I still have an exceptional love for Greece and its past, but I'm sure I can find some avocation as a Grecophile through books, art, travel, and the occasional Greek feast in my kitchen.

I zoom in with the camera on the Virgin in the indigo robe over the door, on the gold polychromatic spattering behind her, then on her outstretched hands. I notice she has a yellow star on her forehead and one on each shoulder, just like the Queen of Heaven fresco I saw in the monastery at Meteora during my college trip. That fresco had initiated me into a world of Mary that I didn't know. Now, she has become part of a trinity for me, along with Athena and Joan.

Last year, I found a lump in my breast. I was in the shower and there it was, a tiny hard lump. I turned off the water and, wrapping a towel around me, stood at the sink trying not to panic. I recalled every story I'd ever heard about breast cancer striking women early in their lives. In their twenties.

After examining me, the doctor ordered a mammogram. After that, an ultrasound. Hardly believing the lump had taken me all the way to the radiologist's office, I lay on the table that day, perspiring despite how cold the room felt. *You do not have cancer*, I told myself. *You are not going to die.* But I didn't know, and the longer I lay there not knowing, the more I started to pine for all the things I wanted that hadn't happened yet. My wedding. My first anniversary. Motherhood. Writing. Another trip with Mom. I felt incapable of calling up the strength I needed to keep me from falling apart.

The treatment room was dark and quiet. I listened to the nurse's comfortable shoes barely making noise on the floor and felt dizzy with fear. I wanted to feel loved. To be reassured and comforted. To find the resources inside myself to hold it together.

"This won't hurt. Just relax," the nurse told me. "Think about the beach."

I closed my eyes, but I didn't see waves and sand. Spontaneously, I pictured my mother on one side of me and Mary on the other. It was no surprise that my mother turned up in my image and no big shock Mary was there either. Since I'd felt her presence bent over my life in the cathedral at Le Puy, I'd thought of Mary as my spiritual heart, my ability to love myself.

You're scared, I know, but the three of us can handle this, I imagined Mary telling me. Gradually I felt myself grow calm. Mary and my mother held my fear until the doctor was able to tell me the lump was benign.

I'm hesitant to say this incident became a huge turning point in my life, but afterward I was very conscious of life's gifts. I seemed to cherish the people I love more. I was a little more forgiving and appreciative, for a while anyway, though I don't think the new cherishing I felt ever wore off completely. My writing pursuits intensified, too. Life seemed fragile, and this knowledge may have been in the back of my mind when I left my job at *Skirt!* a couple of months before this trip in order to write full-time. It was a risky decision—Scott and I would have to sacrifice financially. But life seems too short now not to pour myself into the work I love.

After the breast lump, I also felt more aware of my connection to Mary. I have faith that when I approach the icon in the tree and ask Mary for what lies in my heart, someone is listening. I don't believe every prayer I toss out will be answered, but I like the idea of handing it over to someone. In my case, Mary. Whenever I pray now, it's second nature to turn to her.

As I walk through the wooden doors beneath the tympanum of Mary, I keep the video camera running, lingering on the stone pavement in the courtyard, cracked like the bottom of a swimming pool. Lush, tropical-looking flowers bulge around the base of palm trees and spill over earthen jars. Looking at them, ROY G BIV crosses my mind—the word trick for remembering the colors of the rainbow.

Assembled on the stoops where the nuns live are wooden chairs with extra seat cushions, baskets of yarn, and knitting needles. A nun sits in the shade of a grape arbor holding a ball of black yarn in one hand and pulling a strand of it with the other, as if conducting a piece of music. It reminds me of a print I bought at a consignment shop that depicts Mary pulling a red thread from a spindle as the angel Gabriel surprises her.

Even with Mom's description of the myrtle tree, there are some things you have to see for yourself. It's decorated with tin votives the size and shape of playing cards. There's a fence around the trunk, but I get as close as I can and discover the votives are etched with hearts, legs, arms, eyes, infants, and torsos of grown women. On one side of the myrtle, white twine zigzags through the limbs like a web, like the work of the mythical spider Arachne. I cannot figure out if it's to hold the branches together or if it's another offering. My favorite ornament is a row of sculpted clay birds strung between two limbs.

After I complete one revolution around the tree and turn off the camera, I see Mom sitting on a nearby bench looking at me, like part of her delight in being back is observing me take it in. I don't know what to say, so I purposely make my eyes as big as spoons when I look back. We will go to great lengths to make one another laugh, resorting even to idiocies such as this one. I watch Mom's expression, the way she teasingly lifts her hand and pinches the back of it, our family code for how to compose yourself during church: pinch the back of your hand as you imagine the suffering face of Mother Teresa.

Remembering the last time we were in Greece and how I struggled with sharing my pain about the rejection letter and the worst indictments about myself, it's clear the partition between us has dissolved, replaced with an openness in which Mom feels like my best friend. And while I guess I don't tell her everything, I feel I could tell her anything.

As I put the camcorder into my bag, a nun shuffles along the courtyard clutching loaves of bread under both arms like footballs. The sight of her returns me to why I'm here. I drop a drachma into the donation box near the tree and light a spaghetti-thin candlestick. Slipping away from the women clustered around the tree, I pull myself up onto a low wall, take out my spiral-bound journal, and begin to compose the prayer I want to say to Mary in the tree. I want to see the words in ink.

When I return to the myrtle, I stand in front of the icon, taking in the dried bougainvillea and palm fronds which have been draped across the top of it. Above the Virgin's head is a small cross molded out of candle wax and smooshed onto the frame. Staring into the Virgin's eyes, I tell her what is in the bottom of my heart.

I want to write a book about my travels.

The prayer is a green, unopened bud. And for once, it's not about arresting my fears, but about fulfilling conviction and a desire that has been building in me. Inside, though, it seems like more than a single prayer; it feels like an induction.

Sue

Palianis Convent—Crete

꙰ The convent at Palianis is just as I remember. Flowers in hot, sunburned colors. Grapes sagging heavily under arbors. Walls whitewashed from cleanliness to godliness. Passing three black-clad nuns in the courtyard, I peer at their faces, hoping one of them might be the nun from seven years ago, but none looks familiar.

Coming around the back side of the church, I spot the myrtle tree still festooned with dangling rosaries and ribbons and the glittering clotheslines of tin votive offerings, and of course, the icon of the brown-faced Mary tied to a gnarly old limb.

"You mean the icon stays in the tree all the time?" Ann said, when I first described it to her back home. I told her the legend of Mary repeatedly escaping from the church to the tree until the nuns gave up and let her live there. Happily ever after, it turned out.

As I gaze at the tree from across the courtyard, I realize why I love that story. It's partly because I relish the cautionary note in it about severing divinity from nature and the rightness of grafting it back, and partly because it features Mary slipping out the back door of the church, shedding sectarianism and making off to the tree and the wide world.

Last night, I opened the shutters in our hotel room in Heraklion and saw the moon, bright-white, over the Venetian harbor and a cruise ship pulling out, strung with lights from bow to stern, and the sight brought back shards of memory from my first trip here. I told Ann about swimming in the Libyan Sea and hiking the gorge at Kato Zakros, about the lightbulb that went off in my head when I saw a fresco of Mary in Krista, holding a snake in the same pose as the ancient Minoan snake Goddess. I launched into a full-scale story about Terry and me being invited into the home of an elderly woman on the Lasithi Plateau, where she served us tea and octopus sandwiches and told us (in Greek) about her dead husband, repeatedly using the word "kaput," and our slow realization that we would not be released until we bought her handmade doilies.

Ann followed my stories by pinpointing their settings on her map, making a geography lesson out of it. "The Lasithi Plateau is here," she said, circling it in red. When I ran out of adventures and spots for her to highlight, she said, "What was your favorite place?" And I immediately thought of *this* place, of the unhurried world inside the courtyard, of the tree, and Mary out on her limb. "Palianis," I told her, and the realization carried the sharp pang that accompanies homecoming.

Now, standing in the midst of the convent, I understand that in a way Palianis *is* a point of origin for me. It's the place where I composed my prayer to Mary about becoming a novelist. It's where my *new* creative life began—at least that's how I've framed it for myself. That's how it *feels*. I could also say the moments I spent in the Tate, contemplating Rossetti's painting of Mary's annunciation, are a point of origin. Both events allowed me to acknowledge a desire and a potential I'd held in abeyance and to finally state my intention out loud. Naturally, there would be nostalgia and homecoming attached to that.

The women in our group pool beneath the tree, circling the

white iron fence around the trunk, taking in the twisting limbs with all the trimmings, then one by one stepping over to the icon for their private conference with Mary. I find a shady nook in the courtyard and sit down to watch from beneath the brim of my black straw hat.

There's a particular scene in my novel that is always drifting back to me, like a radio song or a church litany one grows up repeating, and it comes now, just as it did in France in the chapel at Rocamadour: Lily is standing before the figurehead statue of the Black Madonna, pressing her hand to Mary's heart, saying, "I live in a hive of darkness and you are my mother. You are the mother of thousands."

I'm not sure why I go back to that fragment of the book in this recurring way. The obvious answer is that Lily's words are my own avowal. *You are my mother* could be my own secret confession of faith, I suppose.

And the phrase *You are the mother of thousands*—that could be me groping for hope in the symbol of a loving, divine Mother. I do fantasize about what might happen if such a feminine symbol actually began to function in the big spiritual picture—in the minds and hearts of people, in cultural and political institutions. What if there's truth to the theological notion that our picture of God offers a revealing glimpse of what we secretly value most in life, in ourselves, and in one another? What would happen if the picture widened out to include a creative, loving Mother or Sister who is all about compassion and relationship? Would it help invest us in the wise arts of the heart?

But I believe the real reason that particular scene from my novel gets caught in my thoughts so often is not because of either one of those two phrases. I believe it's because of their preamble: *I live in a hive of darkness.*

When I wrote those words for the novel, I wasn't thinking about a global hive. I was focused on Lily's private pain. It was only later, recently in fact, that I began to associate "the hive of darkness" with the world at large.

The year 2000 had dawned with so much hope, yet at the same time, it seemed no different from any other year. Threats of terrorism, wars, environmental disasters, religious and cultural clashes, ethnic cleansing, human rights violations . . . the images streamed across the television. Watching them made me sad, then angry, and sometimes sick to my stomach. When I grew tired of my senses being assaulted, I resorted to cynicism. "*Humans,*" I would mutter, as if we were a hopeless species. When the cynicism began to veer into bitterness, I would turn to denial. "Cut off the TV," I would say to Sandy. Maybe there is wisdom in limiting one's daily intake of bad news, but out of sight did not entirely prove out of mind for me.

Was the hive actually growing darker, or did seeing so much ceaseless news just make it seem so? Or, was this some newly heightened sensibility emerging from inside of me? So yes, I find myself brooding more about the planet these days. I believe all this new concern of mine is partially age-related, as if my biological clock is resetting itself for grandchildren and I'm disturbed about what sort of place it will be for them. It's as if my developmental clock is resetting itself, too, demanding to know what I plan on leaving behind, what drop of light, what response to the darkness in the hive.

And *that's* why the scene in the novel flares up so regularly, and why it flares up now. I look around for Ann's blue shirt and spot her on the ledge of a wall near the myrtle tree, her journal open, her pen sweeping over the page, and my memory lights upon a similar moment in France when she sat with her journal outside the chapel at Rocamadour, trying to come to terms with what to do with her life.

She has been writing for nearly a year, doing it with commitment and steady, hard work. That does not surprise me, but it is quite something to witness this sort of maturation in your *child*— the adult settling-in, the taking-on of life. You raise them for it, but honestly, when it happens, you can't help marveling a little. I've been reading pieces of her writing and each time she hands me the pages, she prefaces it: *Tell me the truth, give it to me straight, I want the good, the bad, and the ugly.* She read in one of her writing books that a writer's job is to serve his or her work—not the ego, but the writing itself. She took this to heart.

As I sit here with twenty-two years of writing behind me, thinking of Ann and the way she has plunged into her apprenticeship, which is what she calls it, I mull over the idea that a writer's job is to serve her work. This notion consumed me for most of my writing life—for nearly the first two decades. But now it flips over in my mind and I find myself wondering what the *work* ought to serve.

~ ~ ~

A breeze swirls up, ruffling the swag of tin offerings in the tree, causing light to dart and scatter. I take out my new black journal so I can set down some of my thoughts on paper, but pause first to read the Rumi quote I recorded on the front page: *We are pain / and what cures pain, both. We are / the sweet, cold water and the jar that pours.*

Putting an epigraph at the beginning of this journal felt compulsory. I did it for the other two trips, I reasoned. How could I not come up with another one? Except every quotation I found seemed artificially induced. Just words I was plucking out of a book and imposing. The lines from Rumi, though, reminded me of the dream I had before Ann's wedding about dispensing water to dying mothers. They sparked against something on the inside of me.

Rereading the words now, it's apparent they also resonate with the brooding I've been doing about the world and the questions that have begun to simmer inside of me: What will I leave behind? What will become of the world? What indentation will my work make? Why do I make myself audible like this? For what purpose?

I've always written because I wanted to. *Had* to. Because it was the necessary fire. I don't imagine any of that will change. But now, with the years moving by so fast and the darkness in the hive growing, I do find myself drawn to this poetic notion of Rumi's about being the water and the jar that pours it.

In my thirties, an apprentice writer myself, I was more concerned with figuring out how to express the truth of my soul than worrying about the suffering world and how I should respond to it. I was focused on that whole matter of serving the work. The burning question back then was whether my work was true to my voice and my vision. Was it *real*? I would go into small agonies about it. I'm sure that's because unvarnished authenticity was always the conflict for me. It was easier and simpler to please the culture and the family that shaped me than to uncover and tell my own truth. When I wrote *The Dance of the Dissident Daughter*, however, that conflict was shattered. The old, burning question died away.

A new overriding question has surfaced now, I realize: What does my work serve? I suspect the impulse to find a purpose for my writing that's larger than myself has grown out of my experience in the burial chamber in Gavrinis, France, when I discovered the need to identify with the "billion lights" and find a simple return to love. And yes, it's accentuated by the grandmothering spirit that rises in the last third of life.

I write all this down in my journal with a certain trepidation. It could sound full of loftiness and heroic delusion to some. I don't want to kid myself. There is wisdom in refusing the role of savior and accepting my limitations. Turning fifty involved making a severe peace with the fact that I cannot give birth to every egg in my ovaries or every potential in my soul. To say nothing of the way motives sometimes get mixed when the scheme is grand: what starts out as serving the world can easily turn into serving one's self. The opposite side of it, though, is the long, slow retreat into indifference and cynicism.

The air gusts up again, and I hear a hollow, echoing sound like the clatter of a bamboo wind chime. Then it dies away, and the walled world is silent. Even my mind shuts down and I *experience* the silence that I'm always reading and writing about. And here is what rises in me: There is a time when you are simply seized by tenderness for the world, that's all. When you come home to it, like Mary finding her way back to the tree and the wide world. When you decide you want your work to serve some part of that, too.

~ ~ ~

When the tree is deserted and everyone in the group has wandered off to visit the church or rummage through the shop where the nuns sell their lace, I open the gate on the iron fence that surrounds the tree. Am I trespassing? Stepping through, I look guiltily over both shoulders, then wade into the shadows around the base of the trunk. I pick my way over the arthritic old roots, circling around to the icon.

Staring at Mary through the plate glass, I'm arrested by how close and personal she feels without the fence between us. I'd forgotten the smoldering brown eyes. I stand there for a few seconds, staring at them, disarmed, self-conscious, listening for footsteps, for the nuns coming to haul me out.

I make myself think back to the prayer I uttered about becoming a novelist when I was here in 1993, back over the circuitous way things unfolded after that, and I get a whole tableau of pictures. The image of bees in the wall that wanted to become a story. The writing teacher pronouncing its potential small. The bee lighting on my shoulder in Ephesus like an epiphany, like a tiny cymbal crash, and all the determination this visitation set off in me. The moment in Rocamadour when I knew I had to send what I'd written out there. The phone call in the optometrist's office. Then trekking from my desk to the dock through the summer as I finally finished the book.

I reach in my bag for the small jar of South Carolina honey I've brought as my thank-you offering, relieved the jar has actually made it over here in one piece in the plastic bag at the bottom of my suitcase.

I unscrew the lid and pour the contents across the tree roots. The air is flooded with the powerful scent of sweetness. I watch the honey ooze over the roots into the dirt, how it leaves dark, glistening stains on the bark. Dipping two fingers inside the empty jar, I scrape a little more from the side and dab it onto the glass over the icon, over the Madonna's heart.

The padded steps of a nun intrude. Compared to the others, she is young and tall, though she's got to be fifty and no more than five foot two. She carries a tubular loaf of bread and what looks like sticks of incense. When she looks at me, I freeze like I've been caught drawing a mustache on Mary instead of dousing her in gratitude. But the nun only nods and breezes by with a scruffy black dog traipsing behind her.

Turning back to the icon, I press my hand onto the smudge of honey on the glass and think how *funny* that I ended up with Mary, with this devotion. As I look at her, though, I know she is not a figure in a tree or in a church, but a presence inside. She is a way to meet the divinity in myself. Even now she fuels the conversation that is trying to form in me about my writing, about Rumi's sweet, cold water and the jar that pours it.

Ann

Restaurant–Delphi
The Acropolis, Plaka, Electra Palace Hotel–Athens

🐾 Gathered at banquet-style tables, our group has just polished off dinner at a restaurant in Delphi. I am stuffed on *dolmadhes*—grapevine leaves filled with rice, lentils, and feta. As the servers clear away the dishes, we push our chairs into a horseshoe. There is no dance floor, but there will be dancing.

The columns around the room are the same burnt-orange color as the pyracantha that bloom all over town like burning bushes. Their berries have rained cinderlike onto the narrow pedestrian streets. Mom and I slogged through them on the walk here from the hotel, cutting through what seemed like people's backyards, past tiny balconies where towels hung to dry beside the geraniums. In ancient times, Delphi was known as the center of the world. As we walked, I told Mom the story of how Zeus located it by sending an eagle from the east and an eagle from the west. They met in Delphi, and the spot was marked by a stone called the Omphalos, or the navel.

As the first notes of a clarinet pipe through the speakers in the restaurant, I push "record" on my video camera. The troupe—three women and four men—springs into the room, holding hands. Forming a circle, they skip—graceful, controlled, perfectly in step with each other. I'm pretty sure I've seen a dance scene like this painted on ancient Greek vases in archaeological museums. I watch the dancers' feet bounce off the smooth stone floor as the tassels on the men's hose whisk the air and their pleated *foustanellas* flutter around their thighs. Costas, the leader of the troupe, is easy to spot in his bright red sash.

The music speeds up. Everyone, including me, sways in their seats. Camera flashes break across the dancers' faces as the song ends suddenly and the women get in touch with their inner cheerleaders, whooping as another dance starts.

Beside me, Mom claps, her camera dangling from her wrist. The sight revives the memory of our night out in Athens two years ago—dinner in the Plaka, the singer in the blue-sequined dress, the electric hurtles of the Greek dancers, and then the one who held his hand out, inviting me to dance. I had revisited the moment a million times in my mind. I thought the dancer's face would become the marker of this memory, the way dismay spread like an inkblot across his bright expression, but it was his outstretched hand I've remembered. The whole incident lasted three seconds, but it's three seconds I wish I had back.

Costas steps to the side of the dance floor as two of the other men make elaborate leaps, then twist themselves into limbo postures. Standing beside the Mythos beer crates stacked by the bar, he bounces on his heels, drums his fingers against his chest, and blows piercing whistles through his fingers. I focus the video camera on him, the Lord of the Dance.

As the two leaping men take their bows, I notice Letta, the Greek guide who's traveling with us, applaud, and I remember what she said when we first started out in Crete: "People do not come to Greece to rest. They come to gain their days."

I'd tried to shield myself from life and inhabit my own small, safe corner. But there is no immunity from life—that's what I've learned. I will never be the kind of person to volunteer from the audience at *Cirque du Soleil*, but I won't be satisfied being draperies either. I don't want to miss out on what the Greeks call *zoe*. Life. I want to live all of it, the whole glorious hazard.

Costas walks straight to me, and I see it coming. He holds out his hand.

I set the video camera on the table.

"You want to dance?" he asks.

I'm on my feet.

He pulls me into the center of the room. As we dance, I try to catch a glimpse of his feet, almost bumping into him. I rely on what Demetri taught me three and a half years ago—step, step, step, hop. When he raises our hands above our heads, my fingers accidentally brush against the dark stubble on his face.

The beat of the music accelerates. Costas yells for Trisha to grab on, and she takes my outstretched hand. Soon a long line snakes through the flame-colored columns in a mood of mild pandemonium. My mother is back there somewhere, but I can't see her. Costas sings along to the music, our hands sweating together, and I feel the heat on my cheeks. On the next pass by the table, I see my video camera still rolling, its red light glowing, capturing me from the waist down as I dance at the center of the world.

~ ~ ~

I guess the second time is the charm—the museum on the Acropolis is open. Finally, I'm going to see the relief that archaeologists have given two names—the *Mourning Athena* and the *Contemplating Athena*. Take your pick.

The whole museum consists of a few white rooms with accenting panels of Mediterranean blue. Every artifact here was found on the Acropolis, many of them offerings to Athena or adornments on the temples. Stopping before a carved owl, Letta explains its role in Athena's mythical story: "It is one of her symbols—a bird with the ability to see all around. It points to Athena's quality of seeing and understanding. She is the Goddess of Wisdom, after all."

Letta tells us that when she was a little girl, there were still owls roosting on the Acropolis, small and gray, like the ones Athena is often depicted holding. I'm reminded of the owl feather that has sat on my desk back home. Before this trip, I dreamed about a gray owl that swooped through the doorway of my apartment and flew into every room. I woke, jolted. In my head I kept hearing what Athena said to me three years ago in an earlier dream: *You can see me anytime you want. All you have to do is dream.* But I never did. This dream, however, felt like a visit from her. The thrilling sensation I got watching the owl fly through my apartment stayed with me all that day.

I walk through the brittle afternoon light that slants through a large museum window, noticing how it illuminates the remnants of muted paint on the Korai, or maiden sculptures. At the end of the hall is the relief I've been waiting to see. It is taller than I expected, more than lifesize. Letta informs us the relief dates to 460 BCE, around the beginning of the Golden Age of Pericles. I stare at the way Athena's forehead is bowed against her spear. She is barefoot, one hand on her hip and a pensive expression on her face.

In 1998, when I saw this image in a book, Athena looked as if the fight had gone out of her. I know now it was I who felt defeated. Today, two years later, I have a different impression. The cast of her face strikes me as contemplative rather than mournful. To me now, this is a look of contentment.

~~~

At 5:00 P.M. I wait in the lobby of the Electra Palace Hotel for Demetri. Swinging my bag onto my shoulder, I walk to the end of the lobby desk and look out the front door. I'm a little jumpy about meeting him, only because it has been so long since I've seen him and I don't know what to expect—how much he will have changed, whether meeting him now as a friend is a reasonable idea, or whether, once a romance is over and done, it is better to just walk away. I'm pretty sure it's the latter, but the relationship was significant to me in a way that went far beyond Demetri himself, and I cannot shake the feeling that what I wish for by this encounter is closure.

I glance again at the door. It occurs to me that he may not even show up.

During the past year, Demetri and I exchanged Christmas cards, Easter cards, and infrequent letters. I wasn't accustomed to receiving Easter cards, and he wasn't accustomed to Christmas cards depicting ice-skating nuns. "Your card was unusual," he wrote.

Our letters were the efforts of two people trying to be friends, but stuck in pen-palish language: *Hi. How are you? The weather here is . . .* I continued to write because I wanted his friendship, and because I felt badly about what happened before—failing to show up or even answer the phone when he called. I wanted to make it right.

In my last letter to him, six months ago, I told him I was getting married and also that I was coming to Greece with my mom this fall. Months passed and I heard nothing back. Then in late August, a battered letter arrived, having endured an arduous, three-month postal excursion to our new apartment.

Dear Ann,
I have finished school. I took some time for holidays on Zakinthos and now I am in Athens and attend further courses. I will stay here until December when I will move. . . .

He wrote about his plans, his friends, his car. It went on for two pages. Then he closed with this:

Congratulations about the wedding. I truly hope you are happy. I am glad you will be back in Greece in October. I would like to see you again, but because of what happened last time—it is up to you.

Demetri

P.S. If you decide to see me, bring your wedding pictures.

I wrote back suggesting five o'clock, October 19, in the lobby of the Electra Palace Hotel—it was the only free time I had in Athens.

I told Scott about the meeting and that I hoped I had his blessing, explaining how badly I felt for avoiding Demetri last time. "Besides," I said, "how often is a person in Greece anyway?"

"Apparently every other year," he joked, and then, "I'm okay with it."

Scott did seem unconcerned, but I wasn't sure *Demetri* was up for the meeting. When I left for Greece, I had not heard a word from him. Did he get the letter? Did he ignore it?

Demetri walks into the lobby ten minutes late, wearing a thin leather jacket. He looks taller. A more grown-up version of the lanky nineteen-year-old I met on a sidewalk in the Plaka.

"You look the same," he says. "Your hair is shorter, but still . . . the freckles."

"And you're taller," I tell him.

We walk toward Apollonos Street, into the sound of motor scooters sputtering like chain saws. He says, "The weather is nice."

"It's a lot like home," I respond.

When we arrive at Mitropoleos Square, Demetri gestures to a table at an outside café near the cathedral, not far from where

•

Mom and I were once besieged by hungry cats. After we've dispensed with the awkward small talk, he leans his elbows on the table and looks at me. "So, are you happy?"

"I am," I say, and it's not a pleasantry. I actually am.

As the server places two small cups of coffee in front of us, I think about Scott, how I could not imagine my life without him. About the puppy we want to get. The book I want to write. The trinity of Athena, Mary, and Joan, who travel with me now. I think how my experience in the underworld has brought me to a new sense of myself, the way my self-rejection has turned into acceptance and a new way of valuing myself. As painful as that was, I wouldn't change any of it.

"What about you?" I ask.

"I'm studying this summer. It's okay." I listen as he elaborates, noticing more ways he has and has not changed. His hair is just as dark, his eyes as brown, his manners as courteous. But there seems to be a serious quality about him that I didn't notice before. He throws a pack of cigarettes on the table, and that's a marked difference from the person who told me cigarette smoke made his head hurt. Perhaps we both have a shorthand version of each other.

"Did you ever learn any Greek?" he asks.

"A little."

"Let me hear."

I toss out random phrases I remember from my language tapes. *Ine oreo.* It's beautiful. *Nomizo.* I think so. *Alithia?* Really? *Dhen katalaveno.* I don't understand.

"It's good," he says, and sips his coffee. "Did you bring pictures of your wedding?"

"A few." I reach for the envelope in my bag and spread the photos on the table. Me in my wedding dress, standing with my mom, then dancing with my dad, and finally Scott and I cutting the cake.

"He might look a little Greek," he says, pointing to Scott. I laugh at that. I want to ask him if he knows the phrase "As American as apple pie." Sliding the photos back into the envelope, I say, "Will you be getting married anytime soon?"

"I have a girlfriend, Helen," he tells me. Of course, Helen—the face that launched a thousand ships. He looks at his watch. "I have to meet her shortly."

After the bill comes, I pull out my map of Athens and ask him to pinpoint the restaurant where we danced. It has bothered me that I've forgotten its name and location. I want to always know the spot where I danced on a tabletop.

"I'll take you," Demetri says. "It's not far."

We walk to the corner of Mnisikleous Street. "The restaurant used to be up there," he says, pointing. We stand beside kiosks of sunglasses and leather belts and stare at a narrow lane leading to a building painted antique gold.

I recognize it the instant I see it. "Did you say it *used* to be there?"

He nods and leads me up the steps, to the door. "It's an art gallery now."

I peer through the windowpanes, remembering how Demetri and I slipped outside after dancing. We kissed in the spot where we are standing right now, and where I'd looked up to see the Acropolis in the distance.

He is quiet. His hands find their way into his coat pockets.

"*Signomi*," I say. I'm sorry. "I wrote it in a letter, but I wanted to say it in person. I never wanted to make you feel like you didn't matter to me."

He puts his hand on the back of my arm. "I know."

Back at the hotel, we stop outside the doors. He gives me a hug.

"Good-bye, then," he says.

"Bye."

He walks back in the direction we came from.

I watch him for a few moments, then head through the lobby and onto the elevator, pressing the button that will take me to the rooftop.

~ ~ ~

Soon this spot atop the hotel will be crowded with people sipping drinks and watching the sun slump over Athens, but right now I have the place to myself. I have the whole city and a postcard view of the Acropolis.

I take the chair by the rail. Propping my feet on a planter of marigolds, I gaze at the eastern end of the Parthenon. The bare rock of the Acropolis seems to pare things down to what feels irreducible and true.

I picture Demetri walking away on Nikodimou Street and try to understand just who he was to me.

I feel some sadness. This visit with him was an ending—I know I'll never see him again. I feel a strange happiness, too, as I begin to see my relationship with Demetri for what it is: an event in time *and* an event in the soul. Our experience together is more than moments in a restaurant or on a dance floor, more than a brief romance. It's about what I learned that night and what became freed inside of me. Demetri helped me break through my self-imposed limitations, my smallness, my pathological safety. I cherished him because he introduced me to myself, he caused me to fall in love with my own life. *That's* what carries the charge, and that's what will go on in me. It's so easy to mix that up with the person.

The sun has slipped behind the clouds, hidden except for a haze of yellow. As the beeping of car horns fades on the streets below, I rummage through my bag until I find the graduate school rejection letter I've been carrying around since we arrived in Greece.

Two years ago, the letter felt like a dead end. It eventually came to represent my entire historical collection of rejections and failures. I brought it all the way over here in order to tear it up. I wanted to do it *here*. That seemed fitting. But now that the letter is in my hands, I see that it was really a catalyst, a beginning, and I decide I will keep it. I am who I am because of what the letter set off in me.

The tint over the city turns to bronze. As the lights around the Parthenon blaze, I feast on the sight, then head downstairs, thinking of home and everything waiting.

Sue

———

Sanctuary of Demeter–Eleusis

∾ Trailing Ann into the ruins in Eleusis, I study the green velvet ribbon on which she has strung her red pomegranate, how it's tied at the back of her neck, green like spring foliage. I'm wearing my pomegranate, too, but on a plain silver chain, drab by comparison.

I touch the tiny glass orb with my finger, remembering when I spied the charms through a store window on our first trip, how later our matching necklaces seemed to magically convince the taxi driver to bring us to this same site, when our verbal pleading failed. After that, we joked that we were wearing our myth on our sleeves—Demeter, Persephone; mother, daughter; the saga of loss, search, return—though, honestly, no one except the Greek driver ever seemed to notice it. Once, a woman in a restaurant asked us quite seriously if we were promoting pomegranate juice.

Ann's green ribbon is a brand new touch, just for this trip. I cannot stop telling her how pretty it is. She told me she got the idea from *Little Women*—meaning, I supposed, that it was inspired by the pendants that dangled on velvet ribbons around the March girls' necks. Ann loves *Little Women*. Especially Jo March, the feisty one who wants to be a writer. But as I take in the shoots of green breaking over the back of Ann's coat collar, I ask her if she wasn't also thinking about Persephone.

"She's why I chose the color green," she tells me.

We've had numerous conversations about Persephone's so-called "green fuse," a catchphrase we use to describe her regenerative essence.

It is the chilliest day of the trip. Overhead, cloud patches have pieced themselves into a gray quilt with scraggly blue seams. The light glooms noticeably as we cross the broken pavements with the other women, moving past the toppled columns and tympanums. Wind whips up the scent of dry weeds and musty old stones, pulling me back once again to our first visit . . . to Ann and me roaming this bonepile of ruins.

I wish I did not remember how lost and depressed she was then, but it wells up suddenly and a sharp sensation twists through my stomach, as if the memories are archived in the cells of my body and have been viscerally retrieved. I look at Ann striding ahead of me in her Persephone–Jo March ribbon and remind myself that while the memory of that period still stabs, she's no longer in the dark place she was two years ago.

Ann has told me that when we visited Eleusis before, she began to view her confusion, disillusion, fear, and depression in light of the myth, identifying them with Persephone's sojourn in the underworld. She began to see meaning in her descent. It became a search for a new sense of herself and a place for that self in the world. She found them, it seems to me now, in the daily confrontations with her darkness.

Just ahead, the women have begun to gather around the Well of the Beautiful Dances, peering into the dry, empty hole where I previously tossed a lock of my hair. The place where I capitulated.

I have another pang, though considerably milder, as I recall my own feelings of loss the last time I was here—the pulverizing moments I spent by the well, pondering the lost daughter: Ann, yes, but also the one inside.

Slipping into the circle of women, Ann and I stare at the stone well like two people gazing at the ocean, hushed by the sight of it.

"It is so different, being here this time," Ann says.

I nod, aware that the sadness and angst I felt here before are gone. Used up. What is left is the emotion stirred up by memory. And even that seems spent at the moment. Those natural losses of womanhood had craved expression and I am glad now for giving in to them. A kind of contented acceptance has grown up in their place, and this is a knowledge I have not fully possessed until now.

~~~

Earlier this morning during breakfast, while reviewing the itinerary, I realized today was our tenth day of traveling. That would have been an unremarkable fact except that I also remembered that in the myth, Demeter searched for Persephone for nine days and on the tenth, she found her.

I looked across the table at Ann, who was munching her toast, and I had the feeling there was meaning in the small synchronism. Where was I now in the scheme of the myth? Had I arrived not just at the tenth calendar day of the trip, but at the mythic "tenth day"?

As the waiter cleared our plates, I suddenly thought of the gift Ann had given me two years ago for my fiftieth birthday. It was a photograph she'd taken at Eleusis, one of the many she took of me when I wasn't looking. In it, I stand in the cavelike opening where Persephone returned to her mother, my white sundress no bigger than a postage stamp in the stark shadows. In the matting of the framed picture, Ann had inserted a paraphrased passage from the Demeter-Persephone myth in Edith Hamilton's *Mythology*:

As Persephone emerged from the underworld, Demeter ran out to meet her daughter as swiftly as a Maenad runs down the mountain side. Persephone sprang into her arms and was held fast there.

For twenty-six months that photograph and caption had hung on the wall of my study. After a time, I hadn't really seen them any more, in that way familiarity breeds invisibility, but sitting at the breakfast table, I realized the picture was an image of the "tenth day"—of me in the role of Demeter as she arrives at the entrance of the underworld at the end of her quest, knowing the deal for her daughter's return has been struck with the Gods.

I told Ann about "the tenth day" as we left the hotel dining room. Smiling, she paused in the middle of the room, and the two of us stood there for a long moment and looked at one another, seeming to comprehend together that the seeking had turned into finding.

~ ~ ~

We comb the jigsaw of ruins, as our guide Letta points out the remains of this and that—the inner sanctuary, the ruts worn into the floor over the centuries by massive doors—hundreds of moldering objects passing by as if on a conveyor belt, bearing history. I try to concentrate on each one, but the feeling at breakfast—the vision of Persephone bounding into her mother's arms and the awareness of a similar convergence happening in me—bleeds through all of it. I walk along as cameras click, and voices murmur, and the wind jousts with the cypresses on the hill, and I am . . . elsewhere.

I think about my mother. I phoned her not long ago and asked if she would like to go to France with Ann and me next spring. Recently, I decided to co-lead one more of these trips just for that possibility. "It could be a grandmother-mother-daughter trip," I told her.

"Well, isn't *that* nice," she said, using the tone she always gets in her voice when she's simultaneously astonished and pleased. I pictured her standing with the phone in the kitchen, over at the window where she could see the scuppernong vines looping along the fence.

I waited for her to say something more. When she didn't, I asked, "Do you need to talk to Dad first before you decide?"

"Oh no, I'm *going*," she replied. "I wouldn't miss this for anything on earth."

"Me either," I told her, and the words felt large inside, not just something to say.

At breakfast this morning, when I thought about the photograph Ann gave me, I was picturing myself as Demeter, identifying with the mother part of the myth, but now that I'm here, it has also flipped around and I'm the daughter. *I'm* the one returning to my mother. If I confided this to her, I feel like she would say: *Returning? But I never felt like you left.* She would be right, I was always there, but this is a different kind of closeness. As if a hidden aperture has opened. It's entirely possible that some of the new intimacy I perceive between us comes from a subtle variation in myself—the shift that began when I opened myself to her Hestia world.

The next time I called Mother, just to say we were off to Greece, she was at the gym. As our group processes past the ruins of Hecate's temple, I get a vision of my mother, seventy-nine years old now, going to town on the treadmill in her Reeboks and light blue warmup pants, and it provokes a spontaneous promise to myself: *I will grow young like that.*

Bending down, I pick up a stone the size of my thumbnail and squeeze the vow into its white surface. I'm leery of New Year–ish pledges to exercise and eat right, as I've left most of them behind like a trail of broken crockery, but this one seems forged in a deeper place. Since turning fifty, I've been initiated into a whole new relationship with my body. All that concern about what I see in the mirror has begun to leave; more and more what remains is simply the powerful need to take care of myself.

The high blood pressure readings have not returned. I did not even bring the blood pressure machine on the trip this time. "What? You didn't bring the Alarm Clock?" Ann asked the first morning in Crete. She bestowed this pet name on the machine last year in France because the whining and beeping woke her nearly every morning.

"I'm afraid you'll have to wake without the benefit of my medical equipment," I told her.

Her face rearranged into seriousness, and she said, "Do you think it will come back—your hypertension, I mean?"

Did I? I told her my blood pressure spoke fluently to me about the struggle between doing and being that was lodged at my core, and I imagined it would always be my severe teacher, spiking when I lapsed into my old bad habits. Several nights later I had an oddly terse dream—just a voice speaking out of the silence, making a surprising pronouncement: *When you become an old woman, you won't have blood pressure problems anymore.*

The irony was that our group was in Delphi when I had the dream, the land of oracles and Sybils. In actuality, we had tromped up the mountain earlier that day to what's left of Apollo's temple, composing questions for the Delphic oracle in our heads—the sacred game that pilgrims there always engage in. Something about all this must have primed me to dream what sounded like a foretelling.

I recounted it to Ann when we woke. The dream was hopeful to me, but cryptic, too. I suppose I wanted to take it literally. Now, though, I understand the voice was not referring to chronological years, but archetypal ones. It was talking about the Old Woman.

Dropping the rock into my bag, I slide out my journal. I scribble questions awkwardly, standing up, while the group moves on, leaving me behind. *What was it about the Old Woman that could be healing for me? Freedom? The repose of belonging to oneself? Was it the wise and curative ways of being? The release that happens when you suspend the ego and turn your attention to the soul of the world? Was it simply coming to the tenth day, no longer driven by "what else," but a finder of "what is"?*

~ ~ ~

I hurry to catch up with the others at the grotto where Persephone returned from the underworld, where Ann and I ate pomegranate seeds last time.

From a distance, the cave opening appears like a half-moon shadow painted crudely onto the rocks. When I draw closer, I find Ann standing in the center of it. Her back is to me, her hair blowing in static wisps around her head, the hood of her teal nylon windbreaker flapping between her shoulder blades. The way she is framed in the cavernous opening halts me.

I plop down on a block of mottled stone that was once part of a temple wall to Hades, picking an out-of-the-way spot where I can observe my daughter unaware. I watch her inspect a niche in the rock where offerings are left. When she turns, her face is caught in the midday glare and I'm struck by a sweet, choking feeling— that way love blindsides.

She returned. I form the words deliberately in my mind, knowing there was no single point when it happened, only that this is the moment I choose to acknowledge it. We made a reunion.

For over two years, ever since these expeditions of ours started, I've tried to understand what the embrace between Demeter and Persephone means. I have come to believe it's really about that aperture opening. It's the channel where the souls of a mother and a daughter open and flow as two separate adults, woman to woman. It is, I know now, a place created through necessary loss and necessary search, and a reinvention of the whole relationship.

Spotting me on my perch, deep in my vigil, Ann wanders toward me. As she crosses the grotto, she reaches behind her neck and unties the green velvet ribbon. She slips the pomegranate off and pockets it.

I cannot register what she is doing. I get to my feet, curious, tilting my head to the side in a question.

She holds the ribbon out to me. "You should wear it," she says.

"Oh no, I couldn't—" I answer automatically, then break off.

"I want you to," she says.

And I'm aware suddenly how much *I* want to, too. "All right, thank you," I tell her.

I have the feeling Ann's gift is motivated by the conversation we had this morning at breakfast when I told her that today is the "tenth day," when Persephone returns to her mother. The ribbon must be Ann's token of that, her way of acknowledging to me that *she* has returned. It takes me a moment longer to grasp another, more hidden implication, one perhaps Ann doesn't see at all. That the ribbon is also the Young Woman returning to me.

As I unclasp my own silver chain, remove the pomegranate, and thread it onto the ribbon, my mind tumbles back to a different conversation Ann and I had in Paris about Picasso's painting *Girl Before a Mirror*. The way the Young Woman reaches for the Old Woman in the glass. I haven't thought about that for a very long time. Or how the reunion of Demeter and Persephone conveys a similar image: the essence of Young and Old coming together in a woman to create new life. A new self.

Ann ties the ribbon for me. "There," she says, and steps around to look at it. "You have to see it, too."

I wait while she plows through her backpack for a compact. She pries it open and holds it up to my face. I rise on my toes a little in order to see the V of plush green, the red pomegranate suspended at the hollow of throat. Then my face bounces into the mirror, accompanied by a flash of meeting myself.

As Ann tucks the mirror away and zips the backpack, I hold this moment inside with all the others. All that has happened. All that Ann is to me. This belonging.

AFTERWORD

September 2008

Ann

❧ When Mom and I returned from our final trip to Greece, I plunged into writing the travel book I had announced to the Madonna in the tree at the Palianis convent. In effect, this very book became my "apprenticeship." Over the years, I worked steadily on it in a small, L-shaped study over the garage of our new house, surrounded by images of my female triptych—a picture of Mary, a statue of Athena, and an icon of Joan of Arc. My desk was constantly buried beneath travel journals, trip photographs, postcards, research books, and dozens of notes I'd scribbled to myself. Much of the time, I felt like I had no idea what I was doing. I deleted five hundred sentences for every one I kept and lost count of how many outlines I created as I struggled to find my voice and probe the places I'd visited—not just the ones on the map, but those in my own interior landscape.

Gradually, as my work progressed, I came to feel that only half the story was being told. I thought about my mom's experiences during our trips, how she'd defined what it meant for her to become an older woman, discovered a new spiritual focus, and regenerated her whole creative life. It seemed a shame for her not to write about her own metamorphosis. Not to mention, our travels contained not just her individual story, and not just mine, but *our* story—a mother-daughter one that had happened in unison. Our experiences were tightly braided. Just as I could not imagine taking the trips alone, it became impossible to imagine the book without her voice. Mom, however, was immersed in writing her second novel and I had no idea whether writing about our travels even interested her.

In the spring of 2003, shortly after my twenty-seventh birthday, I finally brought the matter up, calling Mom one morning as I lingered at my desk. I told her there was more to the book than just my story. "Why don't you write it with me?" I said on impulse.

To my surprise, she didn't hesitate. "I would love to, but I want you to be sure."

"I've been sure," I told her, and immediately set about trying to re-conceive the book as a joint project.

In September of that same year, I was propped in bed watching *My Big Fat Greek Wedding* over my Big Fat Pregnant Belly. As the character Toula was prevaricating to her date about her family, I felt our baby deliver four hard, even kicks. *That was different.* I glanced over at the wooden cradle across the room. Earlier that day I'd had a feeling the baby was ready to come, and I'd put clean sheets and a blue blanket on the little mattress.

My intuition was right. Later that night, Ben was born. Motherhood was something I'd always wanted, and I fell in love with it the moment Scott put Ben into my arms, not to mention falling in love with Ben himself.

During his first year of life, I wrote very little, content to concentrate on Ben and my new role as his mother. But slowly the pull to work on the book reasserted itself, and I began the long, classic struggle to balance the tensions between tending Ben and tending my creative life. Finally, when he was two, I enrolled him in a preschool program, allowing me time to write other than during his sporadic naps.

I rarely thought about the rejection letter from the university, though I still keep it in a file folder in my desk, slotted between "Future Trips" and "Hurricane Evacuation Plan." One day, I hope Mom and I will travel together again—I've had an idea of taking a Jane Austen tour of England. As for Greece, I imagine returning with Scott and Ben one day, showing them the place that changed me.

The best part of writing *Traveling with Pomegranates* was the time I spent with my mother, brainstorming, editing, and veering off sometimes into completely unrelated topics, discussing the books we read or sorting through fabric samples for sofa pillows.

When I told the Virgin in the myrtle tree that I wanted to write a book about my travels, I did not imagine I would run *over* my seven-year apprenticeship, that it would take eight years from that day in 2000 when I said the prayer at the Palianis convent until this day in 2008, when I sit here at my desk and write the last few lines. But I've discovered being a writer is an ongoing apprenticeship, just like everything else in life that matters to me—being a mother, a wife, a daughter, or simply a woman alive in the world, content to be myself. Today at thirty-two, I am glad to wake up each day and begin.

Beyond the window of my study, Scott and five-year-old Ben are playing T-ball in the backyard, our black lab, Luke, chasing after them. Having come to the end of this book, I push back in my desk chair, feeling grateful, and think about the irony of me—the girl who wanted to be invisible—putting my story out there in the world, and aware, too, of the red shoe box beside my desk that holds the collection of images and ideas I contemplate writing about one day. For now, though, I slip on my shoes and head outside.

Sue

⟋◌ Back home from Greece, I happily observed Ann at work on her travel book and concentrated on planning the tour I would co-lead to France in the spring of 2001. I entertained no thoughts of writing about the trips myself—indeed, I was eager to start a second novel the moment some compelling idea occurred to me. During the tour of France, however, while standing with Ann and Mother beside an exalted old Black Madonna in the crypt of Chartres Cathedral, I felt a sweep of wonder at my connection to each of them and at the traveling that had helped me forge those connections. In that moment, I realized I wanted to write about my search for the Old Woman and finding not only her but Demeter, Persephone, the Black Madonna, Ann, my mother, and myself.

The desire to explore that passage of my life and translate it into story did not leave, but the passage was inextricable from our travels and the trips were Ann's to write about, a reality that brought me a great deal of pleasure, even as I put aside the idea of writing about them myself.

Soon, I was at work on my next novel, *The Mermaid Chair*, a project that would consume me for the next few years, along with tending the publication of *The Secret Life of Bees*. The last thing I imagined was that *Bees* would find the success it did. In fact, I don't think I realized the popularity of the novel until one evening when I was watching *Jeopardy!* and an answer that popped on the screen was: "Sue Monk Kidd's debut novel is about these insects." I blinked at the television, dumbfounded, before shouting "What is bees?" to the contestant, who luckily did not need my help.

I got a lot of on-the-job-training in learning to be the "contemplative writer" I first envisioned when Ann and I were at Mary's House in Turkey. As I worked on *The Mermaid Chair*, I honed a rhythm in which I wandered back and forth between my desk and the marsh, as I'd done the summer I finished *Bees*. I've come to value simply being as much as working, and my hypertension stays away as long as I keep them balanced.

Mary continues to be the primary icon of devotion in my life, functioning as a vibrant symbol of the divine feminine, and also as my muse. In a painting over my desk, the Black Madonna sits enthroned, presiding over my work.

By the time I was fifty-eight, I'd become a grandmother three times over. Not only was there Ben, but our son, Bob, got married the year after Ann, and he and his wife, Kellie, brought Roxie and Max into the world. Grandmotherhood initiated me into a world of play, where all things became fresh, alive, and honest again through my grandchildren's eyes. Mostly, it retaught me love.

When I finally began work on this book in May 2006, I felt like the stark and beautiful truths I'd met at the turn of my fifth decade had become a deep part of me. Over the next two and a half years, I sat at my desk, trying to render memory and perception into narrative, while several miles away, Ann did the same. We fell into a pattern of writing the first drafts of our individual chapters separately, then reading each other's work, followed by long sessions during which we reminisced, probed, divulged, discovered, laughed, wept, challenged, commiserated, and encouraged.

So it went.

"We write to taste life twice," Anaïs Nin wrote, "in the moment and in retrospection." Living the experiences in this book and then writing them was a privilege and a gift, but what I savored most was doing so with Ann. Tasting life together. Twice.

ACKNOWLEDGMENTS

We would like to express our gratitude to our agent, the amazing Jennifer Rudolph Walsh; to Molly Stern, our fabulous editor, along with all the exceptional people at Viking Penguin who supported this book and worked so hard on its behalf; to Trisha Sinnott and Terry Helwig, who traveled with us; to Leah Monk, extraordinary mother and grandmother in these pages; and to Scott, Ben, Sandy, and our family for the love and happiness they bring.